The Jews in Weimar Germany

The Jews in Weimar Germany

Donald L. Niewyk

LOUISIANA STATE UNIVERSITY PRESS   Baton Rouge and London

To my parents

Copyright © 1980 by Louisiana State University Press
All rights reserved
Manufactured in the United States of America
Designer: Patricia Douglas Crowder
Typeface: VIP Sabon
Typesetter: The Composing Room of Michigan, Inc.

The author gratefully acknowledges permission to reprint, in revised form, the following articles: "The Economic and Cultural Role of the Jews in the Weimar Republic," *Leo Baeck Institute Yearbook,* XVI (1971), and "Jews and the Courts in Weimar Germany," *Jewish Social Studies,* XXXVII (1975).

LIBRARY OF CONGRESS CATALOGING IN PUBLICATION DATA

Niewyk, Donald L.   1940–
   The Jews in Weimar Germany.

   Bibliography: p.
   Includes index.
   1. Jews in Germany—Politics and government. 2. Germany—Civilization—Jewish influences. 3. Antisemitism—Germany. 4. Germany—Ethnic relations. 5. Germany—Politics and government—1918–1933. I. Title.
DS135.G33N44   943/.004/924   79-26234
ISBN 0-8071-0661-5

Contents

Preface

Many of the problems experienced by Germany during its troubled initial experiment with democracy, the Weimar Republic, have been integrally related to the history of Germany's small Jewish minority. Willy-nilly, the Jews were thrust into the center of controversies between liberal democrats and radical authoritarians that ultimately tore Germany's first republic apart. Hence the study of German Jewry has been essential to understanding the fate of Weimar democracy and the rise to power of National Socialism. Several existing studies have clarified some of the fundamental issues. This book seeks to make a further contribution by viewing the "Jewish question" from the inside, as an issue for the Jews themselves as well as for the German people as a whole. By focusing on the Jewish response to radical anti-Semitism, it attempts to enlarge our understanding both of the German Jews and of Weimar society and culture.

Many individuals and institutions assisted me in writing this book. I owe a special debt of gratitude to Professors William Sheridan Allen and Werner T. Angress, who gladly agreed to read the manuscript and offered ideas for its improvement. I also profited considerably from the advice and encouragement of Dr. Ernest Hamburger, Dr. Arnold Paucker, and Professors Wolfgang Sauer and Hans A. Schmitt. Dr. Marion A. Kaplan, Professor Klaus J. Herrmann, and Dr. Carl J. Rheins kindly shared the results of their unpublished research with me. To Dr. S. Adler-Rudel, Dr. Friedrich Brodnitz, Dr. Werner J. Cahnmann, Dr. Ernest J. Cohn, Dr. Fred Grubel, Dr. Max Grünewald, Hans Jaeger, Dr. Herman Pineas, Dr. Eva G. Reichmann, Dr. Hans Steinitz, Gabriele Tergit, and Dr. Robert Weltsch I am grateful for interviews and letters that allowed me to benefit from their recollections of Jewish life in Weimar Germany. I would also like to thank Diane C. Risser and Robert J. Holland for assisting with the progress of the manuscript at different stages.

I am particularly grateful to the staffs of the Leo Baeck Institute and the Yivo Institute for Jewish Research (New York), the Institute of Contemporary History and Wiener Library (London), the German Federal Archives (Koblenz), the State Archives in Hanover, Koblenz, and Münster, and the Central Zionist Archives (Jerusalem) for their patience and cooperation. The publishers of the *Leo Baeck Institute Yearbook* and of *Jewish Social Studies* have given me permission to use, in modified form, parts of two articles listed in the bibliography. Finally, I wish to thank the Penrose Fund of the American Philosophical Society and the Council of the Humanities, Southern Methodist University, for financial assistance granted during the course of my research.

The Jews in Weimar Germany

Introduction

For the Jews of Germany, as for the rest of Europe's Jews, the modern age began with the eighteenth-century Enlightenment and with the French Revolution. Both of these historical developments contained liberating messages that touched everyone, but none so profoundly as the persecuted and the disinherited. Throughout the nineteenth century and later, the fate of the Jews would be linked inextricably with that of liberalism itself. Their loyalty to liberalism would be intense and abiding, nurtured on gratitude for rights received and determination to establish a permanent place for the Jews in the modern European world. Liberals, although scarcely ecstatic over persistent Jewish religious and social particularism, would reciprocate with toleration and increasing measures of equality before the law. Both parties, but especially the Jews, would be acutely aware that Jewish emancipation stood or fell with the fortunes of liberalism.

That the fortunes of liberalism in Germany were less than prosperous requires little commentary. Initially, classical liberalism—and that is the minimal sense in which the word *liberalism* is to be understood here—won growing numbers of Germans to its program of individual liberty, constitutional government, and free political and economic institutions. But the failures of 1848 and the capitulations of the 1860s became juxtaposed in the German mind with the triumphant authoritarianism of Bismarck's "blood and iron" policies. Later, the liberal Weimar Republic, conceived in defeat and born in revolution, never achieved a stable liberal consensus and succumbed after only fourteen years of life to Nazi barbarism.

This is a study of the Jewish response to that approaching nightfall. It focuses on the dilemma of a liberal minority, genuinely committed to the Republic and the principles upon which it was founded, that was gradually but effectively isolated by defections from liberalism on the part of the non-Jewish middle class during the closing years of the Weimar experiment. To use Peter Gay's words,[1] the Jews were "outsiders" who became "insiders" as a result of

1. Peter Gay, *Weimar Culture: The Outsider as Insider* (New York and Evanston, 1968).

the collapse of the Wilhelminian empire, occupying important and influential positions across a fairly broad spectrum of German life. Although the Jews were never fully accepted by German society, such full acceptance might well have taken place if history had taken a different, less tragic, turn.

If German Jews willfully remained in the liberal camp in the face of oncoming disaster, they may have misapprehended the dangers that confronted them and fatally blinded themselves to the full extent of anti-Semitism in Germany. Or, conversely, they may have found themselves without alternatives, barred from following their natural proclivity to join the rest of the middle class in supporting the political right by its anti-Semitism, and unable to ally themselves with the left due to its anticapitalism. A third possibility is that they understood the threats to their safety as well as those threats could have been apprehended at the time and yet chose, deliberately and voluntarily, to reject readily available alternatives in order to hold fast to liberalism. No attempt to explain the behavior of the Jews in Weimar Germany can afford to ignore any major aspect of their position: their place in German economic and social life; their understanding of and responses to anti-Semitism; their attitudes toward religion, patriotism, and ethnicity; their confrontation with rival versions of Jewish life; and, above all, the sources and strength of their commitment to the liberal credo.

The era of emancipation that stretched from the late eighteenth-century revolutions to the completion of German unification in 1871 forged the link between liberalism and Germany's Jews. Before that their communities were legally and emotionally distinct from their Christian neighbors, neither group wishing more than passing business relations with the other. Christian distrust of "Christ-killers" and "deliberate unbelievers" and Jewish fears of conversion and assimilation combined to build spiritual walls as effective as any made of stone that had surrounded the medieval ghettoes.

The secular and humanistic spirit of the Enlightenment began to undermine those spiritual walls late in the eighteenth century. In ethnic and religious hatreds the spokesmen of the new age saw lamentable vestiges of ancient barbarisms, whereas differences based on such considerations they viewed as doomed to fall before the liberating onslaught of reason. In the early 1780s a young liberal archivist in the Prussian War Office, Christian Wilhelm Dohm, became the first German liberal to express himself in favor of granting virtual equality to the Jews. In a book entitled *On the Civic Improvement of the Jews,* he dwelt at length on the narrow and degenerate characteristics of the typical Jew in order to argue for their elimination through removal of Gentile hostility, the primary cause of Jewish otherness. Emancipation, combined with a new spirit of toleration, would hasten the day when the Jews would set aside their anxieties and affirm the essential unity of the human race.[2]

These views, advanced for their day, took on new urgency a few decades later as Germany girded itself to resist Napoleon's conquering armies. To save themselves, Germans would have to modernize and set aside their differences. Every ounce of creative energy was required to end French domination of Central Europe. In Prussia the liberal reformers Wilhelm von Humboldt and Karl August von Hardenberg emancipated the Jews in 1812, but three years later, at the Congress of Vienna, Hardenberg failed to persuade the other German states to follow suit. He had stumbled on the forces of a newly resurgent conservatism that had tolerated liberal ideas only during the national emergency and now returned to its old habit of despising Jews as religious and social outsiders. In Prussia itself the emancipation decree was watered down by interpreting it in such a way as to exclude Jews from a wide variety of occupations, and it was not applied at all in the territories newly acquired by Prussia at the peace table.

The Jews, although dismayed at this setback, remained confident that full equality would ultimately be theirs. They attached themselves to the liberal movement, and they retained that association until well into the Weimar years. A few grew impatient with the slow progress toward emancipation and converted to Christianity or else became atheists. Certainly some of these conversions to the majority religion were entirely serious; the music of Felix Mendelssohn and the conservative politics of Friedrich Julius Stahl exemplified profound identification with Christian and German values. Whatever the motivating impulse, conversion quickly opened all the doors closed by the law; the prevailing animus was religious, not racial. But most German Jews optimistically assumed that it was only a matter of time before they would progress along the lines of their emancipated coreligionists in France and England, proudly aware at the same time that their own disabilities were as nothing compared to those suffered by the great masses of Jews in Poland, Galicia, and Hungary.

The commitment of German Jews to political liberalism helped to spark liberal trends in the Hebrew religion during the nineteenth century. Reform

2. Jacob Katz, *Out of the Ghetto: The Social Background of Jewish Emancipation, 1770–1870* (Cambridge, Mass. 1973); Klaus Epstein, *The Genesis of German Conservatism* (Princeton, 1966), 220–29.

Judaism sought to strip religious life of its most separatist and "oriental" characteristics without tampering with the essential core of the faith. It acknowledged marriages between Jews and non-Jews, introduced the organ, choir, and use of the vernacular into services, allowed men and women to sit together in the same pews, and dropped all claims to a separate Jewish civil law. Reform Jews, deeply influenced by the classical German literature of the first half of the century, gladly left behind the old cultural ghetto as well as much of the old religion. Reform Judaism went so far in that direction that it failed to find a secure doctrinal basis in Germany and lost most of its mass following late in the century. However, before its decline it gave birth to a less radical compromise with the modern world, Liberal Judaism, which became the creed of the great majority of German Jews by about the time of the First World War.

Orthodox Judaism responded to the new *Zeitgeist* with profound changes of its own. Most Orthodox Jews were repelled by their leaders' stubborn refusal to make concessions to the modern age and turned to the Neo-Orthodoxy advanced by Samson Raphael Hirsch, chief rabbi of the Orthodox Jewish community in Frankfurt-am-Main. As willing as Reform Jews to shed all pretensions to political and national identity, Hirsch distinguished Orthodoxy from Reform and Liberal Judaism in terms of its commitment to divinely inspired law that could not be reasoned away by demonstrating its historical evolution or by appealing to higher ethical laws. By the end of the nineteenth century the vast majority of German Jews belonged either to Liberal or to Neo-Orthodox congregations, both of which, for all their differences, conceived of Judaism as a religious and a cultural heritage, and nothing more.[3]

It would be a mistake to view the abandonment of Judaism's national traits primarily as a concession to pressures to assimilate and convert or as a conscious or unconscious demonstration of Jewish eagerness for emancipation. It is better explained as part of a larger movement among the various European religious bodies to adapt faith to science and the prevailing spirit of rationalism. The "higher criticism" of Christian scholars liberated educated Christians from literal belief in Holy Writ in a development that closely paralleled Judaism's jettisoning of anachronisms and archaisms. Moreover, in

3. Isidor Grunfeld, *Three Generations: The Influence of Samson Raphael Hirsch on Jewish Life and Thought* (London, 1958); David Philipson, *The Reform Movement in Judaism* (Rev. ed.; New York, 1931), 1–89, 107–269, 284–328, 382–402; W. Gunther Plaut, *The Rise of Reform Judaism* (New York, 1963); Max Wiener, *Abraham Geiger and Liberal Judaism* (Philadelphia, 1962).

affirming the modern world and their purely confessional role in it, German Jews declared their allegiance to liberal ideals that promised the emancipation of all mankind, not just the Jews. Theirs was a philosophy of hope, not of fear or self-seeking.[4]

The Jews' faith in liberalism was not unfounded. In that great outpouring of the liberal spirit at the revolutionary Frankfurt Assembly in 1848–1849, Jewish emancipation was adopted as a self-evident constitutional right in the form of a general statement of nondiscrimination on religious grounds. The assembly's Jewish vice-president, Gabriel Riesser, helped avert a more specific statement about the rights of Jews by insisting that they were neither a race nor a nation but simply another religion. In the individual German states, revolutionary liberals sponsored similar constitutional statements of equality òr else pressured their monarchs into promulgating statutes of emancipation. Many of these gains were whittled down or erased in the reactionary decades that followed 1849, but in 1850 the Prussian crown sought to steal some of liberalism's thunder by handing down a constitution that recognized no distinctions between Jews and Gentiles. Baden followed suit in 1862, and Württemberg did the same two years later. In 1869 the North German Confederation adopted emancipation, which was extended to the German empire as a whole upon its creation two years later. That these were concessions to liberalism was an unmistakable fact, further tightening the association of Jews and liberal politics in the minds of Germans of all faiths and parties.

For all of the gains that this association with political liberalism had brought to the German Jews, there were significant weaknesses in German liberalism that limited further Jewish progress. Although it was stronger and more influential than similar movements in other countries of Central and Eastern Europe, German liberalism never matched the vigor of that political philosophy in France and England, countries more favored by geographical isolation, advanced economic development, or positive revolutionary traditions. The Prussian liberals' initial opposition to Bismarck's flouting of the Prussian constitution during the struggle over army reforms in the early 1860s melted away following the war with Austria in 1866. With the achievement of unification five years later, Bismarck triumphed all along the line. He had succeeded where the liberals had tried and failed. His enormous popularity and his willingness at first to work with the liberals in evolving a pseudoconstitutional structure for the German Reich made opposition appear impolitic and

---

4. But for another point of view, see Ismar Schorsch, *Jewish Reactions to German Anti-Semitism, 1870–1914* (New York and London, 1972), 5–10.

unattractive. Hence most German liberals made their peace with the Iron Chancellor's semifeudal authoritarianism. In their impatient zeal to consolidate national and spiritual unity, many of them came to view the Jews as intentional outsiders.[5] Only a few liberals held fast to the old trilogy of unity, justice, and freedom.

Especially following the "liberal era" of the 1870s, the new German state was characterized by a conservative authoritarianism that was not entirely congenial to the Jews. The old ruling class continued to practice social discrimination against unbaptized Jews and, infinitely more damaging, thwarted the spirit of emancipation by effectively blackballing Jews from positions at all levels of Germany's enormous civil service. No Jew could hope to enter the army officers' corps, and it was extremely difficult for one to secure a professorship at a German university.

This conservative discrimination against Jews, based as it was on principles of social privilege and religious exclusivity, was less potentially damaging than attempts that were made in Imperial Germany to revive anti-Jewish prejudices among the masses and supplement them with racism. As Reinhard Rürup has pointed out, modern anti-Semitism had its genesis in the reaction against liberalism that developed in Germany during the last third of the nineteenth century. The economic depression and subsequent agricultural crisis of the 1870s, widely regarded as the "social costs" of rapid economic growth, occasioned attacks on the Jews as synonymous with materialism, liberalism, and modernism.[6] To be sure, there had been earlier attempts to link the Jews with materialism. George Mosse and Jacob Katz have shown how some German literature of the eighteenth and nineteenth centuries mirrored a popular image of the Jews as greedy self-seekers who were capable of dishonorable deeds because they were without roots in Germanic soil.[7] This was precisely the stereotype of the Jews employed by anti-Semitic agitators in their unsuccessful efforts to found mass movements of the political right during the economic depression that began in 1873. Their diatribes attempted to pin responsibility for closed factories, unemployed workers, and lost investments on "alien swindlers"—the Jews. Elements of the conservative and Roman Catholic press echoed their charges.

5. Uriel Tal, *Christians and Jews in Germany: Religion, Politics, and Ideology in the Second Reich, 1870–1914* (Ithaca, 1975), 31–120, 296. Tal may exaggerate somewhat when he concludes that these liberals regarded Jews as the *chief* impediment to unity.
6. Reinhard Rürup, *Emanzipation und Antisemitismus: Studien zur "Judenfrage" der bürgerlichen Gesellschaft* (Göttingen, 1975), 81–111.
7. George L. Mosse, *Germans and Jews: The Right, the Left and the Search for a "Third Force" in Pre-Nazi Germany* (New York, 1970), 61–76; Katz, *Out of the Ghetto,* 81–83.

The best-known of these early anti-Jewish agitators was Court Chaplain Adolf Stöcker. Following his failure in the middle of the 1870s to found a workers' movement on the basis of patriotic and Christian socialism, Stöcker turned his attention to the lower middle classes with a message of social justice combined with anti-Semitism, holding the Jews responsible for the abuses of capitalism. In 1881 he managed to get himself elected to the Reichstag, where he joined the Conservative party, but no mass following ever materialized, and hostility from the crown and from Bismarck combined with economic recovery to kill his Christian-Social movement within four years.

A second wave of anti-Semitism in the early 1890s drew its support largely from impoverished rural districts where Jewish moneylenders and cattle and grain dealers were identified as the culprits of economic decline. It also imported Gobineau's racialist ideas from France and denounced Jews, not for their religion, but for something they could never change—their race. In 1893 it managed to send sixteen deputies to the Reichstag. However, as Richard S. Levy has shown, this comparatively impressive showing was determined less by Judeophobia than by strong opposition to the economic policies of Imperial Chancellor Leo von Caprivi. The anti-Semites themselves, constantly quarreling and dividing, were no more successful than Stöcker had been at producing a mass movement against the Jews. The crowning achievement of political anti-Semitism—on paper, at least—was the Conservative party's adoption of an anti-Jewish plank in its 1892 Tivoli Program. Hence, although the small anti-Semitic parties themselves all but disappeared in the years that followed, one of Germany's largest and most influential parties had declared its intention to "fight the multifarious and obtrusive Jewish influence that decomposes our people's life." In practice, however, the Conservatives were highly opportunistic in pursuing the anti-Jewish line. By 1913 they had dropped it as ineffective. In the long run, the influence of such conservative intellectuals as Heinrich von Treitschke, Julius Langbehn, and Paul de Lagarde probably had far greater impact than did political anti-Semitism. All three denounced Jews as typical representatives of capitalism, liberalism, and secularism, which were breaking down traditional German values. Their diatribes helped reinforce conservative prejudices and gave a measure of intellectual respectability to anti-Semitism in university circles and among the educated middle class.[8]

8. Richard S. Levy, *The Downfall of the Anti-Semitic Political Parties in Imperial Germany* (New Haven and London, 1975), esp. 85–102, 254–65; Paul W. Massing, *Rehearsal for Destruction: A Study of Political Anti-Semitism in Imperial Germany* (New York, 1949); Peter G. J. Pulzer, *The Rise of Political Anti-Semitism in Germany and Austria* (New York, 1964); Tal, *Christians and Jews in Germany*, 223–89, 303–305.

The reaction of German Jews to this hostility was increasingly defensive. After some hesitation and several false starts, they established the Central Union of German Citizens of the Jewish Faith (Centralverein deutscher Staatsbürger jüdischen Glaubens) in 1893. The Centralverein's mission was to fight anti-Semites by giving the lie to their allegations, prosecuting them in court, and helping to defeat them for public office. At the same time it worked within the Jewish communities to strengthen both German and Jewish consciousness and to warn Jews against behaving in ways that their enemies might use to embarrass them. Alone among the Jewish organizations in Imperial Germany, the Centralverein enjoyed the support of virtually all German Jews. Its effectiveness is difficult to assess, but its growing militancy proved that its members and supporters were not prepared to abandon the field to their opponents.[9]

Self-defense, as important as it certainly was, hardly monopolized Jewish interests. Far from preoccupied with the obstacles that still stood in their path, German Jews took advantage of the opportunities available to advance in the economy and to make positive contributions in a variety of fields, especially in law, medicine, and journalism.[10] Nor did many of them lose confidence that progress was inevitable and that it would culminate in the complete victory of liberalism. They had come a long way in the hundred years since Hardenberg and Humboldt had taken the first steps toward granting Jewish emancipation. A few more decades were not too long to wait for the old prejudices to die and for liberalism to find new sources of strength. In the minds of most Jews in Imperial Germany, gratitude for opportunities extended and progress made far outweighed any bitterness over rights still withheld.[11]

Perhaps no Jewish leader better articulated the feeling of intimacy with which German Jews contemplated their Fatherland than did the great Marburg philosopher Hermann Cohen. Among Cohen's chief interests were the origins of Jewish ethics, which he identified in rational sources capable of being subjected to systematic analysis, the authority of the Talmud having been overthrown by the Reform and Neo-Orthodox movements. Protestant Christianity, which had undergone a similar process of humanization, stood on virtually the same ground now that it, too, had been forced to fall back

9. Schorsch, *Jewish Reactions to German Anti-Semitism*, 103–48.
10. Monika Richarz, *Der Entritt der Juden in die akademischen Berufe: Jüdische Studenten und Akademiker in Deutschland 1678–1848* (Tübingen, 1974), 172–217; Schorsch, *Jewish Reactions to German Anti-Semitism*, 13–16.
11. Jacob Toury, *Die politischen Orientierungen der Juden in Deutschland: Von Jena bis Weimar* (Tübingen, 1966), *passim*, esp. 202–45, 276–94.

on ethical monotheism as the basis for all moral culture. The Kantian Enlightenment and the humanistic idealism of Goethe and Schiller, the highest expressions of German culture, were in no way to be distinguished from the essential qualities of Jewish ethics. Although Cohen grew increasingly concerned about the trend toward amalgamation during his last years (he died in 1918) and hence laid more emphasis on issues separating Christians and Jews, he never abandoned his conviction that there existed a special kinship between Judaism and German humanism. His intense German patriotism gave concrete expression to that belief, as did the love of Fatherland displayed by countless German Jews in all of Germany's wars through World War I.[12]

Germans, too, had come a long way since the reforms of Stein, Hardenberg, and Humboldt. Most continued to harbor unflattering stereotypes of Jews and to regard them as unassimilated outsiders, but rarely was any of this translated into overt hostility. Indifference was in far greater supply than antagonism. Acts of violence against Jews comparable to the pogroms in Russia and the riots that accompanied the Dreyfus Affair in France were unheard-of in Germany. The Jews thrived in this atmosphere of imperfect toleration; their coreligionists throughout the world, and especially those in Eastern Europe, looked to them for support and leadership. Political anti-Semitism persisted, it is true, but it had become a virtual monopoly of the Conservatives, who, although solidly entrenched, could not hold out forever against the forces demanding change. The most vigorous of these, the Social Democratic party, had grown less radical as it had gained more support. By the time it became Germany's largest party in 1912, it had set aside most of its traditional view of Judeophobia as an immature form of anticapitalist revolt that could be rechannelled into Marxist politics. Now the Social Democrats attacked anti-Semitism as an evil in and of itself. It seemed only a matter of time before they, together with other progressive elements in the liberal and Roman Catholic parties, would give Germany a new political emphasis, one that would bring about the full and final realization of Jewish emancipation.

Germans and Jews, having drawn progressively closer together for more than a century, cemented their bond with a common enthusiasm in defending the Fatherland in 1914. For the first time Jews were made officers in the army, and a Jewish businessman, Walther Rathenau, was placed in charge of allocating Germany's precious and limited supplies of strategic raw materials.

12. Hans Liebeschütz, "Hermann Cohen and His Historical Background," *Leo Baeck Institute Yearbook*, XIII (1968), 3–33; Nathan Rotenstreich, *Jewish Philosophy in Modern Times: From Mendelssohn to Rosenzweig* (New York, 1968), 52–105.

Ironically, this war, which at the outset seemed to strengthen German-Jewish solidarity, was to set back the cause of full emancipation by decades and to open the way to disaster. The army's failure to win a quick victory or to make a decisive breakthrough on the western front had to be explained. To anti-Semites of all stripes, the guilty parties were known. Accusations of Jewish shirking and war profiteering began to be heard with increasing frequency, and the army was taken to task for tolerating both while at the same time claiming that it had mobilized German strength to the hilt.

In October, 1916, the Prussian war ministry responded to this agitation by ordering a census of Jews in the army for the first of November. It justified the census as a means of defusing charges that Jews were successfully dodging the draft and avoiding service at the front. In fact, it seems far more likely that the charges it was meant to defuse were those against the war ministry for complicity in Jewish shirking. In addition, the German officers' corps feared that the Jews would push for the appointment of Jewish officers at higher ranks on the basis of their enthusiastic service to the nation; the census, by casting doubt on the extent of that service, would be likely to maintain the homogeneity of the officers' corps. Hence, although the census was hardly intended to give major impetus to a revived anti-Semitism, it focused hostility on the Jews as symbols of unpatriotic elements that allegedly stood in the way of total mobilization and victory. When the census was actually taken, there were so many irregularities in compiling the statistics that it provoked a storm of protests from Jewish, liberal, and socialist circles. The census figures were never published, either because of the protests or because the military never intended to reveal them in the first place.[13]

Nevertheless, the damage had been done. A third wave of anti-Semitism had been set in motion, one that was to prove more dangerous and more durable than its predecessors. Soon it was to be reinforced by defeat, humiliation, inflation, and depression. The German Jews, not entirely unprepared for this phenomenon, were about to be put to the hardest of tests.

---

13. Franz Oppenheimer, *Die Judenstatistik des preussischen Kriegsministeriums* (Munich, 1922), 5–45; Egmont Zechlin, *Die deutsche Politik und die Juden im ersten Weltkrieg* (Göttingen, 1969), 524–37; Werner Jochmann, "Die Ausbreitung des Antisemitismus," in Werner E. Mosse and Arnold Paucker (eds.), *Deutsches Judentum in Krieg und Revolution 1916–1923* (Tübingen, 1971), 425–27; Werner T. Angress, "Das deutsche Militär und die Juden im Ersten Weltkrieg," *Militärgeschichtliche Mitteilungen*, Nr. 19 (1976), 77–146.

II

The Role of the Jews in the Economic, Political, and Cultural Life of Weimar Germany

To survive yet another storm of hostility, German Jews would require more than determination and optimism. Money would be essential to finance intensified defensive actions and to cope with attempted boycotts while maintaining the bourgeois standard of living to which most Jews had grown accustomed. If the old anti-Semitic charges were to be believed, this should have posed no problem since vast segments of the capitalist economy were at their disposal.

As usual with such charges, there was at least a grain of truth to it. One does not have to agree with economist Werner Sombart's charge that the Jews invented capitalism [1] to recognize strong Jewish proclivities for free enterprise and the comforts and security of middle-class independence. The reasons for this association are well known. For centuries virtually all German Jews had been obliged to live in urban ghettos and to work as peddlers and moneylenders and in such other occupations as Christians found undesirable. Often the very survival of local Jewish communities depended on their ability to provide the princes with substantial taxes and compulsory loans, and Jews therefore became adept at accumulating capital against the day of arbitrary official harassment. Having been freed from all legal disabilities comparatively recently—less than fifty years before the establishment of the Weimar Republic—insufficient time had passed for them to have lost their characteristic economic predilections. And, indeed, there was no compelling reason why they should have wanted to do so. Certainly there were Jewish artisans and retailers whose incomes compared unfavorably with those of their non-Jewish competitors or even of some skilled industrial workers. But the comfortable niches that a great many Jews occupied in the machinery of German capitalism provided them with a degree of social prestige and wealth that few of them could have held in contempt. Moreover, they experienced little difficulty in finding a measure of security from Judeophobia in the independence

1. Werner Sombart, *The Jews and Modern Capitalism*, trans. M. Epstein (Glencoe, Ill., 1951).

of self-employment or the semi-independence of managerial positions.[2] By 1914, therefore, the great majority of German Jews appeared to be reasonably content in the bourgeois occupations that history seemed to have prescribed for them.

The fact that the prewar prosperity persisted, at least in a relative sense, for much of Weimar Germany's Jewish middle class has tended to obscure the evidence of decline, both of income and of power. The role of Jews in the economy and, indeed, in the culture of Weimar Germany has been exaggerated by both Nazi and anti-Nazi writers, the former to disparage alleged Jewish decadence and domination, the latter to praise Jewish achievements and to identify anti-Semitism as being rooted in part in jealousy and envy.[3] And yet, there can be no question that Jews contributed to some aspects of German life between 1919 and 1933 in numbers disproportionate to their representation in the population. The roughly 600,000 Germans of the Jewish faith constituted just under 1 percent of the German population before 1933, and there was a smaller number of Jews who had broken all ties with the Hebrew religion.[4] The census figures, on which most economic analysis must rely, provide information only about Jews who adhered to Judaism. In identifying Jews in Weimar society, however, it is essential to include all who had Jewish ancestors and who were therefore regarded as Jews by anti-Semites. A great many Jewish intellectuals and businessmen had long since ceased to think of themselves as Jews, and it was in large part the persistence of Judeophobia that prevented their full amalgamation. Indeed the tension between social discrimination and opportunities for advancement in German economic and cultural life was instrumental in forming the productive pattern of Jewish participation in German society before 1933.

The statistical record offers convincing evidence that the overwhelming

2. Salo W. Baron, "Modern Capitalism and Jewish Fate," in Arthur Hertzberg and Leon A. Feldman (eds.), *History and Jewish Historians* (Philadelphia, 1964), 43–64.

3. Typical of the Nazi point of view are two publications of the Institut zum Studium der Judenfrage: F. O. H. Schulz, *Jude und Arbeiter: Ein Abschnitt aus der Tragödie des deutschen Volkes* (Berlin, 1944); and *Die Juden in Deutschland* (Munich, 1939). Anti-Nazi sources erring in the same direction are Arnold Zweig, *Bilanz der deutschen Judenheit 1933: Ein Versuch* (Amsterdam, 1934); Marvin Lowenthal, *The Jews of Germany* (New York, 1936); and Sidney Osborne, *Germany and Her Jews* (London, 1939).

4. For detailed demographical and sociological information about the Jews of Weimar Germany, consult Erich Rosenthal, "Trends in the Jewish Population in Germany, 1910–39," *Jewish Social Studies*, VI (1944), 233–74; Esra Bennathan, "Die demographische und wirtschaftliche Struktur der Juden," in Werner E. Mosse and Arnold Paucker (eds.), *Entscheidungsjahr 1932: Zur Judenfrage in der Endphase der Weimarer Republik* (Tübingen, 1966), 87–131; and Arthur Ruppin, *The Jews in the Modern World* (London, 1934), 182–85, 218–20, 329–31.

majority of German Jews was engaged in bourgeois occupations between 1918 and 1933. Almost three-quarters of them made their living from trade, commerce, banking, and the professions, especially medicine and law. At the same time only about one-quarter of the non-Jewish population of Germany was similarly employed. Although professed Jews made up at most 0.9 percent of the German population in the Weimar period, they held slightly more than 3.5 percent of all positions in these trades.

More than 61 percent of all gainfully employed Jews in Weimar Germany were engaged in some form of trade or commerce. Of these, slightly more than one-half were self-employed and nearly three-quarters were retailers. Strong Jewish proclivities for economic independence kept most of these firms small or medium in size. Jewish business houses were of particular importance in the textile and clothing trades. In 1930, Jews owned four thousand of Germany's wholesale textile firms, or 40 percent of the total, and nearly 60 percent of all wholesale and retail clothing businesses were in Jewish hands, again divided among many hundreds of concerns. Around a quarter of all wholesalers of agricultural products were Jewish, although they and all other agricultural middlemen were increasingly challenged by farmers' cooperatives in the 1920s. Jews were also important in the wholesale metal trades and the retail grocery business.[5]

Although most Jewish firms were neither large nor individually conspicuous, Jews were highly visible as owners of great department stores and chain stores. In 1932 department stores owned by Jews accounted for 79 percent of all business done by such enterprises. Just before the turn of the century the Jewish brothers Hermann and Leonhard Tietz had introduced department stores to Germany in conscious imitation of the American model. Later the brothers separated. Leonhard operated a chain of department stores in southern Germany and the Rhineland, while Hermann Tietz established his concern in Berlin and, together with his nephew, Oscar Tietz, made it into the city's largest in 1926, when he purchased the KDW (Kaufhaus des Westens) from another Jew, Adolf Jandorf. The brothers Franz, Georg, and Wilhelm Wertheim operated three large department stores in Berlin, as well as branches in Breslau and Rostock. Outside the capital, Salman and Simon Schocken ran a chain of thirty department stores; two important chains of shoe shops, the Salamander and Leiser companies, were also Jewish-owned.[6]

5. A. Marcus, "Jews as Entrepreneurs in Weimar Germany," *Yivo Annual of Jewish Social Science,* VII (1952), 175–203.
6. For brief biographies of these and many other Jewish businessmen, consult Daniel

Jews were similarly prominent as bankers in Weimar Germany. Almost half of all private banks, the number and importance of which declined after 1920, were owned by such famous Jewish banking families as the Mendelssohns, Bleichröders, and Schlesingers. On the other hand, Jews directed fewer than 1 percent of Germany's more numerous and increasingly important credit banks, although those with Jewish managers included some of the largest and most successful of these financial institutions. Arthur Salomonsohn directed the Disconto-Gesellschaft and engineered its fusion with the Deutsche Bank just before his death in 1930, thus creating the famous DD Bank. Salomonsohn employed his considerable skills to consolidate the German potash industry and to help revive and rebuild Germany's heavy industry and merchant navy after the First World War. The equally important Dresdner Bank was directed by Eugen Gutmann and, after his death in 1925, by Henry Nathan. Jakob Goldschmidt, director of the Darmstädter and Nationalbank, was largely responsible after 1923 for acquiring substantial loans of working capital for German industry from Holland, Sweden, and North America. The University of Heidelberg in 1927 awarded him an honorary doctorate for his "services to the reconstruction of the German economy."[7]

Jews were less prominent in the leadership of German industry, although they were well represented in a few fields. Two major areas of Jewish participation were the mining and chemical industries of Upper Silesia, a region where Jews had encountered few barriers to careers in industry as a result of the relative indifference of the great landowners to Silesia's industrial potential. By 1919, the Friedländer coal concern had branched out into the coke, petroleum, and coal-tar industries. The largest of the Silesian iron and steel concerns, founded more than thirty years earlier by Georg von Caro, was ably directed until 1930 by Leo Lustig. Indeed, in contrast to conditions in the Rhineland, more than half of Upper Silesian industry was owned or directed by Jews before 1933.[8] Elsewhere the proportion was much smaller. After the murder of Walther Rathenau in 1922 and the retirement in 1927 of Paul Mamroth, Jewish influence in the Allgemeine Elektrizitäts-Gesellschaft virtually disappeared; in 1933 the firm required no official "aryanization." While a number of skillful Jewish scientists worked for the I. G. Farben trust,

Bernstein, "Wirtschaft: Handel und Industrie," in Siegmund Kaznelson (ed.), *Juden im deutschen Kulturbereich* (Rev. ed.; Berlin, 1959), 760–97; Siegfried Moses, "Salman Schocken: His Economic and Zionist Activities," *Leo Baeck Institute Yearbook*, V (1960), 73–104.

7. Bernstein, "Wirtschaft: Handel und Industrie," 747.

8. F. R. Bienenfeld, *The Germans and the Jews* (New York, 1939), 16–17; Osborne, *Germany and Her Jews*, 18–19; Zweig, *Bilanz der deutschen Judenheit*, 166–67.

the only Jewish member of its board of directors was the distinguished chemist Carl von Weinberg. Only in the publishing industry were Jews unquestionably leaders. The two largest publishing houses in Germany, the Ullstein and Mosse concerns, published large numbers of books, magazines, and newspapers; Jewish journalists were notable across almost the entire spectrum of the liberal and left-wing press.

Since most Jews had been excluded from the judiciary, the civil and diplomatic services, and many corporative posts before 1918, large numbers of them concentrated in law and medicine, both then and during the Weimar years. In 1933, they made up 11 percent of Germany's doctors, more than 16 percent of its lawyers and notaries public, and around 13 percent of its patent attorneys.

Not all Jews in Germany enjoyed more or less comfortable middle-class lives. Almost one in five of them was a refugee from Eastern Europe who was forced to eke out an existence as an industrial worker, minor artisan, or itinerant salesman. Of all the Jews in postwar Germany, these Eastern Jews suffered the hardest lot. Some had been enlisted by the wartime German military government in Poland as workers for war industries, whereas others had taken refuge in Germany both before and after the World War from pogroms and political upheavals in the countries of their birth. Crowded in the industrial centers of Upper Silesia, Berlin, and the Rhineland, they were subject to chronic unemployment, sporadic official harassment, and the resentment of both Jewish and non-Jewish Germans.[9] Anti-Semitic agitators quickly discovered that they could be exploited for political purposes and alternately carped on the nation's inability to absorb the Eastern Jews and sought to obscure the distinctions between the newcomers and German Jews. Characteristically, these detractors had nothing to say against the much more numerous White Russian refugees who lived in Germany illegally.[10]

The Eastern Jews had little chance to better their conditions or to erase their alien identity. Germany's naturalization procedure, involved and time-consuming in the first place, permitted any of the German states to block the granting of citizenship subject only to ultimate review by the upper house of parliament, the Reichsrat. The right-wing governments of Bavaria in the early years of the Republic, and Thuringia in its later years, made ample use of this

9. Jacob Toury, "Ostjüdische Handarbeiter in Deutschland vor 1914," *Bulletin des Leo Baeck Instituts,* 21 (1963), 81–91; S. Adler-Rudel, *Ostjuden in Deutschland, 1880–1940* (Tübingen, 1959), 60–119; *Jüdische Rundschau,* December 16, 1930.
10. *Allgemeine Zeitung des Judentums,* January 21, 1922.

provision.[11] Given the obstacles, few alien Jews even applied for naturalization, with the result that some Eastern Jews had been born in Germany and had fought for her in the World War without ever becoming citizens.

The typical urban German Jewish community was divided into four fairly clear strata. At the very top were the wealthy old families of bankers or lawyers, proud of their high cultural milieu and of their contacts with non-Jews of similarly exalted status. Many of them had had their children baptized and had gladly seen them married to non-Jews. A few proudly flaunted honorary titles acquired from the prerepublican regimes in return for their generous services to charity.

Just below them stood a far larger stratum of well-to-do businessmen, doctors, lawyers, journalists, and other professionals whose families had been urbanized for three or more generations. A somewhat less cosmopolitan group, its members associated primarily with other Jews. Variations of wealth were marked among them, ranging from downwardly mobile salesmen to newly rich owners of department store chains. Wealthy elements among them helped form the popular image of the "Kurfürstendamm Jew," the elegant and meticulous inhabitant of that fashionable street on Berlin's west end who would leave no mistake in people's minds about the cost of his attire. Their sons were sometimes able to live lives of independent wealth, as in the case of Aby Warburg, who employed his family's banking fortune as a springboard to dabble brilliantly in art history. It was thanks to the prosperity of much of this group that the average income of Jews in Weimar Germany was 3.2 times that of the total population.[12]

Considerably lower in the pecking order were the Jews who had only recently moved from small town to city, most of them former cattle and grain dealers who had become small urban businessmen. They wanted nothing more ardently than to be accepted into the established groups. At the bottom stood the Eastern Jews, commonly referred to simply as "Polacks" by Jews and non-Jews alike. Both lower groups furnished the bulk of workmen employed by the Jewish religious communities. They often constituted a militant, class-conscious challenge to the financially strapped big-city communities.[13]

If most Jews seemed prosperous to the ordinary German, they saw their

11. *Jüdische Rundschau*, February 6, 1931.

12. *Central-Verein Zeitung*, December 4, 1931; E. H. Gombrich, *Aby Warburg: An Intellectual Biography* (London, 1970); Ernest Hamburger, "One Hundred Years of Emancipation," *Leo Baeck Institute Yearbook*, XIV (1969), 62.

13. Maria Zelzer, *Weg und Schicksal der Stuttgarter Juden* (Stuttgart, n.d.), 104–106; *Israelitisches Familienblatt*, September 2, 1920, August 2, 1923.

own economic status in less rosy light. Both long- and short-range trends appeared to conspire against them at least as much as against other middle-class Germans. Most likely to be downwardly mobile were the very large numbers of independent Jewish tradesmen of all kinds, the victims of a worldwide trend toward concentration and rationalization. Developments in the metal industry typified the problem. Most Jewish investment there was limited to commerce, as opposed to production, and progressively fell victim to the amalgamation of the copper, zinc, and aluminum industries, which began to buy and sell raw materials and finished goods directly. Between 1923 and 1930 the Jewish share of the metal trade dropped from 71.7 percent to 57.3 percent. Similarly, in the scrap metal trade, at one time a virtual Jewish monopoly, direct trade between suppliers and industries began to freeze out Jewish middlemen during the Weimar years. In the retail trade, small independent Jewish businessmen were as likely as their Gentile competitors to be threatened by the big, often Jewish-owned department stores. Some manufacturers began to sell their products directly to the consumer. In the agrarian sector, consumers' and producers' cooperatives increasingly made inroads into the business of small-town Jewish businessmen.[14]

Some members of this endangered species of tradesmen clung tenaciously to marginal existences, but increasingly they found themselves obliged to give up their prized independence and seek employment in the burgeoning industrial and commercial concerns. In this their Jewishness sometimes stood in the way. Jewish employers were frequently reluctant to hire large numbers of their coreligionists for fear of calling attention to themselves or of giving an impression of partiality. Non-Jewish employers, too, often shied away from hiring Jews, occasionally out of blatant hostility, but much more commonly out of anxiety that militant racists might call for boycotts against their firms.[15]

An eroding standard of living for much of the Jewish middle class became most starkly evident during the years of uncontrolled inflation at the begin-

14. Alfred Marcus, *Die wirtschaftliche Krise der deutschen Juden* (Berlin, 1931), 33; Ruppin, *Jews in the Modern World*, 118–21; Gerhardt Bauer, "Die Beteiligung der Juden an der deutschen Eisen- und Metallwirtschaft," *Der Morgen*, III (1927), 86–98; Hans Goslar, "Eine sterbende 'jüdische' Branche?" *Israelitisches Familienblatt*, February 9, 1928; *Central-Verein Zeitung*, March 9, 1928; Max Tischler, "Wirtschaftliche Neuorientierung," *Jüdische Rundschau*, September 9, 1930.

15. Kurt Zielenziger, "Die wirtschaftliche Umwälzung," *Central-Verein Zeitung*, July 4, 1930; Ludwig Holländer, "Gesperrte Berufe," *ibid.*, July 30, 1926; Ernst Behrendt, "An die Angestellten!" *ibid.*, May 11, 1928; S. Adler-Rudel, "Die Erwerbslosigkeit unter den Juden und die Bedeutung der Jüdischen Arbeitsnachweise," *Gemeindeblatt der Jüdischen Gemeinde zu Berlin*, XVIII (1928), 110–12; *Israelitisches Familienblatt*, August 21, 1924; Arno Herzberg, "Der jüdische Arbeitgeber," *ibid.*, July 25, 1929.

ning of the Weimar Republic and the years of depression at its end. In those difficult times marginal existences became unviable, forcing those who had led them to rely on public and private welfare. In the twelve years between 1912 and 1924, the proportion of Berlin Jews with taxable incomes of more than 5,000 marks fell from 10.6 percent to 5.8 percent, while during the same period the number of Jews with annual taxable incomes under 1,200 marks rose from 73.3 percent to 83.6 percent of the city's Jewish population.[16] Jews who lived on fixed incomes from savings or investments were ruined during the inflation. By the end of 1923, the Berlin Jewish Community had established nineteen soup kitchens, seven shelters, and an employment information and placement office for the destitute Jews of the city.[17] Other big-city communities did the same.

These measures had to be renewed on an even larger scale in the years 1930–1933. Overtaxed Jewish communities hired as many of their own destitute members as they could and provided food, coal, and clothing for the rest.[18] By 1933, they were groping their way toward establishing a voluntary agricultural labor service program for young Jews. Pilot projects had begun in Berlin, Leipzig, Cologne, Essen, Breslau, and Munich, but severe shortages of funds kept their three labor service camps small. The largest, Neuendorf, near Fürstenwalde, accommodated only about fifty men and women under the age of twenty-five.[19]

Just how hard hit by the depression the German Jews were is difficult to determine with any exactitude. There is no confessional information included in government jobless statistics, which are of limited value anyway since a good many workers were on short time or else had given up hope of finding employment. Certainly much of Jewish welfare was absorbed by proletarian Eastern Jews rather than by German Jews themselves. And yet, Ernest Hamburger's estimation that significantly fewer Jews than non-Jews were unemployed in 1932 may be open to question. If the Orthodox journal *Der Is-*

16. L. A. Loeb, "Wo ist der jüdische Wohlstand geblieben?" *Central-Verein Zeitung,* February 5, 1926.

17. *Israelitisches Familienblatt,* February 14, 1924.

18. Alexander Szanto, "Im Dienste der Gemeinde 1923–1939: Erinnerungen" (Typescript in Leo Baeck Institute Archives, New York), 17; Heinrich Stahl, "Unsere Wohlfahrtsaufgaben im kommenden Winter," *Gemeindeblatt der Jüdischen Gemeinde zu Berlin,* XXIII (1933), 37–39; *Jüdische Rundschau,* January 6, 1931; *Israelitisches Familienblatt,* September 22, 1932; *Verwaltungsblatt des preussischen Landesverbandes jüdischer Gemeinden,* July 1, 1932.

19. Max Kreutzberger, "Freiwilliger Arbeitsdienst und seine Auswertung durch die jüdische Gemeinschaft," *Gemeindeblatt der Jüdischen Gemeinde zu Berlin,* XXIII (1933), 37–39; *Jüdische Rundschau,* January 6, 1931; *Israelitisches Familienblatt,* September 22, 1932; *Verwaltungsblatt des preussischen Landesverbandes jüdischer Gemeinden,* July 1, 1932.

raelit's 1932 estimate of 50,000 Jewish unemployed was anywhere near to being correct, it suggests that almost as great a percentage of adult Jews as non-Jews were jobless.[20]

Signs of decline within the Jewish middle class were by no means confined to the years of inflation and depression. In Berlin, where about one-third of Germany's Jews lived, the Jewish unemployment rate stood at around 3,500 during the "good years" of the Republic (1924–1929).[21] Rabbi Leo Baeck of Berlin noted in 1928 that, whereas before 1914 most Jewish welfare efforts cared for Eastern Jews in Germany, since 1918 German Jews had come to absorb one-third of social aid furnished by the religious communities.[22] Fewer Jews could afford to send their sons and daughters to university; in two areas of traditional Jewish concentration, law and medicine, enrollments of Jews in Prussian universities declined from 10.3 percent to 5.2 percent and from 12.8 percent to 6.9 percent respectively between 1911 and 1930. Nor was the decline in those areas atypical of the general trend. While total university enrollments increased slightly in Prussia between 1911 and 1925, the number of Jewish students declined from 2,212 to 1,675.[23]

Least likely to be threatened by unfavorable economic trends were those Jews fortunate enough to be established in the professions. The expanding public health insurance system, operated through the labor unions and employee associations, gave special advantages to young Jewish doctors who might otherwise have encountered difficulties in setting up practices.[24] On the other hand, overcrowding of the legal and journalism professions all but closed those traditional avenues to new Jewish blood. Recent Jewish university graduates who lacked special talents or advantageous contacts had little to look forward to but menial labor or unemployment. In the tight labor market their Jewishness, normally a marginal consideration, could be a decisive drawback.

20. Hamburger, "One Hundred Years of Emancipation," 62; *Der Israelit*, February 25, 1932.

21. Max Kreutzberger, "Die jüdische Arbeitslosigkeit in Berlin," *Israelitisches Familienblatt*, August 1, 1929.

22. Leo Baeck, "Die jüdischen Gemeinden," in *Zehn Jahre deutsche Geschichte 1918–1928* (Berlin, 1928), 440.

23. Julius Rothholz, "Rückgang der jüdischen Studierenden Preussens," *Central-Verein Zeitung*, July 2, 1926; Margot Melchior, "Die Zahl der jüdischen Studierenden nimmt ab," *ibid.*, January 30, 1931; E. Lewin-Dorsch, "Rückgang der jüdischen Medizinstudenten .... Ein Symptom?" *Der Schild*, VII (1928), 249.

24. Ernst Feder, *Heute sprach ich mit ... Tagebücher eines Berliner Publizisten 1926–1932* (Stuttgart, 1971), 84–85; Paul Tachau, "My Memoirs" (Typescript in Leo Baeck Institute Archives, New York), *passim*; interview with Dr. Friedrich Brodnitz, July 12, 1975.

Fears of creeping proletarianization were frequent subjects of Jewish comment after 1918.[25] Rabbi Max Dienemann stood virtually alone when he welcomed them as spurs to renewed interest in Judaism. Far more common were expressions of concern that economic insecurity discouraged Jews from having large families; the drop in the Jewish birth rate was so dramatic during the twenties that fears were voiced of a drastic, even disastrous numerical decline. Late marriages and birth control, already regarded as desirable practices among virtually all middle-class Germans, became necessities in conditions of actual or incipient ruin. In the largest German state, Prussia, Jewish deaths began to outnumber births as early as 1922, and by 1928 there were ten deaths for every seven births among the Jewish population.[26]

Economic pressure also contributed to the high Jewish suicide rate during the Weimar years, prompting the Berlin B'nai B'rith to mobilize itself against what it called "the suicide epidemic among the German Jews." Their savings dissolved and their livelihoods threatened or destroyed, the less flexible among them took their own lives in numbers disproportionate to their share of the population. In Berlin the suicide rate for Jews during the year 1925 was 68 per 100,000, while the comparable figures for Protestants was 45 and for Catholics 32. In 1922 there had been 61 Jewish suicides in the capital; three years later there were 117, which amounted to 12 percent of all suicides there, or roughly four times the Jewish proportion of the population. The figures for Prussia as a whole showed an even more dramatic disproportion between Jewish and non-Jewish suicide rates. The statistics for German Jews were also significantly higher than those for Jews in large cities of Eastern Europe such as Warsaw, Lodz, and Budapest, where Jews took their own lives less frequently than did non-Jews.[27] This suggests that the deeply wounded self-esteem of declassed German Jews was a more significant cause of suicide than anti-Semitism per se.

Middle-class Jews who were threatened with economic extinction found

25. Tischler, "Wirtschaftliche Neuorientierung," *Jüdische Rundschau*, September 9, 1930; Alfred Marcus, "Wirtschaftswende—auch für uns?" *ibid.*, October 21, 1932; Marcus, *Die wirtschaftliche Krise, passim; Israelitisches Familienblatt*, October 23, 1919.

26. Max Dienemann, "Die Proletarisierung der deutschen Juden," *Der Morgen*, VII (1931), 115–26; *Der Israelit*, September 24, 1923; Stefan Behr, *Der Bevölkerungsrückgang der deutschen Juden* (Frankfurt, 1932), 44–51; Felix A. Theilhaber, *Der Untergang der deutschen Juden: Eine Volkswirtschaftliche Studie* (Rev. ed.; Berlin, 1921), *passim*.

27. *Central-Verein Zeitung*, February 21, 1924, November 27, 1925, February 12 and 19, 1926; *Jüdische Rundschau*, February 9, 1926; Fritz Salomon, "Erschütternde Selbstmordziffern," *Der Schild*, IV (1925), 453–54; *Jüdische Rundschau*, October 21, 1927; Arthur Ruppin, *Soziologie der Juden* (2 vols.; Berlin, 1930), I, 247–48.

that a more hopeful sign pointed them toward radical occupational reorientation in agriculture and the skilled trades. It was spoken of in almost messianic
terms by virtually all segments of Jewish society. Liberal Jews usually stressed
its economic necessity. They identified agriculture and, to a lesser extent, such
trades as gardening, electronics, and carpentry as the only segments of the
economy that were expanding and capable of absorbing new productive
forces. The more far-sighted among them looked to occupational reorientation as a means of elaborating a system of social politics that would make
Jews economically unexceptional vis-à-vis the rest of the German population.
Others spoke of the need to give new life to the Jewish community by breaking with the artificialities of urban existence in favor of direct contact with
nature and the soil.[28] But all gave primacy to saving Jewish children from the
fate of proletarianization.

Zionists joined in supporting the new occupational directions, purportedly
for quite different reasons. Retraining for more "practical" occupations
would prepare Jews to make positive contributions to the Palestinian economy at a time when the depression in Germany was breaking down their resistance to emigration.[29] And yet, while Zionist youth groups trained small
cadres of their members to make the great transition from Europe to Asia
Minor, most German Zionists frankly admitted that in the foreseeable future
Palestine could absorb only a small fraction of the Jews threatened by changes
in the industrialized world. In the short run, most German Jews, including the
Zionists, would have to find ways of surviving in Germany. Hence Zionists,
too, used arguments of economic survival similar to those of their liberal rivals, although they studiously avoided the impression that occupational
reorientation was a response to anti-Jewish attacks. Instead they placed
greater emphasis on agriculture's capacity to regenerate a Jewish communal
spirit and rekindle national and ethnic identity. In practice, most Zionist vocational retraining programs aimed at preparing Eastern Jews for new lives in
Germany or abroad.[30]

28. Norbert Bachrach, "Berufsumschichtung und produktive Arbeit," *Israelitisches
Familienblatt*, August 21, 1924; E. Jungermann, "Jüdische Siedlung in Deutschland,"
Gemeindeblatt der Jüdischen Gemeinde zu Berlin, XXII (1932), 207–209; *Central-Verein
Zeitung*, September 28, 1922; Felix A. Theilhaber, "Berufsproblematik der Juden," *Central-
Verein Zeitung*, December 6, 1923; Ludwig Holländer, "Das Handwerk Lebt!" *ibid.*, September 9, 1932; Ernst Wolff, "Wählt feste Berufe," *Von deutsch-jüdischer Jugend*, V (1929),
5–6; Henny Lin, "Der Weg zur Scholle," *Von deutsch-jüdischer Jugend*, I (1925), 9; Leo
Baeck, "Mensch und Boden," *Der Schild*, X (1931), 68.
29. Tischler, "Wirtschaftliche Neuorientierung," *Jüdische Rundschau*, September 12,
1930.
30. Hugo Rosenthal, "Schule und Umschichtung," *Jüdische Rundschau*, July 8, 1930; J.

Rebuilding the Jewish sense of community on the land appealed to Orthodox Jews as much as to the Zionists, but for religious rather than nationalist reasons. Orthodoxy was aware of the close relationship between urbanization and the decline of traditional religious ways. It hoped for a return to the Law, to family, and to community in the healthier environment of rural existence.[31]

No single individual did more to popularize the idea of agricultural training for young Jews than the great Jewish sociologist Franz Oppenheimer. A former Zionist, Oppenheimer enjoyed cordial relations with nearly all segments of the Jewish community. Both before and after his retirement from the University of Frankfurt-am-Main, he took every opportunity to plug his idea of "liberal socialism," which involved offering the workers an agrarian alternative to urban wage-slavery while ending food shortages through intensive agriculture. The Jews, he argued, ought to show the way, because for them to settle on the land would demonstrate their capacity to put down roots into the German soil both literally and figuratively, disproving anti-Semitic claims that they were capable only of parasitic relationships with urbanites.[32]

These efforts to alter the Jews' allegedly unhealthy social and vocational patterns were not without precedent in Germany. In the eighteenth and early nineteenth centuries, similar interest in occupational reorientation had aimed at promoting emancipation and creating new economic opportunities. More recently such efforts had concentrated on helping Eastern Jews and Jewish orphans. In 1880 the Association of German Jewish Communities had founded the Alliance for the Propagation of Skilled Trades among the Jews. Seventeen years later it was joined by the Alliance to Promote Agriculture among the Jews of Germany. By the end of the 1920s each of these and a few similar organizations could claim that their training programs had graduated a few hundred young people, at least half of whom had chosen to practice their new skills outside of Germany.[33]

Lestschinsky, "Wirtschaftskrise und deutsche Juden," *ibid.*, November 20, 1931; Israel Tunis, "Zum jüdischen Berufsproblem," *ibid.*, July 12, 1932; *Gemeindeblatt der Jüdischen Gemeinde zu Berlin*, XXII (1932), 306–307; interview with S. Adler-Rudel, August 14, 1973; Walter Preuss, *Ein Ring schliesst sich: Von der Assimilation zur Chaluziuth* (Tel Aviv, n.d.), 173–74.

31. *Der Israelit*, March 28, 1929, June 18, 1931.

32. Adolph Lowe, "In Memoriam Franz Oppenheimer," *Leo Baeck Institute Yearbook*, X (1965), 141–43; Franz Oppenheimer, "Genossenschaftliche Siedlung," *Bayerische Israelitische Gemeindezeitung*, III (1927), 213–18; *Israelitisches Familienblatt*, October 5, 1927, May 2 and December 4, 1930.

33. Sucher B. Weinryb, *Der Kampf um die Berufsumschichtung: Ein Ausschnitt aus der Geschichte der Juden in Deutschland* (Berlin, 1936), 42–46; Tamar Bermann, *Produktivierungsmythen und Antisemitismus* (Vienna, 1973), 56–59; E. G. Lowenthal, "The Ahlem

As valuable as these efforts were, they were clearly too small to have a significant impact upon German Jews. Chief impetus for supplementing them with an agricultural training program tailored to the needs of young middle-class Jews came from the Jewish veterans' organization, the National League of Jewish Frontline Veterans (Reichsbund jüdischer Frontsoldaten). Founded just after the end of the World War, it worked to document Jewish contributions to the war effort and to dramatize Jewish patriotism. What better way to promote the latter than to seal the Jews' attachment to the paternal soil with plow and scythe? This sentiment was reinforced by enthusiasm for broadening economic opportunities for Jews while helping them to escape from the deleterious influences of urban life. Encouraged by a program of government aid to prospective farmers that helped establish thousands of new agricultural settlements after 1919, it acquired in 1925 the Buckow estate near Berlin from the Alliance to Promote Agriculture as a place to fulfill its plans to train young Jews and retrain wounded war veterans in agricultural and related skills. This attempt did not succeed, however, and Buckow had to be taken over by the Berlin Jewish Community.[34] Undaunted, two years later the veterans' organization inaugurated a vigorous fund-raising campaign under the slogan, "Jewish Farmers on German Soil!" The campaign entered a new phase in November, 1928, when the veterans secured the cooperation of virtually every important German Jewish political and administrative body in forming two new organizations: "Jewish Agricultural Labor, Limited" to provide technical assistance in founding new settlements; and the "National League for Jewish Settlement in Germany" to finance them.[35]

The veterans' efforts culminated in 1931 with the founding of the cooperative agricultural training settlement Gross-Gaglow near Kottbus, which was heavily underwritten by the Berlin Jewish Community. By 1933, Gross-Gaglow was a thriving community of twenty-four Jewish families. Although small and subjected to occasional Nazi harassment, it was regarded as a promising beginning and almost universally applauded by the Jewish press. The leader of the ruling liberal party in the Berlin religious community, Kurt Fleischer, spoke of expanding the retraining program to involve 100,000

Experiment," *Leo Baeck Institute Yearbook*, XIV (1969), 165–79; *Allgemeine Zeitung des Judentums,* October 31, 1919.

34. Jakob Ledermann, "Land!" *Der Schild*, IV (1925), 1–2; Bruno Woyda, "Arbeit," *Gemeindeblatt der Jüdischen Gemeinde zu Berlin*, XXII (1932), 209–11; Ulrich Dunker, *Der Reichsbund jüdischer Frontsoldaten 1919–1938: Geschichte eines jüdischen Abwehrvereins* (Düsseldorf, 1977), 81–88, 93–95.

35. *Der Schild*, VI (1927), 33–36; *ibid.*, VII (1928), 378.

Jews.[36] Smaller retraining centers were founded in the early 1930s by the separatist Orthodox Jewish communities and by wealthy Jewish philanthropist Simon Schocken.[37]

Amid all the enthusiasm for training Jews to be small independent farmers, a few skeptical voices could be heard. These noted the great problems that urbanized Jews would encounter in adjusting to rural life. Berlin Professor Eugen Wolbe went to the heart of the matter when he noted the absence among most bourgeois Jews of an emotional drive to become farmers similar to the drive impelling young Zionists to prepare for Palestine.[38] Evidence supporting Wolbe's doubts came from a source within the Jewish veterans' organization that revealed a drop-out rate of 50 percent in the retraining settlements; abstract idealism melted quickly in the clear sunlight of agrarian existence. Other skeptics observed that the German land was already over-populated, that landless farmers stood first in line for whatever land might be available, and that farming communities had produced one of Hitler's first and most fanatical mass followings.[39]

The skeptics' points were well taken. Ideological rigidity and utopianism were hallmarks of the drive to prepare Jews for life on the land. How many of its supporters must have assumed that farming was a calling that some *other* Jews' sons should follow! The scarce resources of the day could have been used more profitably in giving greater emphasis to training Jews to be tailors, mechanics, upholsterers and the like.

Much has been made here of the economic decline of significant portions of the Jewish middle class in Weimar Germany. Whatever elements of tragedy were present in these developments, they were partly offset by the advantages

36. Dunker, *Der Reichsbund jüdischer Frontsoldaten*, 88–91; *Gemeindeblatt der Jüdischen Gemeinde zu Berlin*, XXII (1932), 306–307; Moritz Rosenthal, "Schicksalswende des deutschen Judentums," *ibid.*, XXI (1931), 195–96. Carl J. Rheins oversimplifies somewhat when he concludes that the veterans' settlement program demonstrated that they "implicitly accepted the argument that Jews, in their present occupations, were parasites." Carl J. Rheins, "German Jewish Patriotism 1918–1935: A Study of the Attitudes and Actions of the *Reichsbund jüdischer Frontsoldaten*, the *Verband nationaldeutscher Juden*, the *Schwarzes Fähnlein*, *Jungenschaft*, and the *Deutscher Vortrupp*, *Gefolgschaft deutscher Juden*" (Ph.D. dissertation, State University of New York at Stony Brook, 1978), 46.

37. *Der Israelit*, May 26, 1932; *Jüdische Rundschau*, February 21, 1933.

38. Eugen Wolbe, "Die Schwierigkeiten der jüdischen Siedlungsbewegung," *Israelitisches Familienblatt*, October 27, 1927. See also *Central-Verein Zeitung*, April 1, 1927.

39. Hermann Rosenthal, "Das Landproblem in RjF," *Der Schild*, V (1926), 117; Werner Cahnmann, "Die gesellschaftliche und wirtschaftliche Zukunft der jüdischen Jugend in Deutschland," *Bayerische Israelitische Gemeindezeitung*, VII (1931), 206–207; Martin Götz and Alfred Marcus, "Von der Grossstadt aufs Land?" *Central-Verein Zeitung*, February 20, 1931; *Der Israelit*, March 5, 1931; Ernst Holzer, "Deutschjüdische Bauernsiedlung?" *Der Morgen*, IX (1933), 42–48.

accruing from the less exceptional Jewish social and economic patterns they might have produced under less stressful political conditions. By no means would all German Jews have been proletarianized, but it seems likely that the plausibility of attacks on the Jews for their role in the economy would have declined along with the one-sided Jewish engagement in a few mercantile and professional vocations.

In 1928, one Rudolf Kaulla published a booklet entitled *Liberalism and the German Jews: Jewry as a Conservative Element.*[40] Its thesis, that Jews were political moderates committed to the democratic status quo, was unexceptional, to say the least. That it required stating at all illustrates the gap between popular image and concrete reality on this point, too; for some Germans were as prepared to assume that Jews were left-wing revolutionaries as they were to believe that they were mostly rich capitalists.

The impression of Jewish radicalism had been established rather firmly in the nineteenth century. Liberalism, with its promise of emancipation for the Jews, had been forced into a revolutionary position in the reactionary days after Napoleon. Somewhat later, Jewish intellectuals who preferred to merge their conception of emancipation with militant leftist visions of general human emancipation had taken prominent places in the growth of German socialism. The names of Karl Marx, Ferdinand Lassalle, and Eduard Bernstein come to mind almost automatically.

Far more important in fixing the image of radical Jews in the popular mind, however, were the revolutionary events in Germany at the end of World War I and just after. The moderate Marxists in the Social Democratic party (Sozialdemokratische Partei Deutschlands) were determined to fill the vacuum left by the collapse of the monarchy with genuinely free political institutions. They were accused by right-wing Germans of having assisted the nation's defeat by "stabbing Germany in the back" with strikes and other forms of internal dissension; now that their treachery had brought it low, they were saddling it with a political system that Germans neither wanted nor understood.

These detractors were not slow to publicize Jewish involvement in the Social Democratic leadership and to remind Germans of that party's ultimate allegiance to the ideas of the Jew Karl Marx. In fact, a surprisingly large number of Jewish intellectuals had risen to leading positions in the party. The Social Democratic party, as a working class party, lacked trained journalists,

40. Rudolf Kaulla, *Der Liberalismus und die deutschen Juden: Das Judentum als konservatives Element* (Munich and Leipzig, 1928).

propagandists, and parliamentary representatives. It was only natural that educated Jews, part of a minority deprived of full rights under the monarchy, should have filled this need in substantial numbers. One measure of their involvement in Socialist politics was provided by Eduard Bernstein, who estimated in 1921 that 10 percent of the participants in party conferences were Jews. Throughout the Weimar years, Jews made up a similar percentage of the Social Democratic Reichstag deputies.[41]

Jewish participation in the Socialist-dominated provisional government established following the collapse of the imperial regime was considerable, although far from decisive. The Socialist leader Friedrich Ebert (a non-Jew) appointed a Jewish comrade, Otto Landsberg, to the Council of People's Commissars, the government's central decision-making organ. For Ministry of the Interior, Ebert chose Hugo Preuss, a bourgeois-democratic expert on constitutional law who was charged with the additional task of preparing a draft constitution for the new Germany. Jewish Social Democrats were also instrumental in establishing revolutionary governments at the state level. Most prominent among them were Paul Hirsch in Prussia and Georg Gradnauer in Saxony.[42]

While Socialist and liberal Jews helped to set the basis of a representative democracy in Germany, other Jews actively promoted more radical alternatives. Members of the Independent Social Democratic party (Unabhängige Sozialdemokratische Partei Deutschlands) who had broken away from the mother party in 1917 to oppose continued support for the German war effort promoted a utopian scheme of workers' democracy based on the revolutionary workers' and soldiers' councils. Among their leaders were the Jews Hugo Haase, who for a time sat on the Council of People's Commissars, and Kurt Eisner, an idealistic Socialist journalist who had taken over the leadership of the revolution in Munich.

In Berlin the left wing of the Independent Social Democrats, inspired by revolutionary events in Russia and dismayed by the Social Democrats'

41. Eduard Bernstein, "Jews and German Social Democracy," *Die Tukunft*, XXVI (1921), 145 ff., quoted in Massing, *Rehearsal for Destruction*, 329; Donald L. Niewyk, *Socialist, Anti-Semite, and Jew: German Social Democracy Confronts the Problem of Anti-Semitism 1918–1933* (Baton Rouge, 1971).

42. A brief but extremely useful summary of the most important Jewish participants in the revolutionary governments is to be found in Hamburger, "One Hundred Years of Emancipation," 28–31. For a more comprehensive treatment of the same subject, consult Werner T. Angress, "Juden im politischen Leben der Revolutionszeit," in Werner E. Mosse and Arnold Paucker (eds.), *Deutsches Judentum in Krieg und Revolution 1916–1923* (Tübingen, 1971), 137–315.

Kareski, on the Center party's list of Berlin Reichstag candidates for the September, 1930, elections helped to spark an "Organization of Jewish Center Party Voters" headed by another Zionist, Dr. Max Kollenscher.[48] Ironically, the Center party's association with prominent Zionists may have hurt its chances with liberal Jews, who were far more numerous.

The Social Democratic party, perennially handicapped by an image that was more radical than its policies, made up for it in Jewish eyes by keeping the proletariat relatively free from anti-Semitism and by combating the Nazis more militantly than anyone else. The orthodox *Der Israelit,* which had castigated the Socialists as late as 1930 for being intolerantly atheistic, softened its tone until, by 1932, it placed them on the same high level of acceptability with the Center party. The Zionists, who had always harbored a faction sympathetic to the German left, likewise published at least one pro-Socialist essay.[49]

Hence it seems likely that the Center and Social Democratic parties divided most of the Jewish vote between them after 1930, although the ratio cannot be determined with any precision. There is suggestive evidence, however, that at least a substantial minority voted Socialist. Arnold Paucker has made an informal poll of approximately one hundred surviving German Jews, the great majority of whom had been solid middle-class supporters of the Democratic party before its decline. The results suggest that after 1930 around 62 percent of Jewish voters chose the Social Democrats, while only about 19 percent voted for the State party (Staatspartei—formerly the Democratic party) and a mere 5 percent cast ballots for the Center party. Paucker notes that few Bavarians could be included in his poll and speculates that the more conservative Bavarian Jews may have voted for the Bavarian People's party both before and after 1930.[50] Moreover, if Jewish business people were somewhat underrepresented in his sampling, as seems likely, it may well be that the Catholic parties did much better among Jewish voters than his poll indicates.

If many adult Jews moved to the moderate left during the last years of the Weimar Republic, they did so primarily in response to the increasing danger of nazism and the absence of a suitably militant party of liberal persuasion. The situation among Jewish youths was somewhat different. Although most

circulation figure of around 80,000 copies. *Sperlings Zeitschriften- und Zeitungs- Adressbuch,* LVII (1931), 399.

48. *Jüdische Rundschau,* August 5, 1932. Kareski had been put in the tenth place on the Center party list, a hopelessly low position that gave him no chance of being elected. Hence the gesture was purely symbolic.

49. *Der Israelit,* July 3, 1930, July 7, 1932; *Jüdische Rundschau,* November 4, 1932.

50. Arnold Paucker, "Jewish Defense against Nazism in the Weimar Republic," *Wiener Library Bulletin,* XXVI (1972), 26–27; interview with Dr. Arnold Paucker, July 4, 1973.

of them held fast to the liberal and assimilationist views of their parents, a minority joined other young Germans in feeling alienated from the values of the older generation.[51] Some, impatient with the persistence of German anti-Semitism and/or parental materialism, abandoned the Hebrew faith and moved to the political left or else to Zionism. A Communist journalist and propaganda expert during the Weimar period, Hans Jaeger, has estimated that in the immediate postwar years only 3 out of roughly 240 members of the Socialist student group at the University of Frankfurt-am-Main were non-Jews. Dr. Hans Steinitz recalls that somewhat later at least 25 percent of the Social Democratic students at Heidelberg University were Jewish, whereas the figure at Berlin University was twice that.[52]

Crisis conditions brought on by the depression only intensified the generation gap. Communist inroads were especially deep among young Zionists and Eastern Jews.[53] Shrewdly the Communist party established "independent" organizations, usually called "Jewish Workers' Study Groups," to entice them to Marxism. So troubled were Zionists by these developments that they held special anti-Communist meetings for young audiences and in general stepped up their agitation against Soviet treatment of the Jews and against what they contemptuously labeled "red assimilationism."[54] The great danger presented by this growth of communism in some Jewish circles was driven home when the editor of the *Israelitisches Familienblatt,* Esriel Carlebach, was shot and badly wounded early in 1933. Carlebach had written a series of articles critical of Stalin's treatment of the Jews following a tour of Russia during the summer of 1932. The articles brought forth a flurry of anonymous threatening letters and a vile pamphlet attack upon him from Hamburg's "Jewish Workers' Study Group." Although there is no record of the assailant ever having been apprehended, it seems likely that he was inspired by this issue.[55]

Jewish parliamentarians and governmental office holders also stood some-

51. See, for example, the lament over tensions between the generations made by Rabbi Hugo Hahn of Essen, "Ein Fest jüdischer Jugend," *Israelitisches Familienblatt,* March 14, 1929.

52. Gustav Löffler, "Religiöse Not," *Der Morgen,* II (1926), 259–71; Fritz Friedländer, "Zur Entwicklung unserer Weltanschauung," *Central-Verein Zeitung,* June 21, 1929; interview with Hans Jaeger, June 16, 1974; interview with Dr. Hans Steinitz, July 16, 1975.

53. M. Findling, "Zur Lage der ostjüdischen Jugend in Deutschland," *Der Israelit,* November 12, 1931; Walter Mecklenburg, "Deutschjüdische Jugend und Zionismus," *Jüdische Rundschau,* March 4, 1930; Siegfried Kanowitz, "Kommunismus und Zionismus," *ibid.,* October 27, 1931; Fritz Löwenstein, "Zur Auseinandersetzung mit Kommunisten," *ibid.,* January 26, 1932.

54. *Jüdische Rundschau,* February 9, 1932, June 21, 1932.

55. *Ibid.,* January 10, 1933.

what further to the left than the masses of Jewish voters. Ernest Hamburger has provided a useful summary of the most important of them, and it is not proposed to repeat it here.[56] It remains only to underline the leading role of the Social Democratic and Democratic parties in providing Jews with the most political opportunities. Most of the Jews elected to the Reichstag and to the Prussian Diet represented the former party, and it continued to nominate them as candidates, sometimes placing their names at the head of the ballot, until the Republic's bitter end. They included several former Independent Socialists who returned to the mother party when their own ranks broke apart in 1922. Most prominent among these former Jewish schismatics was the brilliant Marxist economist Rudolf Hilferding, who became minister of finance in the coalition governments of Gustav Stresemann in 1923 and of Hermann Müller in 1928–1930. In general, the appointment of Jews to posts of authority depended on the presence of the Social Democrats and/or the Democrats in the ruling coalition. The same was true at the state level. In Prussia, always the most progressive of the German states during the Weimar years and a stronghold of the two parties, Jews could be found in virtually all administrative departments and in all kinds of civil service positions. Where the Democrats and Social Democrats were frozen out of state governments, as, for example, in Bavaria, Jews stood little or no chance of attaining high office.

The Democratic party, the one for which most Jewish voters opted, was rather more timid than the Social Democrats in promoting Jews for parliamentary or governmental roles. Certainly it did stand behind them in a few cases, most conspicuously in that of Eugen Schiffer, prominent Democratic Reichstag deputy and minister of finance and of justice in several early Weimar cabinets, and a baptized Jew. On the other hand, the Democratic party was more susceptible than the Socialists to fears of seeming too friendly to the Jews. Hence it placed Hugo Preuss, the father of the Weimar Constitution, among its deputies in the Prussian Diet rather than in the Reichstag. In 1930, after its merger with the right-wing Young German Order to form the State party (Staatspartei), Georg Bernhard, Jewish chief editor of the *Vossische Zeitung* in Berlin and a Democratic Reichstag deputy since 1928, was dropped from the party's list of candidates.[57] Due to its virtual demise in the polar-

56. Hamburger, "One Hundred Years of Emancipation," 46–58.
57. *Jüdische Rundschau*, August 15, 1930. Two baptized Jews, Oskar Meyer and Gustav Stolper, were elected State party Reichstag deputies in 1930. The Young German Order (Jungdeutscher Orden), founded in 1918 by Lieutenant Artur Mahraun for the purpose of fighting the "Bolshevik peril," had occasionally associated the Jews with communism and consistently excluded them from its ranks.

ized conditions after 1930, the moderate Democratic (alias State) party was spared the ultimate test of its commitment to equal treatment for the Jews.

The German Communist party's treatment of the Jews is most fascinating. As a radical opposition party it had no chance to promote Jews for high office, but it did enjoy the services of several able Jewish intellectuals, a number of whom it sent to the Reichstag and the state diets in the 1920s. By 1932, however, when the party was winning more votes than ever before, most Jews had vanished from its lists of candidates. Not a single Jew was among the one hundred Communists sent to the last freely elected Reichstag. Some, like Paul Levi, had been expelled from the party for resisting its domination by Moscow. Others had joined Berlin historian Arthur Rosenberg in defecting to the Social Democrats or to leftist splinter groups to protest the heavy hand of Stalinism. And yet several Jews remained. Ernest Hamburger's speculation that they were passed over for public office in order to enhance Communist appeals to the Nazis' constituency and to disprove the Hitlerite claim that communism was Jewish may yet be proved correct.[58]

To sum up, Jewish confidence in the parties of the center and the moderate left proved generally well founded in terms of the opportunities they offered Jews in politics and government service. In the case of Walther Rathenau, the foreign minister assassinated by racists in 1922, it had been possible for a Jew to attain high office without party sponsorship. It had also been possible for another independent Jew of moderate outlook, Curt Joel, to occupy a less visible and less exalted, but still influential, position as the dominant figure in the Reich Ministry of Justice from 1920 to 1931. In little more than a decade since the flowering of full emancipation, an impressive number of Jews had been elected to parliamentary bodies and appointed to positions of authority. The regional and administrative impediments that remained probably would not have survived a similar period of normal development. Both the fascination for communism evinced by some young Jews and the Communists' reluctance to nominate Jewish candidates are best attributed to the distinctly abnormal conditions that prevailed in the Republic's period of decline.

There is no question that the Jews' ability to control or influence Weimar economic and political life was overrated. Their role in Weimar culture is another matter. Jews were enormously important and creative in almost every branch

58. Hamburger, "One Hundred Years of Emancipation," 46–58.

of cultural life from 1918 to 1933. The mediocrity of the culture in *judenrein* post-World War II Germany has not gone unmentioned, although Walter Laqueur has stretched the point considerably by asserting that "without the Jews there would have been no 'Weimar culture.'"[59]

Jewish interest in intellectual achievement is usually traced to the Hebrew religion's long-standing affirmation of the life of the mind and to Jewish longings to overcome discrimination and to attain security and social esteem. It is the latter influence that deserves close analysis, for their position as "outsiders" sometimes encouraged Jews to question popular ideas and to take risks in defying authority. Moreover, past oppressions had left Jews better able than most to understand the problem of rootlessness and alienation that plagued post-Versailles Europe.

Both alienation and empathy contributed to the ambivalence of Jewish intellectuals towards the culture of the Weimar Republic. Undeniably many of them were enthusiastic about its emphasis on rationality and its faith in human progress, the strength and vigor of German cultural institutions, and the degree of emancipation that permitted Jews to use these institutions without giving up their identity as Jews. Not greed, but respect and love—if so far unrequited—encouraged unquestioning adoration of and service to established cultural values. But acute awareness that German Jews enjoyed less than full social equality struggled to neutralize that attraction, and, undoubtedly, consciousness of rejection was a major stimulus to creativity. As outsiders, Jews were in a position to view popular assumptions without reverence, and as a minority deprived of full social equality, they were unlikely to accept the status quo with equanimity. Hence ambivalence expressed itself on the one hand in overt criticism of majority values and radical departures from established cultural and artistic norms. On the other hand it stimulated some Jews to excel in accepted forms and modes of thought.

Weimar theater accurately mirrored the diverse ways in which alienation impelled some German Jews towards innovation and criticism. It would be no exaggeration to describe the Weimar stage as decisively influenced by Jewish directors, actors, and playwrights. Max Reinhardt, already Berlin's most influential director, further developed an expressionist technique that integrated music, dance, pantomime, and other related arts into the obsessive

59. Peter Berglar, *Walther Rathenau* (Bremen, 1970), 308; Walter Laqueur, *Weimar: A Cultural History, 1918–1933* (New York, 1974), 73. The point that this was hardly a new phenomenon has been made by Peter Gay, "Encounter with Modernism: German Jews in German Culture, 1888–1914, " *Midstream*, XXI (1975), 23–65.

naturalism that had dominated the prewar stage. He also found time to convey his skills to a new generation of disciples, among whom were two Jews who became prominent as directors of expressionist and neo-objectivist theater in the capital: Leopold Jessner at the State Theater and Victor Barnowsky at the House of Comedy. The German screen, too, was profoundly influenced by Jewish writers, actors, and directors, including Carl Mayer, coauthor of *The Cabinet of Dr. Caligari,* and Fritz Lang, who directed *Metropolis* and several other notable expressionist and neo-objectivist films.

Of the five or six leading expressionist playwrights of the Weimar years, three—Ernst Toller, Carl Sternheim, and Franz Werfel—were Jews who stood in the vanguard of the movement, and Toller subsequently went on to become one of the pioneers of the "new objectivity" (*neue Sachlichkeit*) of the mid-1920s.[60] Toller was clearly the most alienated from the norms of German society. The World War had made a leftist and a pacifist of him. His part in the Bavarian Soviet Republic of 1919 led to a five-year prison sentence, during which he wrote several plays that were intended to arouse the masses against capitalism and militarism. Toller's first play, *Metamorphosis (Die Wandlung),* was partially autobiographical in that it told of the conversion of an ardent young patriot into an idealistic revolutionary Socialist by the grotesque horrors of war. Expressionist devices like dancing skeletons and speaking choruses, however effective in *Metamorphosis,* turned into cliches in Toller's subsequent dramas, as did his self-righteous harping on the war and the revolution. Deepening pessimism over his inability to influence the course of events colored his 1927 neo-objectivist play *Such is Life! (Hoppla, wir leben!),* in which a revolutionary leftist commits suicide in despair over mankind, following his failure to assassinate a former Socialist comrade who had been rewarded with a high government post for betraying the revolution. A similar end awaited Toller himself in a New York hotel room in 1939.

Another Jewish critic of German society, Carl Sternheim, was more interested in lampooning old foibles than in prescribing new worlds. Typically, his 1926 play *Uznach's School (Die Schule von Uznach)* carried his pungent satires on bourgeois morality into the Weimar period with cynical mockery of the ethical nihilism and sexual license that postwar German youth took for emancipation. Not excepted from his targets were his fellow Jews, whose sin, as he saw it, was that of having absorbed too enthusiastically the banalities of the German middle class.

---

60. The others, Fritz von Unruh, Georg Kaiser, and Bertolt Brecht, were not Jewish.

Less overtly alienated was yet a third popular Jewish dramatist, Franz Werfel, an Austrian who found his most receptive audience in Germany and hence divided his time after 1918 between Berlin and Vienna. Although perhaps best remembered for his poetry and novels, Werfel turned much of his attention to the theater after publishing a collection of pacifist poems, *Day of Judgment* (*Der Gerichstag*), in 1919. Together with the non-Jews Oskar Kokoschka and Ernst Barlach, he had helped to pioneer the expressionist drama immediately prior to World War I. While Toller fulminated against capitalism and Sternheim lampooned the middle class, Werfel concerned himself with the more personal problem of human wavering between the divine and the demonic. A master of the psychological dissection of characters, Werfel was at his best in the 1920 play *The Mirror Man* (*Der Spiegelmensch*), in which the central figure is made aware of his lower instincts by an implacable mirror-image that induces him to commit suicide in atonement for his sins. Similar themes marked Werfel's historical dramas about the Austrian Archduke Maximilian and the Apostle Paul. Underlying Werfel's preoccupation with ethics was a profound religious mysticism that stemmed from a life-long fascination with Catholicism, although perhaps, in a very general way, from his Jewish background as well.

In literature, the best-known and most popular novelist of the older generation, Jakob Wassermann, was neither angry nor particularly creative. In his own day he ranked with Hermann Hesse and Heinrich and Thomas Mann, but time and the literary historians have not treated him kindly. Although a skillful craftsman who attained international popularity, his style was derived essentially from Balzac and Dostoevski, employing themes that described the attainment of humility and selflessness through suffering. Little of his sentimental fiction has enjoyed lasting appeal, and Wassermann is best remembered as the author of an eloquent autobiographical sketch, *My Life as German and Jew* (*Mein Leben als Deutscher und Jude*), published in 1921. Sometimes mistaken for a pure and simple denunciation of German anti-Semitism, the essay is also an expression of faith that the suffering caused by virulent postwar Judeophobia would purify and reconcile Germans and Jews. Wassermann must have been encouraged about the prospects of reconciliation by the enormous popularity of his 1928 novel *The Maurizius Case* (*Der Fall Maurizius*); this prompted him to deliver public lectures on the future adventures of the main character, Etzel Andergast, before adoring crowds that included the cream of the German intelligentsia.

The new wave of expressionism in German fiction received added impetus from the Jews Arnold Zweig and Alfred Döblin. Zweig's novels denounced German militarism as forcefully as did the plays of Toller. Zweig had experienced the brutality of the Prussian bureaucracy at first hand as a member of the press section of the German high command on the eastern front in World War I. The most successful of his novels, *The Case of Sergeant Grischa* (*Der Streit um den Sergeanten Grischa*), vied with Erich Maria Remarque's *All Quiet on the Western Front* as the outstanding war novel of the Weimar Republic. It told of a Russian prisoner of war who escaped from his German captors and assumed the name of a comrade who had deserted, only to be executed as a spy when recaptured by the Germans. Although made aware of the Russian's true identity and thus of his innocence by a compassionate divisional officer, headquarters heartlessly refused to reverse the sentence. Zweig's personal response to the persistence of Prussian bureaucracy in Weimar Germany was to become an enthusiastic Zionist.

Döblin imitated Wassermann's penchant for subjecting his fictional characters to lengthy psychological scrutiny and added a distinct psychoanalytical twist. As a Berlin neurologist and hence a practitioner of the science that was widely associated in the public mind with Jews, he was perfectly situated to do so convincingly. Döblin produced both historical novels and sophisticated science-fiction stories, but his most popular and enduring novel, *Berlin Alexanderplatz,* was a naturalistic attempt to capture the mental processes of a down-and-out Berlin worker who had become a common criminal out of stupidity and bitterness. Not only is it a remarkable record of the thoughts of a proletarian tough, but it compassionately delineates dehumanized urban conditions from the viewpoint of the political Left. The historical novels of Lion Feuchtwanger and Alfred Neumann similarly attempted to penetrate the minds of their subjects, but with considerably less skill and perception. Popularized psychology also marked the almost universally read biographies by Emil Ludwig of such diverse historical characters as Bismarck, Jesus, and Cleopatra.

No Jewish expressionist is better known today than the poet Else Lasker-Schüler. Well before the Weimar years, she had established herself as the high priestess of German expressionism, a title she would have appreciated rather less than the one she gave herself, that of an oriental princess. More than most expressionist poets, she put her bizarre fancies into ecstatic personal language that excluded all but a small group of initiates from their meaning. Elitist that she was, she would have had it no other way.

Closer to earth, Jews found considerable opportunities to comment on

Weimar society as journalists in the moderate and left-wing press. They edited and contributed to Weimar Germany's best newspapers, including the Mosse concern's *Berliner Tageblatt,* the only German newspaper with a primarily Jewish staff. Substantial numbers of Jewish journalists—twenty-nine, to be precise—were employed in leading positions by the rival Ullstein publishing house. The *Frankfurter Zeitung,* perhaps Weimar Germany's best newspaper, continued to employ Jews after it was purchased by the I. G. Farben trust in the 1920s. Among them was Heinrich Simon, its director until 1934. Jews were to be found at less-exalted journalistic posts elsewhere in the provinces, including some on fairly conservative newspapers. On the whole, however, most of their work was notable for its moderate and democratic attitudes as much as for its terse clarity of style; it trenchantly criticized the Republic's shortcomings without abandoning hope of improvement within the Weimar framework.

The same cannot be said for a small group of Jewish journalists who made up perhaps two-thirds of the circle around the *Weltbühne,* an independent left-wing journal inspired by Kantian ethics rather than Marxist dialectics. Most prominent among them were Kurt Tucholsky, Siegfried Jacobsohn, and Kurt Hiller. All were convinced that Germans and their Republic were hopelessly compromised by capitalism, militarism, and bureaucracy and de-served not the slightest aid or sympathy. On the contrary, their forte was sar-castic attacks on everything that German patriots and moderate republicans held sacred. Tucholsky's 1929 book *Deutschland, Deutschland über Alles* of-fered a photomontage of German generals with the caption "Animals are looking at you" and even a description of German traffic control patterns as sublimated militarism. Elsewhere Tucholsky portrayed the typical German as a repulsive philistine talented only at emptying a beer mug. It is with good reason, then, that Walter Laqueur has named the terminal alienation of these Jewish intellectuals the "Tucholsky complaint," identifying as its chief symp-tom the inability to distinguish the sad imperfections of liberal democracy from fascism. Presumably the victorious Nazis convinced them that, in fact, there was something worse than Weimar politicians, judges, and generals.[61]

The left-wing Jewish intellectuals' biting attacks upon the Republic no doubt helped to disillusion elements of the intellectual left with political de-mocracy, although they offered no practical alternatives. But it would be

61. Kurt Tucholsky, *Deutschland, Deutschland über Alles* (Berlin, 1929), 63, 199–201; Walter Laqueur, "The Role of the Intelligentsia in the Weimar Republic," *Social Research,* XXXIX (1972), 312–27; Laqueur, *Out of the Ruins of Europe* (London, 1972), 447–55.

wrong to exaggerate their positive influence, which was never great. The *Weltbühne,* for example, had a circulation of only 16,000 in 1931.[62] Their negative influence, however, although difficult to quantify, was almost certainly far greater, for anti-Semites gleefully quoted from their destructive criticism of everything German as typical of Jewish opinions.[63] Recent attempts to rehabilitate them notwithstanding, there can be no question that these ideologues helped to discredit free institutions in Germany at a time when they needed every possible support.[64]

The most original musical mind of the twentieth century was that of Arnold Schönberg, a Viennese Jew who chose to make his home in Berlin in 1925. There he received the recognition that Vienna had begrudged him. He was called to succeed Ferruccio Busoni as professor of composition at the Berlin Academy, and there was considerable scope for the performance of his compositions in the German capital. Not that the average Berlin audience found Schönberg's "atonality" particularly assimilable or that he was without professional critics, but Berlin produced little of the widespread petty carping that had plagued the composer in Vienna. In Germany, Schönberg not only completed eight new compositions, but he exerted a strong influence on virtually all Weimar composers, including three young Jews—Kurt Weill, Hans Eisler, and Paul Dessau—all of whom have earned more recognition from their musical settings of the polemical lyrics of Bertolt Brecht than for their abstract compositions. An enthusiastic champion of the new music was the Jewish director of Berlin's Kroll Opera, Otto Klemperer. However, the other major Jewish conductor of the day, Bruno Walter, had difficulty in understanding the postromantic idiom and never included such works in his concerts with the Berlin Philharmonic and Leipzig Gewandhaus orchestras.[65] Of the three great Jewish instrumentalists of the Weimar years, Fritz Kreisler, Arthur

62. *Sperlings Zeitschriften- und Zeitungs- Adressbuch,* LVII (1931), 256.

63. See, for example, the use made of material from the *Weltbühne* in Karl Gerecke, *Biblischer Antisemitismus: Der Juden Weltgeschichtlicher Charakter, Schuld und Ende in des Propheten Jona* (Munich, 1920), 44, 46.

64. For sympathetic treatments of the left-wing Jewish intellectuals, see Istvan Deak, *Weimar Germany's Left-Wing Intellectuals: A Political History of the Weltbühne and Its Circle* (Berkeley and Los Angeles,1968); and Harold L. Poor, *Kurt Tucholsky and the Ordeal of Germany, 1914–1935* (New York, 1968). See also Gordon A. Craig, "Engagement and Neutrality in Weimar Germany," in Walter Laqueur and George L. Mosse (eds.), *Literature and Politics in the Twentieth Century* (New York, 1967), 55; Kurt Sontheimer, *Antidemokratisches Denken in der Weimarer Republik: Die politischen Ideen des deutschen Nationalismus zwischen 1918–1933* (Munich, 1962), 387–90.

65. Walter's memoirs, *Theme and Variations,* trans. James A. Galston (New York, 1946), offer revealing insight into the warmest personality among modern conductors.

Schnabel, and Emanuel Feuermann, only the last named displayed genuine interest in playing the most adventurous of the new compositions.

One of Weimar Germany's most original architects, Erich Mendelsohn, was Jewish. He and Walter Gropius led the frontal attack for modern architecture against the heavy formalism that popular taste had inherited from the Second Reich. Both insisted that buildings, in addition to being functional, ought to fit into their surroundings as organic participants rather than as passive intruders. But while the architects of the Bauhaus fashioned geometric structures, Mendelsohn designed sculptured buildings with boldly curving forms. Arguing that nature abhors the pedantic geometry of man, he proved that steel and concrete can appear plastic with his first and most radical creation, the famous Einstein Tower near Potsdam, which resembles an enormous submarine conning tower with windows and doors, crowned by an observatory. His subsequent designs for a variety of department stores and office buildings pushed structural framework far behind the glass facades, making the upper stories seem to float. In some respects his architecture presaged our own disillusionment with the antiseptically functional, and it has been an important inspiration to the school of contemporary architecture that calls itself "modern baroque."

German Jews furnished no equivalent of the innovative genius of Schönberg and Mendelsohn to the painting of the Weimar years. Max Liebermann, the grand old man of German impressionism and president of the German Academy of Arts, remained the most popular artist in Germany, probably because he never developed beyond the austere techniques he had mastered well before World War I. Among younger Jewish painters only Ludwig Meidner and Jankel Adler departed radically from prewar impressionism, and neither of them approached the boldly abstractionist experiments of Wassily Kandinsky and Paul Klee or the bitter social comments of Otto Dix and George Grosz, all of whom were non-Jews.

The faculties of German universities were opened wide for the first time to notable Jewish scholars after 1918, with the result that Weimar academic life was enormously enriched. Ernst Cassirer, the originator of the philosophy of symbolic forms, verified the compatibility of Einstein's theory of relativity with his own neo-Kantianism, and Edmund Husserl founded phenomenological philosophy. In the field of history, Ernst Kantorowicz earned a professorship at Frankfurt for his brilliant biography of the medieval emperor Frederick II, while Arthur Rosenberg dissected the Second Reich from the standpoint of a left-wing Social Democrat and Gustav Mayer perceptively analyzed the German labor movements from a bourgeois point of view. The sociologist Karl Mannheim fought with some success to preserve his discipline from embracing unreservedly deterministic explanations of human consciousness while he investigated irrational influences on mass behavior. Hermann Kantorowicz argued persuasively in favor of basing German law on sociological concepts rather than on dogmatic legal constructions alone. The Institute of Social Research, founded in 1923 at the University of Frankfurt-am-Main, helped launch the careers of several remarkable, predominantly Jewish, Marxist social scientists, including Theodor Adorno, Max Horkheimer, Erich Fromm, and Herbert Marcuse.[66] Jewish contributions to scientific advancements were hardly less distinguished. No fewer than five of the nine Nobel prizes won by German citizens during the Weimar years went to Jewish scientists, two for medicine and three for physics, and most conspicuously to Albert Einstein in 1921.[67]

A Jewish public that was articulate and prepared to buy books, tickets, paintings, and the like was of no small importance in opening Weimar culture to new departures and to Jewish participation in them. In this it was not alone, for German society as a whole granted Jewish intellectuals considerable recognition. Books by Wassermann, Zweig, Feuchtwanger, and Ludwig made the best-seller lists, while a 1926 poll of the readers of the prestigious literary magazine *Literarische Welt* revealed that Franz Werfel stood second only to Thomas Mann in their affections.[68] Else Lasker-Schüler was awarded the Kleist Prize just a year before Hitler came to power.[69] The anti-Semitic minority always excepted, Weimar Germany provided Jewish intellectuals with a fertile environment and a degree of encouragement that was perhaps unprecedented anywhere.

66. Gustav Mayer, *Erinnerungen: Vom Journalisten zum Historiker der deutschen Arbeiterbewegung* (Zürich and Vienna, 1949). Mayer was made a professor of history at the University of Berlin in 1920. Rosenberg was an instructor there until 1930, when he was named an assistant professor. See also Martin Jay, *The Dialectical Imagination: A History of the Frankfurt School and the Institute of Social Research, 1923–1950* (Boston, 1973), 3–29.

67. The other four were: for physics, James Franck and Gustav Hertz, 1925 (for discovering the laws governing the impact of electrons upon atoms); for medicine, Otto Meyerhof, 1922 (for research in the metabolism of energy in human muscles); and Otto Warburg, 1931 (for discovering the nature of respiratory ferment).

68. Adolf Leschnitzer, "Geschichte der Deutschen Juden vom Zeitalter der Emanzipation bis 1933," in Franz Böhm and Walter Dirks (eds), *Judentum—Schicksal, Wesen und Gegenwart* (2 vols.; Wiesbaden, 1965), I, 271; *Der Schild*, June 7, 1926. Useful information about best-seller figures may be gleaned from Donald Ray Richards, *The German Bestseller in the 20th Century: A Complete Bibliography and Analysis, 1915–1940* (Berne, 1968), but it contains errors and should be used with caution.

69. *Israelitisches Familienblatt*, November 17, 1932.

Without these and other Jewish participants, the cultural life of Weimar Germany would have lost much of its richness and diversity. Their achievements in virtually every area reached a minimum level of first-rate technical competence, and in music, science, and architecture some of their contributions earned them lasting international recognition. Success in almost every case can be attributed to their openness to new ideas and their willingness to attempt bold experiments. Of course, the same thing might be said of non-Jewish authors, artists, researchers, and the like. Jewish intellectuals worked as Germans at tasks that had little or no relationship to religious or ethnic distinctions. Their Jewishness sometimes affected their numbers, but it rarely made for qualitative differences.[70]

It was to be Hitler's achievement to confuse the issue by holding the Jews alone responsible for the cultural modernism that bewildered and antagonized more than a few ordinary Germans: Marxian socialism, pacifism, internationalism, expressionism, psychoanalysis, atonal music, and organic architecture. What made his myth plausible was the disproportionately large number of Jews among the critics and innovators of Weimar culture, supplemented by occasional National Socialist attempts to fasten the Semitic label on non-Jewish intellectuals. In truth, Jews were no more solely responsible for modern culture in Germany than they were for the abuses of capitalism or socialism. The left-wing plays of Bertolt Brecht far excelled those of Ernst Toller and occasioned more controversy than those of any Weimar dramatist. None of the psychological novels by Jewish authors could stand comparison in popularity and quality with the best works of Thomas Mann. Nor were Paul Hindemith and Walter Gropius less controversial and creative than Arnold Schönberg and Erich Mendelsohn. Without the contributions of a single Jewish intellectual, Weimar Germany would still have produced a remarkable and energetic cultural life not substantially different in its broad outlines from the one for which it is known.

In all three areas of inquiry—economics, politics, and culture—the trend was for the Jews to evolve toward the average, toward what was more nearly "typical" of incomes, behavior, and tastes in the larger German society. Already most of them were securely ensconced in the middle class and absorbed by its values, having deliberately divested themselves of all but confessional

70. Peter Gay convincingly downplays the qualitative differences, but he tends to lose sight of important quantitative anomalies. Peter Gay, *Freud, Jews and Other Germans* (New York, 1978), 169–81.

identification with things Jewish. Their tendency to concentrate in a few busi-nesses and professions was waning with the decline of traditional Jewish oc-cupations and the appearance of new opportunities in areas heretofore closed to them. Their political loyalties, never very exceptional in the first place, grew more diverse under the pressure of events, although they never strayed from the essentially liberal path. In cultural life, too, the Jews worked in partner-ship with non-Jews in evolving new values to replace the broken world of the nineteenth century. By 1930, this transition to the typical was well under way. It was perhaps the last possible moment for extremist demagogues to write "Out With The Jews!" on the banner of a mass political movement.

III

Anti-Semitism

The charges that Jews ran the German economy, manipulated anti-German political movements, and fostered decadent cultural trends were patently false. That these accusations were believed wholly or partially by millions of Germans has prompted scholars to seek the roots of anti-Semitism in abnormal psychology. The most common of these explanations, the scapegoat (or displacement) theory, seeks to identify sources of stress that induce individuals to abandon reason and personify their troubles in Jewish form. Hardly a new theory, it goes back at least as far as an 1894 book by an Austrian Jewish Social Democrat, Hermann Bahr, whose obsession with the psychology of anti-Semitism led him to neglect the social and economic ramifications of prejudice.[1] The theory reappeared frequently, with varying degrees of sophistication, during the Weimar years.[2] More recently it has found vogue in group studies of prejudice by social psychologists.[3]

The most successful post-Holocaust reassessment of the psychological roots of anti-Semitism was made by Eva Reichmann, a German Jewish sociologist and journalist. She differentiated between the relatively harmless "objective Jewish question," which pits majority demands for social homogeneity against Jewish separatism, and the potentially explosive "subjective Jewish question," which has its roots in latent personal aggressiveness and group tensions that await only suitable conditions to reach the flash point. The Nazi revolt against the "mythical Jew" unfettered the Germans' primitive impulses against a civilization that seemed to have failed them.[4]

A less overtly Freudian analysis of nineteenth-century anti-Semitism was

1. Hermann Bahr, *Der Antisemitismus* (Berlin, 1894).
2. See, for example, Erich Kuttner, *Pathologie des Rassenantisemitismus* (Berlin, 1930); F. Bernstein, *Der Antisemitismus als Gruppenerscheinung: Versuch einer Soziologie des Judenhasses* (Berlin, 1926); R. N. Coudenhove-Kalergi, *Das Wesen des Antisemitismus* (Vienna and Leipzig, 1929).
3. The classic study of this kind is Bruno Bettelheim and Morris Janowitz, *Dynamics of Prejudice* (New York, 1950).
4. Eva G. Reichmann, *Hostages of Civilisation: The Social Sources of National Socialist Anti-Semitism* (London, 1950).

made by the German sociologist Eleanore Sterling. She postulated the essential continuity of medieval and modern anti-Semitism by finding in the latter a secularized and politicized variation of the former. Jews remained devils to powerless and exploited people of unsophisticated social and political awareness. Their prejudices were fanned by conservatives and reactionaries who blamed the Jews for liberalism, and both for the people's torments. More speculatively, she argued that the Jews became a special target for hatred because their unhappy history mirrored the sufferings of mankind and their elimination symbolized the removal of mass misery.[5]

Critics of the psychological approach to anti-Semitism correctly point out that it offers insufficient insight into why the Jews were singled out for attack. Accordingly, they have concentrated their attention on Jewish conduct as a possible source of Judeophobia. Hannah Arendt's classic study, *The Origins of Totalitarianism,* offers a sweeping analysis of mass revolts against governments that failed to provide security for their citizens, and against the Jews, who had become conspicuously associated with those regimes. Economically overprivileged but politically powerless, the Jews became the objects of universal hatred and contempt as the nation-states with which they were identified disintegrated after 1914. Arendt's thesis promises to remain controversial, but since its appearance it has been harder to deny all Jewish responsibility for anti-Semitism and to avoid specific historical analysis of both the Jews and their enemies.[6]

The conservative German Jewish theologian Hans-Joachim Schoeps has placed even more emphasis than does Arendt on Jewish behavior as a source of antipathy. He has noted that Hebrew religious tradition encouraged a narcissistic self-image and a tendency to self-isolation and indifference to Gentile sensibilities.[7] Where Jews were more nearly assimilated, this problem seldom arose, but in Germany, where society as a whole was somewhat backward compared to most Western European countries, the Jews were in an awkward and exposed stage of development, halfway between the ghetto and full

5. Eleonore Sterling, *Judenhass: Die Anfänge des politischen Antisemitismus in Deutschland (1815–1850)* (Rev. ed.; Frankfurt-am-Main, 1969) especially 12–19, 71–72, 168–69. Originally published as *Er ist wie du: Aus der Frühgeschichte des Antisemitismus in Deutschland 1815–1850* (Munich, 1956).

6. Hannah Arendt, *The Origins of Totalitarianism* (Rev. ed.; New York, 1966), 3–120. Golo Mann's useful study of anti-Semitism is typical of recent efforts to balance the psychological approach with social and political understandings: *Der Antisemitismus: Wurzeln, Wirkung und Überwindung* (Munich and Frankfurt-am-Main, 1960), 10–28.

7. Hans-Joachim Schoeps, *Unbewältige Geschichte: Stationen deutschen Schicksals seit 1763* (Berlin, 1964), 206–207.

membership in the larger society.[8] Munich Zionist Rahel Straus indirectly lent support to Schoeps' analysis when she pointedly included in her memoirs the story of a young Italian Jewish diplomat in Germany during the Weimar years who exclaimed, when informed that most young German Jews routinely learned Hebrew during religious instruction in the public schools, that at last he understood why anti-Semitism was a problem in Germany: it arose from an education that taught Jews to regard themselves as separate and different, unlike that in Italy.[9]

Neither the psychology of anti-Semites nor the conduct of Jews satisfies Marxist historians, for whom Judeophobia takes on meaning only in terms of the class struggle. A fine study of anti-Semitism in Imperial Germany by Paul Massing, a former member of the German Communist party, stresses the economic grievances of downwardly mobile elements of the middle class.[10] Behind the iron curtain, however, the infrequent considerations of anti-Semitism reveal the heavy hand of Marxist-Leninist dogma. Recently East German historian Walter Mohrmann defined Judeophobia onesidedly as "a means of integrating the German people into the struggle against Communism" and faulted the Jews of the Weimar Republic for supporting an economic and political system that was "certain" to turn against them.[11] In West Germany left-wing historian Hans-Joachim Bieber has similarly argued that anti-Semitism was a tool used by reactionaries to manipulate the masses; he equates its use in the Weimar years with the more recent use of anti-communism by a revived political right.[12]

Fortunately, none of these interpretations needs to be embraced as exclusively as some of their proponents might wish. An understanding of German anti-Semitism requires appreciation both of the psychological torments produced by a troubled society and of the vulnerable position that the Jews held in it. Nor can it be denied that some politicians cynically employed anti-Jewish appeals to hitch voters to the political right. However, no considera-

8. *Cf.* Meir Gilon (ed.), *Perspectives of German-Jewish History in the 19th and 20th Century* (Jerusalem, 1971), 20–22, 30.

9. Rahel Straus, *Wir lebten in Deutschland: Erinnerungen einer deutschen Jüdin 1880–1933* (Stuttgart, 1961), 270–71.

10. Massing, *Rehearsal for Destruction.*

11. Walter Mohrmann, *Antisemitismus: Ideologie und Geschichte im Kaiserreich und in der Weimarer Republik* (Berlin, 1972).

12. Hans-Joachim Bieber, "Zur bürgerlichen Geschichtsschreibung und Publizistik über Antisemitismus, Zionismus und den Staat Israel," *Das Argument*, Nr. 75 (1972), 231–74. For a more detailed examination of scholarly research on the subject of anti-Semitism, see Rürup, *Emanzipation und Antisemitismus*, 115–25.

tion of the Jews' conduct and role should suggest that different behavior during the Weimar years would have altered the outcome in any significant way. By 1919 the "mythical Jew" was already an established figure in the minds of those who chose to believe in him. Had the Jews succeeded in attaining perfection itself, they would only have been denounced for yet another demonic plot. Nor should there be too much reliance on the "manipulation of the masses" theme. Not only does it shed little light on why the masses were prepared to be led in a particular direction, but it begs the question of whether anti-Semitism per se was particularly successful in leading them anywhere.

During the early years of the Weimar Republic, anti-Semitism was spread by a variety of small organizations that rarely cooperated and occasionally quarreled. The most important and active of them, the "German *Völkisch* League for Defense and Defiance" (Deutsch-Völkischer Schutz- und Trutz-Bund),[13] was created in February, 1919, by leaders of the Pan-German League, which had been established twenty-five years earlier by supernationalist elements to spur the Kaiser on to a more belligerent foreign policy. The Pan-German League had always been more or less anti-Jewish; in 1912 its chairman, Heinrich Class, had, under a pseudonym, published a book urging Kaiser Wilhelm to recognize that Jews were a dangerous and unassimilable race and therefore ought to be stripped of their citizenship and restricted in their economic activities.[14] After the war Class shrewdly maximized the drawing power of anti-Semitism by creating this new organization, formally free from association with the old imperialism and distinguishable from its rivals, for the moment at least, by the swastika emblem. However, Class and the Pan-Germans, with their excellent sources of support from German industry generously financed the League for Defense and Defiance. Money and the talented propaganda of Alfred Roth, the league's moving spirit, helped to bring about a membership of nearly 110,000 in 250 local branches by 1920, partially as the result of its having absorbed a variety of tiny local racist organizations. At the time of its dissolution by government order following the 1922 assassination by racist fanatics of Germany's Jewish foreign minister, Walther Rathenau, it membership exceeded 200,000.[15]

13. The German adjective *völkisch* cannot satisfactorily be translated into a single English word. At once it conveys a sense of nationalism and racial purity combined with a romantic notion of the collective genius of the common people, and it is therefore used in its German form on these pages.
14. Daniel Frymann, *Wenn ich der Kaiser wär'* (Leipzig, 1912).
15. Friedrich Andersen, *Zur religiösen Erneuerung des deutschen Volkes* (Hamburg,

The League for Defense and Defiance, although by far the largest and best organized of the anti-Jewish groups in the early years of the Republic, never managed to bring all such organizations under its wings. In Leipzig, veteran Jew-baiter Theodor Fritsch represented a direct link to prewar anti-Semitism as head of the 600-member "Community of German Renewal." Its influence was far greater than its small size suggests, for its "Hammer Press" put out great quantities of anti-Jewish literature, most notably Fritsch's *Handbook of the Jewish Question*.[16] Alfred Brunner's German Socialist party combined anti-Catholicism and anti-Semitism to win over radicals dissatisfied with the "moderation" of the League for Defense and Defiance. Its Nuremberg leader, Julius Streicher, was later to become the most fanatical of the Nazi Jew-haters.[17] And, of course, there was a small party of militants in Bavaria that called itself the National Socialist German Workers' party (Nationalsozialistische deutsche Arbeiterpartei) headed by one Adolf Hitler. These and at least a dozen other small *völkisch* groups, envious of the size and fearful of the domination of the League for Defense and Defiance, frequently attacked it as infiltrated by those well-known secret allies of the Jews, the Freemasons.[18]

Even while quarreling among themselves, the *völkisch* bands shared common grievances against the Jews, chief of which was their alleged lack of patriotism. In 1919, Alfred Roth, writing under the pseudonym Otto Armin, published a highly unflattering statistical analysis of Jewish participation in the German armed services during the World War. It was based on the questionable, but supposedly still secret, figures gathered in the 1916 Jewish census and leaked to Roth by General Ernst von Wrisberg, wartime director of the General Affairs Division of the Prussian war ministry and a known anti-Semite. They purported to show that a considerably smaller percentage of Jews than non-Jews had served at the front lines and that the percentage of Jewish war dead was less than half as great as the overall figure. Roth con-

---

1920); Alfred Kruck, *Geschichte des Alldeutschen Verbandes 1890–1939* (Wiesbaden, 1954), 130–97; Uwe Lohalm, *Völkischer Radikalismus: Die Geschichte der Deutschvölkischen Schutz- und Trutz-Bundes 1919–1923* (Hamburg, 1970); Jochmann, "Die Ausbreitung des Antisemitismus," 448–86.

16. Reginald H. Phelps, "Theodor Fritsch und der Antisemitismus," *Deutsche Rundschau*, May, 1961, pp. 442–49; Theodor Fritsch, *Handbuch der Judenfrage: Die wichtige Tatsachen zur Beurteilung des jüdischen Volkes* (Rev. ed.; Leipzig, 1931). By 1931 the *Handbuch*, which had first appeared in 1887 as *Antisemiten-Katechismus*, had gone through thirty editions and sold more than seventy-six thousand copies.

17. Manfred Rühl, *"Der Stürmer und sein Herausgeber"* (Diplom-Volkswirt, Hochschule für Wirtschafts- und Sozialwissenschaften in Nürnberg, 1960), 42–45.

18. Lohalm, *Völkischer Radikalismus*, 255–60.

cluded that Jews had used their decisive influence in the war ministry to get phony medical discharges or behind-the-lines assignments.[19] His allegations formed the basis of repeated charges that Jews had shown their true colors by shirking their patriotic duty in the war. They found their crassest expression in a joke told by a right-wing veterans' publication: a field hospital for Jews was established near the front lines, beautifully equipped with the latest medical gear and an all-Jewish staff. After waiting for eight weeks it treated its first patient, who arrived shrieking with pain because a typewriter had fallen on his foot.[20]

The Jews' alleged willingness to fight for revolutionary, if not for German, causes was linked to their fundamental racial otherness in postwar anti-Semitic agitation. Again the League for Defense and Defiance set the tone. It portrayed the Jews as filled with hatred for every Gentile because they had been deprived of their homeland. Their inability to feel a true sense of Teutonic patriotism had made it simple for them to thrust a foreign system upon Germany; the Weimar government was a Jewish republic. The Germans, inherently good-hearted and tolerant, had allowed pity for the Jews' tragic fate to blind them temporarily. But they could be pushed only so far before striking back. Zionism, on the other hand, earned enthusiastic endorsement for its supposed acknowledgment of the permanent immiscibility of Germans and Jews.[21]

Economic themes were also underlined in the millions of pamphlets and thousands of meetings sponsored by the *völkisch* groups. Accelerating inflation and shortages of essential goods were attributed to Jewish capitalists, as were the astronomical reparations demanded by the Versailles treaty. Occasionally such charges sparked the looting of Jewish shops. Special targets were the Eastern Jews, who were held responsible for taking scarce jobs and apartments and were accused of engaging in shady business deals. They were to be expelled, and Jews who were German citizens would lose their citizenship and be placed in temporary "protective custody."[22]

19. Otto Armin, *Die Juden im Heere: Eine statistische Untersuchung nach amtlichen Quellen* (Munich, 1919), 17–46; Ernst von Wrisberg, *Heer und Heimat, 1914–1918* (2 vols.; Leipzig, 1921), II, 93–95; Oppenheimer, *Die Judenstatistik,* 4–45.

20. *Der Schild,* IV, February 1, 1925.

21. Deutschvölkischer Schutz- und Trutzbund, *Sigfried und Ahasver* (Hamburg, 1919), 2–7.

22. *Mitteilungen aus dem Verein zur Abwehr des Antisemitismus,* July 24, 1919; *Israelitisches Familienblatt,* August 18, 1921; C. B., "Der deutsche Schutz- und Trutzbund," *Mitteilung aus dem Verein zur Abwehr des Antisemitismus,* May 14, 1919; *Jüdische Rundschau,* May 9, 1922. Propaganda against Eastern Jews may have been less effective than the racists intended. A "Nonpartisan Association for a Referendum to Solve the Jewish Ques-

Racist agitation also attempted to rekindle latent religious hatred for Jews by picturing them as implacable enemies of Christian values. No one was more diligent at this task than the League for Defense and Defiance activist, Friedrich Andersen, the pastor of Flensburg's principal Evangelical church, St. John's. Andersen drew a sharp line between the Christian and Hebrew religions and between the New and Old Testaments. The God of the Israelites, Yahweh of the Old Testament, was a tribal god who taught egoism and materialism. Hence Jews sought to emasculate Christians, attacking their religion with secular philosophies and their sense of racial identity with internationalism. Neither Christ nor the Christian God was Jewish, but rather the source of an otherworldly, idealistic religion and the savior of all mankind.[23] Theodor Fritsch, while affirming that Jesus was indeed a Jew, pictured him as a rebel against a dangerously ossified Mosaic ritual.[24]

While competing for new converts to the racist cause, the anti-Semites rarely felt the need to form their own political party in the early years of the Weimar Republic. The German Nationalist People's party (Deutschnationale Volkspartei—Nationalists, for short) welcomed them with open arms. Formed shortly after the end of the World War as a coalition of most of the reactionary elements in Germany, the old Conservatives and anti-Semites prominent among them, it formed until 1930 the only far right-wing party of any size. From the beginning *völkisch* elements made up a sizable, but by no means dominant, wing of the party. Even racists who chose to remain outside its ranks nonetheless sent votes to the Nationalists, preferring to unite behind a party with a chance of making a significant impact on political life. In 1919 the party obliged them by adopting a carefully worded endorsement of anti-Semitism which, as slightly revised for its 1920 statement of principles, called for efforts to strengthen Germany by eliminating "every destructive, un-German spirit, whether originating from Jewish or other circles. We emphatically reject the predominance of Jewry in government and public life, which since the revolution has become increasingly ominous. The influx of aliens across our borders is to be cut off."[25] Also, with rare exceptions, the

---

tion," founded in the summer of 1924 for the express purpose of placing expulsion of the Eastern Jews on the ballot, never got off the ground, even though it was relatively easy to bring about referenda under the Weimar Constitution. *Der Israelit*, August 7, 1924.

23. Friedrich Andersen, *Weckruf an die evangelischen Geistlichen in Deutschland* (Hamburg, 1920); Andersen, *Zur religiösen Erneuerung*; Andersen, *Der deutsche Heiland* (Munich, 1921).

24. Fritsch, *Handbuch der Judenfrage*, 62–64, 109–124.

25. Quoted in Werner Liebe, *Die Deutschnationale Volkspartei 1918–1924* (Düsseldorf, 1956), 115.

Nationalists refused to place Jews on their lists of candidates for election to public office.[26]

On the other hand, the Nationalists refused to bow to *völkisch* demands to expel Jews from the party. In fact, most Nationalist leaders were relatively moderate on the Jewish question. They shared *völkisch* prejudices but were unwilling to give them preeminence or to entertain thoughts of violent actions against the Jews. Indeed, there were always a few Nationalists who specifically repudiated anti-Semitism.[27] However, when tension arose between the moderate majority and the *völkisch* zealots it was not over Judeophobia per se but over the issues of respectability and party discipline. Racists such as Wilhelm Henning, Reinhard Wulle, and Albrecht von Gräfe-Goldebee gave the party a bad name by pushing for revolution against the "Jewish Republic," whereas the moderates increasingly longed to become a mass party of the right, acceptable as a partner in ruling coalitions, rather than remain an impotent sect with one foot in the lunatic fringe. Early in 1921, dissatisfaction among radical anti-Semites with party moderation on the Jewish question prompted several of them to secede, most notably Richard Kunze, better known as "Knüppel Kunze" after his constant companion, a rubber truncheon that he used to settle "intellectual arguments." Kunze formed his own German Social party (Deutschsoziale Partei), which made an issue of supposed Jewish influence in the old imperial government to distinguish itself from the Nationalists, who favored restoration of the monarchy.[28] Racists who remained part of the Nationalist party flouted the principle of strict party unity by announcing plans to form a separate *völkisch* organization within the party. Its purpose would be to push for a tougher party line against the Jews and for the formal exclusion of Jews from the party.

The issue of *völkisch* radicalism in the Nationalist party came to a head as a result of the huge public outcry that followed Walther Rathenau's assassination in June, 1922. The party leadership ordered the radical racists to curtail their anti-Jewish agitation and underlined its displeasure with them by dropping Henning, who had been the loudest critic of Rathenau, from the party's national committee. The radicals refused to bow to party discipline, and they resigned en masse when the moderates stuck to their guns at a party congress in October, 1922. Immediately thereafter they formed the German *Völkisch*

26. *Mitteilungen aus dem Verein zur Abwehr des Antisemitismus,* June 12, 1920; Liebe, *Deutschnationale Volkspartei,* 64–65.

27. *Israelitisches Familienblatt,* June 26, 1919; Scherbel, "Ein deutschnationaler Führer gegen den Antisemitismus," *Allgemeine Zeitung des Judentums,* October 15, 1920; *Mitteilungen aus dem Verein zur Abwehr des Antisemitismus,* February 9, 1921.

28. *Mitteilungen aus dem Verein zur Abwehr des Antisemitismus,* March 19, 1921.

Freedom Party (Deutschvölkische Freiheitspartei), which for a time vied successfully with Kunze's German Social party, often in close cooperation with the Nazis.[29]

Given the stressful conditions in Germany from 1919 through 1923—attempted *Putsche* from both right and left, a harsh peace treaty, runaway inflation, widespread unemployment, and French occupation of the Ruhr—it is perhaps surprising that the response to passionate anti-Jewish appeals was not more enthusiastic. The entire anti-Semitic vote (including the votes for the Nationalists, who were hardly a one-issue party) never exceeded 8 percent of the total.[30] Nor was there much violence against Jews. With the exception of the murder of a Jew by racists in 1920, physical attacks on ordinary Jews were rare.[31] Occasionally racist agitators were able to convince mobs to attack and loot the shops of Jewish tradesmen accused of hoarding essential goods, but as often as not such riots were aimed at non-Jewish shopkeepers as well.

Reports of such isolated riots increased during the summer and autumn of 1923 as the German currency faltered and finally collapsed.[32] The most serious of them occurred in Berlin on the fifth and sixth of November. A great crowd had gathered in front of the Central Labor Office, lured by rumors that unemployment subsidies were to be distributed there and enraged over the six-fold increase in the price of a loaf of bread to 140,000,000 marks. When no money was forthcoming, anti-Semitic agitators lifted the cry that it had been given to "the Galicians" instead. With that, a mob of 30,000 descended upon the "Scheuneviertel" in Berlin's central district where a great many Eastern Jews lived and maintained shops. For two days Jewish passersby and shopkeepers were beaten, and nearly a thousand Jewish-owned stores were looted. The police, many of whom regarded Eastern Jews as a major source of criminal and Communist elements and hence held them in no high esteem, reacted slowly but eventually made hundreds of arrests and brought the situation under control.[33]

29. Lewis Hertzman, *DNVP: Right-Wing Opposition in the Weimar Republic, 1918–1924* (Lincoln, Neb., 1963), 124–64.

30. Reached in the Reichstag elections of May 4, 1924. The racist vote declined dramatically in the second Reichstag elections held on December 7 of that year, when it failed to reach 5 percent of the votes.

31. *Jüdische Rundschau*, March 12, 1920.

32. Sch-r [Arthur Schweriner], "Dunkle Tage," *Central-Verein Zeitung*, November 23, 1923; *ibid.*, December 13, 1923; *Der Israelit*, October 18, 1923.

33. *Frankfurter Zeitung*, November 7, 1923; *Jüdische Rundschau*, November 9, 1923; *ibid.*, May, 1924; *Mitteilungen aus dem Verein zur Abwehr des Antisemitismus*, June 10, 1924.

By the end of 1924, at which time the Germany economy was well on the road to recovery and the Weimar Republic was growing increasingly stable, the radical anti-Semites could claim few successes. Their enormous propaganda effort had brought them hundreds of thousands of new converts, but it had failed to win over the great masses of Germans. The one important political party that once had offered them a home had thrown them out, and, as renewed prosperity and stability shoved the Jewish question further and further into the background, surviving racists deserted their parties and sects to huddle around the charismatic leadership of Adolf Hitler in the Nazi movement. Attempts in 1925 by returned German-Americans to found a German version of the Ku Klux Klan, the "Order of the Fiery Cross," fell flat.[34] By 1930 even megalomaniac Richard Kunze had gone over the Hitlerites; the few diehard holdouts languished for want of a following.[35] The Nationalists retained the anti-Jewish plank in their platform but seldom made an issue of it. Still, their old ambivalence remained. They were only too willing to haul out racist appeals when competing with the "Freedom Party" in the Eastern provinces in 1924 or with the Nazis after 1930.[36] On the other hand, at least one voice was raised against anti-Semitism from within the party as late as 1932.[37]

After 1930, radical anti-Semitism was a virtual monopoly of the Nazis, who used it in their brilliant propaganda campaign as they exploited the depression and fears of bolshevism in order to rise from a small sectarian party to one that held absolute power. Judeophobia always had been an important component of National Socialist ideology, partly because it was one of the most potent ideas on the extreme political right after World War I, but also because Hitler believed in it passionately. The sources of his antipathy for Jews will probably never be known in any final sense, but there seems no reason to doubt his own statement that it stemmed from his years in Vienna (1908–1913). The young, down-and-out Hitler, searching for the reasons why the world ignored his artistic talents, delved deeply into whatever anti-Jewish literature he could find. By September, 1919, when he joined the tiny

34. A. Schweriner, "Die unterirdische Gefahr," *Central-Verein Zeitung*, September 18, 1925; *Mitteilungen aus dem Verein zur Abwehr des Antisemitismus*, September 20, 1925.

35. *Mitteilungen aus dem Verein zur Abwehr des Antisemitismus*, February 21, 1928, April, 1930, November/December, 1930.

36. *Central-Verein Zeitung*, February 21, 1924; Ludwig Holländer, "Peinliches Zwischenspiel im Rundfunk," *ibid.*, May 6, 1932.

37. Friedrich von Oppeln-Bronikowski, *Gerechtigkeit! Zur Lösung der Judenfrage* (Berlin, 1932); Arnold Paucker, "*Gerechtigkeit!* The Fate of a Pamphlet on the Jewish Question," *Leo Baeck Institute Yearbook*, VIII (1963), 238–45.

band that was to become the Nazi party, he was a convinced Jew-hater. His early statements on the Jewish question insisted upon a "rational" anti-Semitism, which he defined negatively as the opposite of pogroms, but during and after his incarceration following the disastrous Beer Hall *Putsch* of 1923, he used increasingly violent language that likened Jews to vermin and parasites.[38]

There was nothing new in Nazi anti-Semitism. It simply repeated all the well-known charges. The Nazi program of February, 1920, known as the "Twenty-five Points," established the party line on the Jewish question that was to remain unchanged throughout the Weimar years. Point Four demanded an end to Jewish civil rights; Point Five, removal of citizenship for Jews; Point Six, denial of the right of Jews to hold public office; and Point Seven, their deportation should the lives of German citizens be threatened by the presence of aliens. These, however, were only the minimum Nazi goals, and they were expanded upon from time to time. A Nazi statement on the Jewish question in 1931 added to the old demands the systematic removal of Jews from economic and cultural life and the designation of miscegenation between Jews and non-Jews as a major crime. It also hinted that the way Jews would be treated in the coming Third Reich would depend largely on whether or not foreign Jews tried to sabotage it.[39] Although leading Nazis never explicitly endorsed the murder of Jews, that final solution was proposed indirectly, especially at lower levels of the party. An analogy that frequently appeared in Nazi propaganda compared Jews to fleas. The flea, which sucks the blood of useful beasts, is not spared although it is, after all, an animal, too; the Jew is indeed a human being, but he is to be treated like a vampire that devours human blood.[40] A Nazi speaker in Nüdlingen, Bavaria, put the threat more bluntly: "When we have the power, the gentlemen [Jews] will have a shovel pressed into their hands so that they can dig a hole that is long or broad or deep, depending on whether they prefer to sit or stand or lie in it. Then one of us will step up, take the shovel, hit him on the head so that it splits right down the middle. Into the hole, earth on top. That's all—the end! Next, please!"[41]

38. Adolf Hitler, *Mein Kampf,* trans. R. Manheim (Boston, 1943), 21, 51–61; Eberhard Jäckel, *Hitler's Weltanschauung: A Blueprint for Power* (Middletown, Conn., 1972), 47–66.

39. Gerbard L. Binz, "Das Judentum in der nat.-soz. Rechtsordnung," *Völkischer Beobachter,* January 28, 1931.

40. Rei. [Hans Reichmann], "Der Jude ist auch ein Mensch!" *Central-Verein Zeitung,* September 23, 1927.

41. *Mitteilungen aus dem Verein zur Abwehr des Antisemitismus,* April, 1932.

Leading Nazis, on the contrary, were more inclined to make comparatively mild statements about Nazi plans for the Jews. Early in 1930, Hitler was asked by an American reporter to comment on his anti-Semitism. He replied that his party did not plan to deny rights to Jews and that it used anti-Jewish phrases because they were expected by the voters.[42] Two years later, and again shortly after Hitler became chancellor, Hermann Göring reiterated the 1920 party program on the Jewish question but added that honest Jewish businessmen would enjoy the full protection of the law.[43] Gregor Strasser said much the same thing in a radio address in June, 1932, stating that the Nazi goal was to restore leadership to Germans, not to persecute Jews.[44]

Not only was Nazi policy on the Jews inconsistent, but it was also mercurial, leaving an impression of opportunism and insincerity. At times National Socialist comment consisted primarily of passing ritual denunciations of the "Jewish press" or "Jewish Marxism."[45] At other times anti-Semitism was employed much more intensively. A statistical analysis of the two major Nazi periodicals, the *Völkischer Beobachter* and *Der Angriff,* made for the six-day period September 5–10, 1932, revealed that together they used the term "Jew" in one form or another 211 times, most commonly in generally demeaning terms, but often in the context of highly specific attacks.[46] Since it was difficult to determine exactly where the Nazis stood on the Jewish question or how important the issue was to them, it was impossible for anyone to anticipate with certainty what, if anything, the Nazis intended to do to the Jews.

Partly because the Nazi stand on anti-Semitism was shifting and unclear, it is far from easy to assess the importance of anti-Semitism as a determinant of Nazi success. The opinions of historians range from those of Golo Mann, who considers it to be of only slight significance, to George Mosse, who thinks it was the key to mass support for the Nazis.[47] Some sense of the distri-

42. *Central-Verein Zeitung,* March 7, 1930, October 24, 1930.
43. *Jüdische Rundschau,* May 31, 1932; *Israelitisches Familienblatt,* March 9, 1933.
44. Eva Jungmann-Reichmann, "Wir fragen," *Central-Verein Zeitung,* June 24, 1932.
45. However, Golo Mann's assertion that anti-Semitic attacks virtually disappeared from Nazi propaganda during the 1930 Reichstag election campaign is not supported by an examination of the official Hitlerite organ, the *Völkischer Beobachter.* During the six-week period from early August to September 14, it made no fewer than twenty-four attacks on the Jews, at least ten of which may be characterized as specific and substantial. Mann, *Der Antisemitismus,* 33. Cf. the word-frequency analysis of twenty-eight Nazi election pamphlets for the 1930 Reichstag election in David A. Hackett, "The Nazi Party in the Reichstag Election of 1930" (Ph.D. dissertation, University of Wisconsin, 1971), 283–85, 290–91.
46. R. Horlacher, "Eine 'Juden'—Statistik," *Mitteilungen aus dem Verein zur Abwehr des Antisemitismus,* XLII (1932), 183–87.
47. Mann, *Der Antisemitismus,* 32–33; George L. Mosse, *The Crisis of German Ideology: Intellectual Origins of the Third Reich* (New York, 1964), 298–99.

bution and intensity of Judeophobia in Weimar Germany may be had from an examination of some of the principal groups and institutions in German society: churches, universities, political parties, and various units and organs of government. Such an examination may also provide clues to the nature of whatever anti-Semitism may have existed there. Thus far most of our attention has been focused on the radical Jew-baiters, those for whom the Jewish question was a leading issue and who wished, at the very least, to turn German Jews into resident aliens. But they had no monopoly on anti-Jewish prejudice. Moderate anti-Semites generally regarded the issue as a marginal one and usually repudiated depriving Jews of civil rights or subjecting them to violence; Thomas Mann sarcastically described this as "cultured anti-Semitism" (*Bildungsantisemitismus*). Hence our enquiry will delve into both the quantity and the quality of anti-Semitism in Weimar Germany.

It is sometimes suggested that in the modern world racial anti-Semitism has replaced the older religious prejudices. In fact, a great many Germans still took religion most seriously in the Weimar years, and the Christian churches spawned much of the Judeophobia of the time. Traditional religious prejudices were reflected in popular superstitions and aphorisms that remained current, especially in rural and small-town Germany. In Franconia there were still those who believed that Jews buried their dead with sacks of stones to hurl at Christ in the next world, and that they killed any friend or relative who might die on the Sabbath and thereby bring shame upon his survivors. In East Frisia, ne'er-do-wells were still described as being "as lost as the soul of a Jew." There, too, one could still hear the doggerel verse "*Jöden und Menisten bedrägen alle Kristen*"—"Jews and Mennonites deceive all Christians."[48] These rather quaint religious antipathies might have remained latent and harmless had it not been for the apprehensive reactions of both Protestant and Catholic clergymen to the politics and culture of the day, and the willingness of a minority of them to identify the Israelite faith as a major carrier of the materialistic bacillus.

A fairly typical statement of this point of view appeared in a 1925 essay by the Jesuit Erich Przywara, who argued that Jews denied Christ's divinity because their religion taught them to look for the eternal working out of God's will in a world in which there can be no perfection. Hence Judaism fostered a this-worldly religion that effectively dethroned God and put man in His place.

48. Jakob Blum, "Juden im Volksaberglauben," *Central-Verein Zeitung*, December 13, 1929; Max Markreich, "Die Juden in Ostfriesland. Zweige sephardischen und askenasischen Judentums 1348–1945" (Typescript in Leo Baeck Institute Archives, New York), 6.

Whereas Orthodox Jews held fast to antiquated laws, Przywara believed that most Western European Jews became restless strivers after secular ideals that placed them eternally in conflict with those who were at peace with themselves. These secularisms, in reality substitute messianisms, included capitalism, socialism, neo-Kantianism, and a variety of relativisms. Anti-Semitism arose ineluctably as "the necessary destiny of Ahasuras for the people that has put itself in the place of the transcendental God." That would remain their fate until one day God would save all of Israel, ending the tragic history of the Jews.[49]

Similar arguments were offered on the Protestant side. In 1930, Adolf Schlatter, professor of theology at the University of Tübingen, advanced the opinion that Judaism was a religion of laws rather than of salvation through grace. Hebrew law made man the measure of all things and, by implication, the ruler of all things. Hence Jews treated God's creation as something to be used rather than as an object of reverence. The rationalistic humanism of Spinoza and the materialistic determinism of Marx in different ways expressed the fundamental secularism of Judaism. To combat it, Christians must lead the Jews to Christ.[50]

The Christian social ethic having been set over against the supposedly materialistic spirit of Jewry, it was but a small step for right-wing Christians to equate the defense of the former with the maintenance of a conservative political order and with opposition to the Jews. In 1920, Bishop von Ow of Passau excused anti-Semitism as a means of defending Germany against "certain manifestations among the Jews."[51] Later a Protestant pastor apologized for the desecration of Jewish graves by anti-Semites as a means of protesting against such "un-German" phenomena as Arnold Zweig's war novel, *The Case of Sergeant Grischa.*[52] As late as 1931, during a discussion of the Jewish question among Württemberg Protestant clergymen, one Pastor Hilzinger expressed concern over the "destructive influence" of irreligious Jews on the press, literature, and sexual ethics, and he concluded that it was perhaps unfair to associate nazism with radical anti-Semitism.[53] There were even a few

49. Erich Przywara, "Judentum und Christentum," *Stimmen der Zeit,* III (1926), 81–99. For a reply to Przywara's argument, see Max Dienemann, "Judentum und jüdische Religionsphilosophie im Urteil heutiger Katholiken," *Der Morgen,* II (1926), 57–70.

50. Adolf Schlatter, *Wir Christen und die Juden* (Velbert-im-Rheinland, 1930), 6–21.

51. *Mitteilungen aus dem Verein zur Abwehr des Antisemitismus,* June 29, 1920. *Cf.* Hermann Greive, *Theologie und Ideologie: Katholizismus und Judentum in Deutschland und Österreich 1918–1935* (Heidelberg, 1969), 33–52.

52. Wilhelm Michel, "Kampf gegen Gräber," *Der Morgen,* III (1927), 423–25.

53. *Mitteilungen aus dem Verein zur Abwehr des Antisemitismus,* May, 1931. See also M.

attempts to revive Stöcker's dream of destroying socialism and reuniting the workers and Christianity by means of anti-Jewish appeals, such as this 1921 outburst by Father Elpidius of the Catholic Workers' Association in Essen: "We ask you, you despisers of Christianity and of Priests—why do you place big Jewish capitalists under your protection? I will tell you: because your founders, Marx and Lassalle, were Jews and important capitalists, because your leaders are mostly Jews. . . . The half million Jews already possess the greatest part of our national wealth."[54]

Even when condemning the anti-Christian aspects of radical racism, Christian spokesmen occasionally endorsed a more moderate version of anti-Semitism. The Franciscan theologian Father Erhard Schlund advised his readers to shun *völkisch* extremists, but he added:

> The patriotic Catholic in the anti-Semitic movement will also analyze matters clearly. He will unite with the anti-Semites in sorrow over the constantly increasing influence of Jewry, especially in Germany, and in the wish to see that influence steadily diminished. Above all, he will deplore and counteract the avaricious struggle for money and material goods, the domination of financial matters, the destructive influence of the Jews on religion, morals, literature, art, and in political and social life. He will always be aware that the Jews are an alien race. But he will not go so far as to combat the Jews and work for their expulsion because of their race alone, and still less will he reject the Old Testament. . . . Rather he will always remember that the Jewish people was God's chosen people and that as a Christian he is duty-bound always to do justice to the Jews, and to all human beings.[55]

Both Protestants and Catholics were inclined to be moderately critical of Jews, but Protestants proved to be more susceptible to penetration by radical racism. A tiny but active minority within the Evangelical church calling themselves "German Christians" attempted to expunge the Old Testament, deny Christ's Jewishness, and combine medieval hatred for the Jews with the new racialist anti-Semitism. Tolerated by the church hierarchy, it openly worked for a Nazi victory.[56] More dangerous was the dissemination of *völkisch* notions by trusted spiritual leaders. There were cases of pastors handing out anti-Jewish pamphlets to members of confirmation classes, or else urging

Spanier, "Eine unausrottbare Legende," *ibid.*, January 15, 1919; Greive, *Theologie und Ideologie,* 61–71.

54. *Mitteilungen aus dem Verein zur Abwehr des Antisemitismus,* December 25, 1921.

55. Erhard Schlund, *Katholizismus und Vaterland* (Munich, 1925), 72, quoted in Greive, *Theologie und Ideologie,* 64.

56. H. Falck, *Wie die Bibel entstand* (Berlin, 1932); Gerecke, *Biblischer Antisemitismus, passim;* Hans-Joachim Kraus, "Die Evangelische Kirche," in Mosse and Paucker (eds.), *Entscheidungsjahr 1932,* 254–56; 263–66.

them not to buy confirmation clothes or photographs from Jews. Occasionally church publications repeated the fantasies contained in the "Protocols of the Elders of Zion," while hateful comments about Jews could be heard from a few Protestant pulpits.[57] Contemporary Jewish observers were unanimous in the observation that anti-Semitism was more likely to be found among Evangelical Christians than in the Roman Catholic church.[58]

If moderate Judeophobia made it easier for Protestants to tolerate radical racism, its most pernicious result was to prepare some of them to endorse nazism. Consider the case of Wilhelm Stapel, the conservative Protestant editor of the monthly journal *Deutsches Volkstum*. Stapel belonged to those right-wing intellectuals who saw in the Jews a typical expression of the materialism and intellectualism that were draining life dry of imagination and instinctive feelings. That Jews were incapable of any genuine sense of German patriotism was proved by their inclination toward pacifism and socialism both during and after the World War. All of these differences were racially determined. But while heaping scorn on the "German Christians" for rejecting the Old Testament and the Jewishness of Christ, and repeatedly and specifically repudiating all forms of violence against the Jews, he rendered Nazi anti-Semitism harmless by asserting that racial issues and Christianity were utterly unrelated and congratulating the Nazis for their defense of "positive Christianity" and their opposition to Marxism.[59] In 1932, he listed his expectations of the Nazis on the Jewish question: ousting unpatriotic Jewish journalists; barring Jews from the armed forces (since, after all, no Jew should be forced to fight against his coreligionists in wartime); creating separate educational institutions and courts for the Jews.[60] In anticipating policies that fell short even of the comparatively mild 1920 Nazi program, Stapel, like so

57. *Mitteilungen aus dem Verein zur Abwehr des Antisemitismus,* October 30, 1919; *Israelitisches Familienblatt,* January 30, 1919; Jochmann, "Die Ausbreitung des Antisemitismus," 479–81.

58. Eduard Lamparter, "Die 'Verjudung' der evangel. Kirche," *Mitteilungen aus dem Verein zur Abwehr des Antisemitismus,* October 1, 1929; German Walch, "Ein 'katholisches Problem'?" *ibid.*, November 1, 1929; *Der Israelit,* May 12, 1932. Werner J. Cahnmann has recalled that when he visited the small Jewish communities of Bavaria as a representative of the Centralverein in the late Weimar period, he found that anti-Semitism was more intense in Lutheran than in Catholic areas. Cahnmann, "Die soziale Gliederung der Münchener jüdischen Gemeinde und ihre Wandlung," in Hans Lamm (ed.), *Von Juden in München: Ein Gedenkbuch* (Munich, 1959), 38–39.

59. Wilhelm Stapel, *Antisemitismus und Antigermanismus: Über das seelische Problem der Symbiose des deutschen und des jüdischen Volkes* (Hamburg, 1928); Wilhelm Stapel, *Sechs Kapitel über Christentum und Nationalsozialismus* (Hamburg and Berlin, 1931).

60. Wilhelm Stapel, "Versuch einer praktischen Lösung der Judenfrage," in Albrecht Erich Günther (ed.), *Was wir vom Nationalsozialismus erwarten* (Heilbronn, 1932), 186–91.

many other Germans, saw in National Socialism only what he wanted to see. It was precisely this kind of thinking that in 1931 led a bishop of the Evangelical church, Heinrich Rendtorff of Mecklenburg-Schwerin, to declare his support for nazism as a movement that promoted the idea of brotherhood![61]

By no means all Protestant leaders endorsed or excused anti-Semitism. On the contrary, a minority of them fought it energetically. For every radical racist, one might find someone like Pastor Eduard Lamparter of Stuttgart, a long-time foe of Judeophobia who retired in 1924 so that he could devote all of his energies to assisting the Association to Resist Anti-Semitism (Verein zur Abwehr des Antisemitismus), an organization founded by Gentiles in 1891 to help Jews defend themselves. As its most energetic figure in South Germany, Lamparter gave countless speeches and wrote at least two pamphlets against Judeophobia. Also prominent in the association was Kiel University theologian Otto Baumgarten, who likewise made lecture tours and wrote pamphlets. The association sent his 1926 "Cross and Swastika" to every Evangelical pastor in Germany. Another association activist was Paul Fiebig, professor of Protestant theology at the University of Leipzig, who specialized in defending the Old Testament and in giving the lie to charges that Jewish Holy Writ authorizes mistreatment of Gentiles. Königsberg University's highly respected Old Testament scholar Max Löhr, working quietly on his own, systematically defended the morality and high ethical teachings of the Jewish religion. Known to be a philo-Semite, he usually spent the High Holy Days in the local synagogue, where a special place was set aside for him.[62] Some pastors courageously took action against racist organizations, while others sermonized against anti-Semitism.[63] The Evangelical High Church Council publicly deplored the desecration of Jewish cemeteries, and in Oldenburg the provincial

61. *Jüdisch-liberale Zeitung*, June 10, 1931; *Der Israelit*, June 11, 1931.
62. Eduard Lamparter, *Evangelische Kirche und Judentum: Ein Beitrag zu christlichem Verständnis von Judentum und Antisemitismus* (Berlin, n.d.); Eduard Lamparter, *Das Judentum in seiner Kultur- und Religionsgeschichtlichen Erscheinung* (Gotha, 1928); *Mitteilungen aus dem Verein zur Abwehr des Antisemitismus*, November/December, 1930; Otto Baumgarten, *Kreuz und Hakenkreuz* (Gotha, 1926); H. Mulert, "Otto Baumgarten," *Mitteilungen aus dem Verein zur Abwehr des Antisemitismus*, February, 1933; Otto Baumgarten, *Meine Lebensgeschichte* (Tübingen, 1929), 367–68, 467, 475–86; Paul Fiebig, *Juden und Nichtjuden: Erläuterungen zu Th. Fritschs "Handbuch der Judenfrage"* (Leipzig, 1921); Paul Fiebig, *Wie stehen wir Christen zum Alten Testament? (Christentum und Judentum)* (Göttingen, 1926); Max Löhr, *Alttestamentliche Religions-Geschichte* (Rev. ed.; Berlin and Leipzig, 1930), 116–38; *Jüdische Rundschau*, October 6, 1931.
63. Ernst Möring, *Gegen völkischen Wahn* (Berlin, 1924); K. H., "Ein mannhaftes Bekenntnis," *Mitteilungen aus dem Verein zur Abwehr des Antisemitismus*, September 18, 1919; Ed. König, "Neue Hilfe im Kampf gegen Delitzsch," *Allgemeine Zeitung des Judentums*, November 25, 1921.

Evangelical church organization went on record against efforts to incite racial warfare.[64]

The antiracist record of the Roman Catholic church was rather more impressive. Although it was as much permeated with moderate anti-Semitism as the Evangelical church, it experienced fewer intrusions of radical Judeophobia. Partly because they were themselves a minority that once had been persecuted by the state, and partly because of their close associations with Catholic political parties that opposed the radical right, German Catholics were increasingly sensitive to the fundamentally anti-Christian nature of racism. This however, was more often the case after 1923 than in the early years of the Republic, and more so in the Rhineland than in Bavaria. Strong anti-Semitism was tolerated or encouraged by some Bavarian clergymen, partially as a result of the disastrous Bavarian Soviet Republic of 1919 and the subsequent anti-Berlin agitation. The situation in Bavaria, always complex, depended largely on local conditions—the attitude of the local priest and the cordiality, or lack of it, in relations between Catholics and their Jewish neighbors. But such provincial prejudices were, for the most part, kept out of statements directed at German Catholics as a whole. Only in the Paderborn journal *Leo* was the radical anti-Jewish banner raised.[65] Elsewhere it was rarely seen, particularly as the threat of left-wing revolution subsided and that from the right increased. Catholic resistance to racialism, encouraged by a 1928 papal decretal that excoriated anti-Semitism, reached its high point in 1930 when Bishop Hugo of Mainz banned members of the Nazi party from the sacraments.[66] Unhappily, no other German bishop followed his example.

Cardinal Faulhaber of Munich mirrored changing Catholic concerns. A conservative monarchist, Faulhaber in 1922 denounced the "Jewish press" for riding roughshod over the Eighth Commandment. But a year later, as the Bavarian government turned popular discontent against helpless Eastern Jews and as the Nazis took on increasingly formidable dimensions, he delivered a series of sermons that placed anti-Semitism and Christian love at opposite poles. His outspoken opposition to Judeophobia persisted through the Weimar period into the dark years beyond. The "Jewish Cardinal," as the Nazis called him, gave added meaning to his convictions by fostering cordial personal relations with Munich's Jewish community.[67]

64. *Jüdisch-liberale Zeitung,* December 29, 1928; *Central-Verein Zeitung,* December 3, 1932.
65. *Mitteilungen aus dem Verein zur Abwehr des Antisemitismus,* September 18, 1919; *ibid.,* March 6, 1920.
66. *Israelitisches Familienblatt,* October 16, 1930.
67. *Mitteilungen aus dem Verein zur Abwehr des Antisemitismus,* September 12, 1922;

Such personal concern was not uncommon among leading Catholics. In 1919 Bishop Sebastian of Speyer threw his considerable influence against racists and animal lovers who wanted to prohibit kosher slaughtering.[68] Cardinal Schulte of Cologne, a generous and tactful friend of Rhenish Jewry, was helpful in restoring an ancient Jewish cemetery unearthed by the state-owned railroad in 1922.[69] Catholic priests spoke at synagogue dedicatory services and anniversary celebrations at least as often as their Protestant counterparts.[70]

In sum, it would appear that among Protestants the radical opponents and defenders of the Jews were about equally balanced, while among Catholics the defenders were somewhat in preponderance. Far more crucial, however, were the great masses of ordinary Christians of both persuasions who were either indifferent to the Jews or influenced to varying degrees by the criticisms of Jews as bearers of secularism. Those criticisms, more than any other single consideration, neutralized much Christian opposition to anti-Semitism and helped open the way to Christian support for National Socialism.

No group of Germans was more susceptible to anti-Semitism than the students. Judeophobia, which had been strong among German students at least since the 1880s, intensified noticeably after 1918. The well-known student penchant for political radicalism, combined with the fact that many students were veterans of the lost war, encouraged widespread endorsement of right-wing notions on German campuses. Included among them was the association of Jews with leftist parties, pacifism, and the policy of fulfilling the harsh terms of the Treaty of Versailles. Economic issues were surely present; stiff competition for jobs in law, medicine, journalism, and theatre—fields in which Jewish students were present in numbers far out of proportion to their part of the German population—enhanced racist appeals. But the fact that anti-Semitism was most intense among students at the technical institutes, where Jews offered little or no threat of employment competition and where

Alfred Neumeyer, "Erinnerungen" (Typescript in Leo Baeck Institute Archives, New York), 166; Franz Rödel, "Zeitgenossischer katholischer Antisemitismus?" *Mitteilungen aus dem Verein zur Abwehr des Antisemitismus*, November 1, 1928; Greive, *Theologie und Ideologie*, 71, 242.

68. Bishop Sebastian to Rabbi Kohn, n.d. [*ca.* April, 1919], in *Dokumentation zur Geschichte der jüdischen Bevölkerung in Rheinland-Pfalz und im Saarland von 1800 bis 1945* (Koblenz, 1971), 306–307.

69. Alexander Carlebach, *Adass Yeshurun of Cologne* (Belfast, 1964), 89–90; *Jüdisch-liberale Zeitung*, April 15, 1932.

70. *Israelitisches Familienblatt*, June 20, 1929; *ibid.*, October 3, 1929; *Bayerische Israelitische Gemeindezeitung*, September 15, 1932.

social and political issues were more often polemicized than studied, suggests that political emotions lay at the heart of campus racism.[71]

The prime goal of anti-Semitic students was to limit the matriculation of Jews in order to minimize their influence on university and professional life and their ability to compete in overcrowded job markets. German Jews probably sent no more of their sons and daughters to the universities than the rest of the German middle class, but their detractors preferred to point out that Jews were at least four times as likely to attend universities as non-Jews, considering their proportion of the total population.[72] Anti-Semites demanded the *numerus clausus* to end this supposed inequality by limiting Jews to a number corresponding to their percentage of the population. In the few cases where they convinced their fellow students to support this demand, government authorities swiftly reminded them that Weimar democracy recognized neither religious nor racial distinctions.[73] The racists were far more successful at intensifying traditional social discrimination against Jews in the fraternities; Jewish students were obliged to find shelter in their own fraternities or among socialist, liberal, and Catholic students. Typically, the anti-Jewish fraternities denied "satisfaction"—acceptance of a challenge to a duel—to Jews who felt themselves insulted, boycotted establishments where Jewish students congregated, barred Jews from membership, and infuriated Jewish student organizations by marching at the greatest possible distance from them in academic processions.[74]

71. The best and most detailed treatment of student anti-Semitism is Hans Peter Bleuel and Ernst Klinnert, *Deutsche Studenten auf dem Weg ins Dritte Reich* (Gütersloh, 1967), 131–72. See also Manfred Franze, *Die Erlanger Studentenschaft 1918–1945* (Würzburg, 1972), 56–58; Laqueur, *Weimar*, 192–93; M. J. Bonn, *Wandering Scholar* (London, 1949), 332–33; Michael H. Kater, *Studentenschaft und Rechtsradikalismus in Deutschland 1918–1933* (Hamburg, 1975), 145–61; Wolfgang Kreutzberger, *Studenten und Politik 1918–1933: Der Fall Freiburg im Breisgau* (Göttingen, 1972), 91–96, 117; Jürgen Schwarz, *Studenten in der Weimarer Republik* (Berlin, 1971), *passim*. The Schwarz volume (pp. 409–14) produces figures showing that 90 percent of German university students served in their country's armed forces during World War I; many of them finished their degrees after the end of hostilities. In 1914 there were 80,167 students enrolled, in 1920 there were 151,077, and in 1925 there were 89,481.

72. Although Jews made up less than 1 percent of the German population, they constituted 5.6 percent of the students in Prussian universities in 1926, and 4.2 percent of all German students in 1930. *Jüdische Rundschau*, January 12, 1926; *ibid.*, June 24, 1930.

73. *Im deutschen Reich*, February, 1919; *ibid.*, April, 1920; *Mitteilungen aus dem Verein zur Abwehr des Antisemitismus*, March 6, 1920; *Jüdische Rundschau*, February 26, 1924; *Der Israelit*, July 3, 1930.

74. The General Confederation of German Students (Allgemeine Deutsche Burschenbund), the largest league of dueling fraternities in Germany, voted to exclude Jews in 1920, ostensibly to preserve the organization's unity. A few of the local chapters, led by the Munich group, threatened secession if the anti-Jewish policy were not adopted. Jews made up at most 2 percent of confederation membership at that time. Joachim Seligsohn, "Der 'Allgemeine Deutsche

Unable to bar Jews from entering the universities or to hound them out once there, the racists attempted to exclude them from membership in the German Students' Organization, a comprehensive federation of local student representative bodies at universities in Germany, Austria, Danzig, and the Sudetenland. Formed shortly after the end of the World War, it enjoyed official recognition and financial aid from most of the German state governments. The moving impulse for exclusion came from the militantly anti-Semitic Austrian section of the organization, which barred Jews from full membership in the student bodies of their universities. In 1927 the Prussian minister of culture, Carl H. Becker, called upon Prussian students to vote on a new constitution for their organization that would have severed ties between German and Austrian students and treated the latter as foreigners in Prussian universities in retaliation for the exclusion of Jews from full rights on Austrian campuses.[75] For years German student leaders had worked with some success to neutralize anti-Semitism as an issue in the organization. Now, faced with the unhappy choice of disrupting the symbolic unity of German students everywhere in Central Europe or losing official recognition and financial aid, Prussian students voted heavily against Becker's constitution.[76] Prussia and the other states cut all ties with the organization, which, however, retained the support of most German students for years to come.

Surprisingly, given the widespread toleration of and support for anti-Semitism among German students, Jewish professors were harassed only when circumstances called special attention to them. Albert Einstein, whose theories of relativity were denounced as "un-German" by right-wing physicists as early as 1920, found his lectures crowded with disruptive *völkisch* students in February of that year. Begged by hundreds of serious students to ignore the troublemakers and determined not to limit his audience in any way, Einstein triumphantly resumed lecturing a short time later.[77] Political state-

---

Burschenbund' und die Juden," *Im deutschen Reich,* February, 1920; *Mitteilungen aus dem Verein zur Abwehr des Antisemitismus,* June 20, 1921; *Israelitisches Familienblatt,* June 1, 1922; Max Mainzer, "Von der Heidelberger Universität," *Central-Verein Zeitung,* July 11, 1930.

75. Becker, a member of the Democratic party, sat on the board of the German Pro-Palestine Committee. *Jüdische Rundschau,* February 10, 1931.

76. In the referendum, held on November 30, 1927, only about 20,000 students bothered to vote, less than half of those eligible to participate. Of those who voted, 77 percent cast negative ballots. Werner Rosenberg, "Das Ende der preussischen Studentenschaften," *Central-Verein Zeitung,* December 9, 1927; Bleuel and Klinnert, *Deutsche Studenten,* 157–62.

77. *Israelitisches Familienblatt,* February 19 and March 4, 1920. At a public meeting sponsored by reactionary physicists in Berlin to heap abuse on his "Jewish physics," Einstein managed to steal the show by making a personal appearance and smiling broadly at the racist

ments, however, could touch more tender spots. The Hanover Technical Institute's volatile Jewish professor of philosophy, Theodor Lessing, aroused a scandal during the 1925 presidential campaign with a tasteless attack on the candidate of the right, General Hindenburg, as a moronic "zero" behind whom lurked a future Nero. The resulting student revolt was so intense that Lessing could be defended only by having his future activities at the institute confined to private research.[78] A similar case occurred in 1921 when Freiburg University law professor Hermann Kantorowicz published an article critical of Bismarck's authoritarian tradition and his seizure for Germany of Alsace-Lorraine after the Franco-Prussian War. While nothing was done to infringe on Kantorowicz's teaching, in his case, as in Lessing's, the rest of the faculty was as outraged at his "unpatriotic" opinions as their students were.[79] But such occasions were rare, and cases in which sensitive political issues were raised probably would have ended the same way even if they had not involved Jews. Most Jewish professors were left unmolested by student racists until after the Nazis came to power.

The alarming popularity of nazism among German students[80] during the early 1930s may have been an expression of hatred for Jews, but if this were true to any significant degree it seems strange that student energies were focused so infrequently on Jewish professors. In the most famous of these cases, that involving Ernst Cohn in Breslau, the Nazis waited until a Jew was newly appointed to a faculty position in order to spread the legend that he was being forced on the university against the will of faculty and students alike. The young law professor, unable to begin teaching because of the presence in his lecture hall of disruptive Nazis, many of whom were nonstudents, ultimately lost the support even of his faculty colleagues when he indiscreetly advocated offering asylum in Germany to Leon Trotsky. On the other hand, not a finger

---

nonsense. *Mitteilungen aus dem Verein zur Abwehr des Antisemitismus,* September 21, 1920; Leopold Infield, *Albert Einstein* (New York, 1950), 125–26.

78. August Messer, *Der Fall Lessing* (Bielefeld, 1926), 17–72; *Jüdische Rundschau,* July 26, 1925; *ibid.,* June 22, 1926; S. Freund, "Der Fall Lessing," *Central-Verein Zeitung,* June 19, 1925. For information on a similar case at Heidelberg, see Hans Peter Bleuel, *Deutschlands Bekenner: Professoren zwischen Kaiserreich und Diktatur* (Bern, 1968), 157–60.

79. *Mitteilungen aus dem Verein zur Abwehr des Antisemitismus,* January 26, 1922; Bleuel, *Deutschlands Bekenner,* 145–46.

80. The National Socialist Student Union became the dominant force in German campus politics well before the Nazis had a major impact on national politics. During the winter semester of 1929/30, the Hitlerite students won majorities on the student councils at Greifswald and Erlangen universities. Two years later they held majorities at thirteen of Germany's twenty-eight universities and technical institutes. Michael Stephen Steinberg, *Sabers and Brown Shirts: The German Students' Path to National Socialism, 1918–1935* (Chicago, 1973), 90–93.

was raised against Jewish professors who were already established on the Breslau faculty.[81] Strangely, a small minority excepted, student anti-Semitism was more bark than bite, aimed principally at the abstract Jewish radical rather than the flesh-and-blood Jewish student or teacher. The opinion of a Jewish student that his colleagues' racism was an irritating tradition, not a militant cause, only slightly underestimated its immediate significance.[82]

The German professoriate has been condemned for harboring outspoken anti-Semites during the Weimar years, and with reason. Resentful of administrative control over education by politicians from the "wrong" parties and outraged that the new democratic age made it hard for them to go on excluding Socialists, Jews, or members of other minorities, most German professors gravitated to the political right. A few were only too eager to trace the problems of Germany in general and of higher education in particular to Jewish sources.[83] Jena sheltered two of the best-known anti-Semitic professors, philosopher Max Wundt and zoologist Ludwig H. Plate. Wundt merged religion and racialism in lectures and books that identified the Jews' rejection of Christ as the source of their supposed base materialism and hate-filled alienation. Over the centuries, he argued, they had deteriorated into "a species of race of the second rank."[84] Plate added scientific plausibility to racialism with a debased version of genetics, informing his students that the offspring of a mixed German-Jewish marriage would display Aryan characteristics, but that those offspring would in time produce "a little Cohn." Brought before a disciplinary committee for repeatedly insulting the Jews in lectures and seminars, he succeeded in draping himself in the robes of academic freedom.[85]

There were other German professors with outspoken anti-Semitic prejudices, including Münster sociologist Johann Plenge, Greifswald philosopher Hermann Schwarz, and Berlin jurist E. von Möller.[86] But they were not typical of the vast majority of their colleagues, who regarded radical anti-Semitism as a political issue, suitable for the street corner and the beer hall,

81. Interview with Dr. Ernst J. Cohn, July 17, 1973; Ernst Fränkel, "Die schweren Unruhen an der Breslauer Universität," *Central-Verein Zeitung,* November 18, 1932; Ernst Fränkel, "Geht der Kampf an der Breslauer Universität weiter?" *ibid.,* December 9, 1932; *ibid.,* December 30, 1932.

82. Kurt Pohlen, "Der Antisemitismus an den Hochschulen," *Mitteilungen aus dem Verein zur Abwehr des Antisemitismus,* July 20, 1929.

83. Bonn, *Wandering Scholar,* 329; Bleuel, *Deutschlands Bekenner,* 188–89.

84. Max Wundt, *Der ewige Jude: Ein Versuch über Sinn und Bedeutung des Judentums* (Munich, 1926), 3–19.

85. *Mitteilungen aus dem Verein zur Abwehr des Antisemitismus,* November 21, 1927.

86. *Central-Verein Zeitung,* November 11, 1927; *ibid.,* November 18, 1927; Bleuel, *Deutschlands Bekenner,* 94–208.

perhaps, but not for the university. The professors occasionally showed reluctance to brave the ire of outraged radical students by recommending Jews for faculty vacancies.[87] To defend the rights of established Jewish colleagues, however, they met Nazi students with expulsions and public statements of opposition.[88] Ernst Cohn, the victim of the Nazi campaign at Breslau University, has credited the faculty there with virtual immunity to anti-Semitism, and Jewish professors at Bonn, Kiel, Marburg, and Berlin universities have paid similar tribute to their erstwhile colleagues.[89] A few university teachers were prepared to make personal statements against Judeophobia, as did Berlin professor of internal medicine Friedrich Kraus, who chose a moment of political disorder to remind his class that the great nineteenth-century pathologist Friedrich von Recklinghausen had once declared his own nobility inferior to the Edenic nobility of his Jewish wife.[90]

The best-publicized faculty resistance to anti-Semitism arose in the case of Hans F. K. Günther's appointment to the Faculty of Mathematics and Natural Sciences at Jena in 1930. Günther, a would-be poet and former journalist, had half-educated himself on the subject of "racial science" and written several works that purported to show the racial origins of human behavior for the right-wing J. F. Lehmann publishing house in Munich. When the first Nazi state minister of education, Wilhelm Frick in Thuringia, appointed him to a vacant chair of anthropology at Jena, the faculty overwhelmingly rejected him as incompetent and his published works as lacking in scholarly merit. Frick bypassed these objections by creating a new chair of social anthropology for Günther and denying the faculty any voice in the matter. Neither the rector of the university nor the dean of his faculty would introduce Günther's inaugural lecture, contrary to custom.[91] Although the faculty's stand did not

87. In June, 1924, Munich University chemist Richard Willstätter resigned in protest against the denial of a faculty post to another Jew, Viktor M. Goldschmidt; Willstätter's colleagues feared that Goldschmidt's appointment would trigger student disturbances. Richard Willstätter, *From My Life,* trans. Lilli S. Hornig (New York, 1965), 360–67.

88. *Der Israelit,* August 4, 1932; *Central-Verein Zeitung,* June 24, 1932.

89. Cohn interview; Paul E. Kahle, *Bonn University in Pre-Nazi and Nazi Times (1923–1939)* (London, 1945), 11; Abraham Fränkel, *Lebenskreise: Aus dem Erinnerungen eines jüdischen Mathematikers* (Stuttgart, 1967), 185; David Baumgardt, "Looking Back on a German University Career," *Leo Baeck Institute Yearbook,* X (1965), 241, 244.

90. *Jüdische Rundschau,* June 15, 1928. For a similar case, see Kurt Sabatzky, "Meine Erinnerungen an den Nationalsozialismus" (Typescript in Leo Baeck Institute Archives, New York), 13–14.

91. Hans F. K. Günther, *Rassenkunde des deutschen Volkes* (Rev. ed.; Munich, 1926); Hans F. K. Günther, *Rassenkunde des jüdischen Volkes* (Munich, 1930); Hans F. K. Günther, *Rasse und Stil* (Munich, 1926); *Central-Verein Zeitung,* May 30, 1930; Bleuel, *Deutschlands Bekenner,* 28–41.

represent a direct attack on anti-Semitism, it repudiated Judeophobia indirectly by equating racism with academic charlatanism.

A year later a less well-known but equally revealing drama played itself out at the University of Munich. Hans Nawiasky, a Jewish professor of constitutional law, became the target of Nazi-led riots after he had remarked to students that the Treaty of Versailles was no worse than the treaties of Brest-Litovsk and Bucharest. His fellow faculty members, most of whom probably disagreed with his statement, stood firmly with him, closing the university for a short time rather than submit to Nazi demands for his ouster. Even the majority of students sympathized with him and issued him a formal apology as he resumed his teaching duties.[92]

With few exceptions, the faculty-elected rectors of German universities took their stand against anti-Semitism. The Frankfurt-am-Main rector, Georg Küntzel, responded to the anti-Jewish slurs of Nazi students by suspending their organization, expelling one of its leaders, and issuing a directive demanding respect for all students.[93] His counterparts at Cologne and Würzburg included denunciations of racist students in their annual convocational addresses.[94] The strongest stand of all was taken by Munich University rector Karl Vossler, who banned all student organizations from participation in the university's 1927 centenary after anti-Semitic fraternities had refused to involve Jewish fraternities in the planning stages. At the same time Vossler pointedly sent a special invitation to leaders of the Munich Jewish Community to attend the festivities.[95]

Although the university faculties repudiated radical anti-Semitism, they were by no means immune to its more moderate counterpart. Fritz K. Ringer has shown how broad sections of the conservative German academic establishment adopted a "cultivated" form of Judeophobia as part of their longing to escape from interest politics and materialism. Before the First World War, and even more so after 1918, the "German mandarins" associated the Jews with aspects of modernity that ranged from Marxism to "cultural decadence." The faculties' repugnance for Jewish modernism expressed itself in reluctance to advance Jewish colleagues through the academic ranks and, less

92. Helmut Kuhn, "Die deutsche Universität am Vorabend der Machtergreifung," in *Die deutsche Universität im Dritten Reich* (Munich, 1966), 36–37.

93. *Mitteilungen aus dem Verein zur Abwehr des Antisemitismus*, January, 1930.

94. *Der Israelit*, May 17, 1928.

95. Neumeyer, "Erinnerungen," 165; Karl Vossler, "Ansprache an die Korporationsausschuss," in Lamm (ed.), *Von Juden in München*, 331–33; *Israelitisches Familienblatt*, January 20, 1927.

tangibly, in social discrimination. It also made the university professors somewhat more tolerant of their *völkisch* students than they might otherwise have been.[96] In sum, it would appear that the Weimar professoriate was at least as interested in fostering its own brand of moderate Judeophobia as it was in isolating the universities from intrusions of radical anti-Semitism.

Using the political parties to measure anti-Semitism presents the special problem already alluded to in our discussion of the National Socialist party line. Since there can be no direct equation between their official attitudes on the Jewish question and the motivations of their followers, it would be folly to assert that the former determined the size of party membership or votes. Not everyone who voted for the Nazis hated the Jews, whereas anti-Semites might conceivably have voted for other parties because of issues that they held in equal or higher importance. And yet, the major political parties—especially those that were not explicitly anti-Semitic—provide a valuable barometer of public opinion on the Jewish question.

Each of the two major left-wing groups, the Communist and Social Democratic parties, shared its Marxist heritage with the other while vigorously denying the other's right to it. The Communists, militantly opposed to Weimar democracy as a hopeless compromise with capitalism, sought to lead Germany down the path charted by Lenin and Stalin. The Socialists, horrified by the totalitarian turn in Russian Marxism, modified their class-conscious dogmas enough to form the backbone of support for the new Republic.

Divergent ideologies brought forth conflicting responses to Judeophobia. The Communists' assurance that the class struggle was the central issue and that anti-Semitism was a peripheral matter led them to underestimate the explosive qualities of racialism while using it opportunistically for electoral advantage. For the "orthodox" Marxists, the moving issues in human history were economic. All others were thought of as rationalizations or diversions that would be solved automatically in the classless society and hence could be debunked or exploited in the interests of achieving that end.

In practice the German Communists both debunked and exploited, but they expended far more effort on the latter, appealing for support from the radical right by spotlighting their opposition to Jewish capitalists. Sporadically throughout the Weimar years, and especially in the crisis years of 1923 and 1930–33, the Communists resorted to this tactic as part of their lar-

96. Fritz K. Ringer, *The Decline of the German Mandarins* (Cambridge, Mass., 1969), 135–39, 224, 239–40.

ger policy of "National Bolshevism," an attempted merger of German nationalism and Russian communism on the basis of common hostility to Western culture and capitalism.[97] Typical was party leader Ruth Fischer's demagogic appeal of 1923 to *völkisch* students to hang Jewish capitalists from the street lamps.[98] Similarly, the 1933 Communist broadside that shouted "SA and SS! You have shot enough workers. When will you hang the first Jew?" contained both the accusation that Nazi anti-Semitism was a fraud and the hope that what the party perceived as nazism's fundamentally healthy anticapitalist instincts could be turned against the class enemies, the Jews not excluded.[99] Coupled with these outbursts were allegations that rich Jews slipped money to the Nazis because both shared the goal of saving capitalists irrespective of creed and race. None of this was intended to further anti-Semitism, but it could not have failed to strengthen the stereotype of Jews as selfish exploiters of the masses.[100]

Far more reliable opponents of Judeophobia were Germany's Social Democrats. Among the ideological baggage they jettisoned was the assumption that Jewish emancipation could be left to the coming Socialist revolution. They portrayed anti-Semitism as one of the key elements in a plot to undermine the Republic and the parties that supported it by pinning every problem on the Jews and the "Jewish Republic." That argument successfully tied the vital interests of the Socialist workers to the fight against anti-Jewish appeals. Their commitment was cemented with a continuing Socialist campaign to ridicule, denounce, and pour moral indignation on *völkisch* words and deeds. Far from emulating the Communist party in its attempts at beating the Nazis at their own game, they specifically condemned its demagogic use of racist phrases. In these ways the marginal penetration of anti-Jewish opinions into the organized Socialist working class was kept to an unmeasurable minimum; anti-Semites who raised their heads in the party either resigned or were expelled. Hence it is hardly surprising that significant numbers of Jewish political activists and rank-and-file voters attached themselves to the Social Demo-

97. On "National Bolshevism," see Otto-Ernst Schüddekopf, *Linke Leute von Rechts: Die nationalrevolutionären Minderheiten und der Kommunismus in der Weimarer Republik* (Stuttgart, 1960); Klemens von Klemperer, *Germany's New Conservatism: Its History and Dilemma in the Twentieth Century* (Princeton, 1957), 139–50; Armin Mohler, *Die Konservative Revolution in Deutschland 1918–1932* (Stuttgart, 1950), 59–65.

98. *Vorwärts*, August 22, 1923; *cf.* Ossip K. Flechtheim, *Die Kommunistische Partei Deutschlands in der Weimarer Republik* (Offenbach-am-Main, 1948), 294; Ruth Fischer, *Stalin and German Communism* (Cambridge, Mass., 1948), 283.

99. *Jüdische Rundschau*, February 10, 1933.

100. Hans-Helmuth Knütter, *Die Juden und die deutsche Linke in der Weimarer Republik 1918–1933* (Düsseldorf, 1971), 174–205; George L. Mosse, "German Socialists and the

cratic party or that the Centralverein secretly gave it more aid in the form of money and propaganda material than any of the other republican parties.[101]

Not that the Social Democrats were in any important sense philo-Semitic. They showed no hesitation in occasionally dropping Jews as candidates in order to defuse racist allegations that they were a "party of the Jews." Jewish capitalists were not spared criticism, especially when they gave the impression of indifference to the great dangers presented by nazism. Nor did the Socialists exempt Jews from their general opposition to organized religion and to the use of state funds for the support thereof. On rare occasions they could be vindictive. In 1930 Bavarian Socialists, angered at Jewish support for the landed nobility in the 1926 plebiscite on the confiscation of aristocratic property, cast the decisive votes in the state parliament to require humane butchering techniques that, in effect, outlawed the kosher slaughter of animals.[102] But if Social Democrats did not love Jews qua Jews, they never made a single notable concession to anti-Semitism, choosing instead to fight it to the last.[103]

The principal weakness of the Social Democrats' stand lay not in any concessions to the nationalist spirit but rather in their "plot theory" of anti-Semitism. As effective as that theory was in mobilizing the workers against Jew-baiting, it also denied that racists seriously intended to harm the Jews. It promoted a view of anti-Jewish leaders as cynical manipulators of public opinion who were more intent upon destroying democracy than Jews. That view was reinforced by real or imagined Nazi ties with individual Jews and by the Nazis' shifting emphasis on the Jewish question. Few Socialists expected anti-Semitic violence in the event of a Hitlerite takeover. As one Social Democratic publication put it in 1932: "Jews who can pay up will have nothing to fear in the Third Reich; they'll be grabbed by the purse, not by the gullet."[104] Hence the most outspoken political opponents of Judeophobia, the German Social Democrats, spread doubts that the Nazis were ideologically committed to anti-Semitism. That impression may have induced some Germans to sup-

Jewish Question in the Weimar Republic," *Leo Baeck Institute Yearbook*, XVI (1971), 134–43.

101. Arnold Paucker, *Der jüdische Abwehrkampf gegen Antisemitismus und Nationalsozialismus in den letzten Jahren der Weimarer Republik* (Hamburg, 1968), 92–99; Donald L. Niewyk, *Socialist, Anti-Semite, and Jew*, 58–59, 106, 190–91.

102. Philip Löwenfeld, "Memoiren" (Typescript in Leo Baeck Institute Archives, New York), 842–51; Niewyk, *Socialist, Anti-Semite, and Jew*, 195–96.

103. *Cf.* Mosse, "German Socialists and the Jewish Question," 132–33, 150–51; Knütter, *Die Juden und die deutsche Linke*, 129–53, 206–13 *passim*. The alleged widespread hostility of German workers toward Jewish Socialist intellectuals has yet to be documented.

104. *Münchener Post*, February 16, 1932.

port or tolerate the Nazis on the assumption that they would become more conservative and responsible once in power.[105]

The Center party and its Bavarian wing, the Bavarian People's party, together constituted the second-largest republican bloc in Weimar Germany. As the parties of Germany's large Roman Catholic minority, they were decisively influenced by the Catholic clergy and hence reflected the Church's ambivalent, but predominantly positive, attitudes towards the Jews. On the one hand, the Catholic parties were critical of Jewish intellectuals who took stands against religion and for such radically secular ideologies as socialism and communism. This was especially true in conservative Bavaria during the revolutionary turmoil of the years immediately after the armistice. Typically, the Bavarian People's party's *Bayerische Kurier* smeared the Independent Socialist revolutionary leader Kurt Eisner as "the Galician Jew Salomon Kosmanowski" and observed that Jews were injecting foreign influences into Germany's politics, economy, press, literature, and theater.[106] Such outbursts grew very much less frequent after 1920, but they did not disappear altogether.[107]

Far more typical of the Catholic parties' attitudes, however, was a speech delivered by Münster University professor Georg Schreiber to the Center party's 1920 party congress denouncing anti-Semitism as un-Christian, beneficial only to the reactionary right, and potentially threatening to all religious minorities, the Roman Catholics included.[108] Before the end of that year the great preponderance of both Catholic parties' comment opposed Judeophobia rather than contributed to it; and so it was to remain.[109] Two prominent Center party personalities, Konstantin Fehrenbach and Heinrich Krone, became active in the Association to Resist Anti-Semitism, while in Bavaria the Centralverein often carried forward its work in cooperation with officials be-

105. Niewyk, *Socialist, Anti-Semite, and Jew*, 200–14.

106. Jakob Scherek, "Umschau," *Im deutschen Reich*, XXV (1919), 13–15; Jakob Scherek, "Antisemitismus im Zentrum," *ibid.*, 420–22; *Mitteilungen aus dem Verein zur Abwehr des Antisemitismus*, April 30, 1919; *ibid.*, July 10, 1919; Klaus Schönhoven, *Die Bayerische Volkspartei 1924–1932* (Düsseldorf, 1972), 27; Jochmann, "Die Ausbreitung des Antisemitismus," 494–95; Rudolf Morsey, *Die deutsche Zentrumspartei 1917–1923* (Düsseldorf, 1966), 118.

107. *Germania*, October 13, 1922; *Der Israelit*, July 31, 1930; *Jüdische Rundschau*, October 4 and 7, 1932; Geoffrey Pridham, *Hitler's Rise to Power: The Nazi Movement in Bavaria, 1923–1933* (New York, 1973), 241.

108. *Mitteilungen aus dem Verein zur Abwehr des Antisemitismus*, February 9, 1920; *Jüdische Rundschau*, January 27, 1920.

109. *Mitteilungen aus dem Verein zur Abwehr des Antisemitismus*, June 29, 1920; *ibid.*, June/July, 1929.

longing to the Bavarian People's party.[110] Former prime minister Josef Wirth was identified as a Center party leader conspicuous in his sympathy for Jewish rights.[111] As the Republic wavered and the middle-class parties faded away in the depression years, the Center and Bavarian People's parties offered political havens for many, and possibly for the majority of Jewish voters.[112]

The German Democratic party, a liberal party of progressive business and professional people, predictably opposed anti-Semitism as incompatible with its ideals of reason, tolerance, and individual freedom. However, as the party that won the great majority of Jewish votes before 1930, it was even more sensitive than the Social Democrats to charges of Jewish domination and hence shied away from putting up as many Jewish candidates for public office as it might have otherwise.[113] As Hermann Dietrich, a prominent party leader in the state of Baden, put it late in 1918, Jewish candidates lost more votes for the party than there were Jewish voters.[114] As early as 1919, the Centralverein funneled money to Socialist rather than Democratic party candidates, partially to protest the small number of Jews among the latter.[115]

Even more significant in dulling the Democratic party's commitment to equal rights for Jews was the aspiration of its conservative wing to win new

110. *Ibid.*, April 18, 1926; Werner J. Cahnmann, "The Nazi Threat and the Central Verein—A Recollection," in Herbert A. Strauss (ed.), *Conference on Anti- Semitism, 1969* (New York, 1969), 33–36; memorandum signed by Dr. Freund, October 27, 1926, in Nachlass Moritz Sobernheim, Manuscript Division, Library of Congress, 1286/348278-9.

111. *Central-Verein Zeitung,* May 23, 1930; *Jüdische Rundschau,* August 29, 1930. On the other hand, Heinrich Brüning, German chancellor and Center party chief, steadfastly ignored pleas from a variety of Jewish and non-Jewish sources to take a public stand against anti-Semitism. Curt Prüfer to Brüning, March 30, 1931, Julius Hirsch to Pünder, and reply, December 29, 1931, and January 11, 1932, Wilhelm Marx to Hermann Pünder, January 21, 1932, all in Reich Chancellery Documents on Jewish Affairs, Bundesarchiv, Koblenz, R 431/2193 L. 382281–84; 382306-7; 382313; Albert Südekum to Pünder, March 24, 1932, in Nachlass Albert Südekum, Bundesarchiv, Koblenz, 160a, 4–6.

112. *Jüdische Rundschau,* September 2, 1930; *Israelitisches Familienblatt,* May 12, 1932; J. Guggenheim, "Warum wähle ich Zentrum?" *ibid.*, November 3, 1932; *ibid.*, February 16, 1933; P. B. Wiener, "Die Parteien der Mitte," in Mosse and Paucker (eds.), *Entscheidungsjahr 1932,* 306–14.

113. Werner Becker, "Die Rolle der liberalen Presse," in Mosse and Paucker (eds.), *Deutsches Judentum,* 117–22; Jochmann, "Die Ausbreitung des Antisemitismus," *ibid.*, 495–97.

114. Hermann Dietrich to Josef Kaufmann, December 31, 1918, in Nachlass Hermann Dietrich, Bundesarchiv, Koblenz, 216/123–24. Dietrich later denied that this constituted a concession to anti-Semitism, stating that his point of view corresponded to that of Dr. Ludwig Haas, a Jewish Democrat and Centralverein activist, Hermann Dietrich to Dr. Sickinger, February 20, 1919, in Nachlass Hermann Dietrich, 216/181.

115. Curt Bürger to Dr. E. Baerwald, January 31, 1919, in Nachlass Georg Gothein, Bundesarchiv, Koblenz, 54/59–63. Bürger, the managing director of the Association to Resist Anti-Semitism, was an active member of the Democratic party, and the association's chairman, Georg Gothein, sat on the party's executive committee.

strength by means of a coalition with moderate right-wing elements. Efforts made in that direction culminated in July, 1930, with just such a union between Arthur Mahraun's *völkisch* "Young German Order" and the Democratic party to become the German State party. Both partners openly repudiated anti-Semitism, the former declaring itself "a-Semitic" but supportive of existing civil liberties, the latter asserting continuity between the old and new parties on the Jewish question. Prominent voices within the Jewish population guardedly took them at their word, but Jews who had been active in the Democratic party often declined to support the State party.[116] It made no difference that the odd liberal-*völkisch* coalition collapsed after only two months. The damage had been done, although it may only have hastened, rather than caused, the party's decline and virtual disappearance at a time when liberal ideas were commonly viewed as irrelevant to a terminally polarized situation.[117]

Weimar Germany's other important middle-class party, the German People's party, stood clearly to the right of the Democrats and frequently permitted its fears of Marxism to blur its vision of other matters, the Jewish question included. A few party locals adopted vaguely *völkisch* resolutions aimed principally at Jewish radicals and Eastern Jews; one even decided to exclude Jews from membership. Only rarely was party discipline imposed on anti-Semites. On at least one occasion, in a case involving Felix Rathenau, party members blocked a Jew's promotion in the civil service for anti-Semitic reasons.[118]

The toleration of individual Judeophobes notwithstanding, the People's party officially rejected anti-Semitism, especially while Gustav Stresemann lived to lead it down the republican straight and narrow. Although he was himself married to a Jew, the party chief rarely spoke out on the racist issue; a speech delivered in Osnabrück on September 18, 1919, was a major exception. In it Stresemann forcefully denied any direct equation between the

116. Eva Reichmann-Jungmann, "Zum Verständnis unseres politischen Seins," *Central-Verein Zeitung*, September 5, 1930; *ibid.*, August 8, 1930; Ludwig Holländer, "Central-Verein und Staatspartei," *ibid.*, August 15, 1930; *Der Israelit*, August 7, 1930; Feder, *Heute sprach ich mit . . .*, 281; Sabatzky, "Meine Erinnerungen," 12–13; *Israelitisches Familienblatt*, May 12, 1932; *Jüdisch-liberale Zeitung*, August 27, 1930.
117. Wiener, "Die Parteien der Mitte," 289–306.
118. L. H. [Ludwig Holländer], "Wahlen," *Im deutschen Reich*, XXVII (1921), 91; Arthur Schweriner, "Der Centralverein im Wahlkampf," *Central-Verein Zeitung*, December 12, 1924; Paul Nathan, "Die Wahl des Reichspräsidenten," *ibid.*, March 13, 1925; Hans Moywod, "Gleiches Recht für alle," *ibid.*, January 23, 1925; *Mitteilungen aus dem Verein zur Abwehr des Antisemitismus*, November 24, 1919; *ibid.*, May 15, 1920; *Jüdische Rundschau*, October 15, 1920.

Jews and such radical manifestations as anarchism, bolshevism, and cosmopolitanism. He credited the vast majority of German Jews with themselves opposing extremist movements, and he closed with an unambiguous injunction: "A liberal party cannot champion anti-Semitic principles with their one-sided view of the question of guilt and its excrescences."[119]

Most of the time, however, the People's party passed over the Jewish question in silence. Not only did it not want to upset intraparty relations, but it seems likely that the widespread underestimation of the danger presented by anti-Semitism had penetrated deeply into this party, too. German Jews reacted ambiguously, unable to excuse the party's toleration of Judeophobes but equally unwilling to abandon it to the racists. Several prominent Jewish conservatives, including Kurt Alexander of the Centralverein and the bankers Jakob Goldschmidt and Max Warburg, chose to remain in the party and fight the spread of anti-Semitism from within.[120] For the Centralverein itself and for most Jews, however, the People's party was at best a questionable case. After Stresemann's death in 1929, its rapid decline and movement toward the extreme right robbed it of most of whatever Jewish support it may have enjoyed.[121]

The three major arms of government service that are included in this survey, the courts, army, and police, were also vulnerable to some racialist penetration. This is hardly surprising, given their sympathies for conservative and superpatriotic causes. The courts were sometimes handicapped by local prosecutors who refused to take action against Jew-baiters out of sympathy for their cause.[122] When brought to trial, Judeophobes occasionally were acquitted or assessed trivial fines by judges of a similar bent, as in the 1921 case of a teacher who was tried for having insulted the Hebrew religion by instructing

119. *Mitteilungen aus dem Verein zur Abwehr des Antisemitismus,* September 18, 1919. See also *Central-Verein Zeitung,* May 18, 1928.

120. Feder, *Heute Sprach ich mit . . .,* 122; Kurt Alexander, "Mitarbeit, kein Abschluss," *Central-Verein Zeitung,* July 9, 1926; Paucker, *Jüdische Abwehrkampf,* 90–91.

121. *Central-Verein Zeitung,* December 4, 1924; *ibid.,* October 28, 1932; Hans Goslar, "Zwischen zwei Reichstagen," *Israelitisches Familienblatt,* July 24, 1930; Wiener, "Die Parteien der Mitte," 314–20.

122. *Mitteilungen aus dem Verein zur Abwehr des Antisemitismus,* April 26, 1922; Paucker, *Jüdische Abwehrkampf,* 77–78; Thilo Ramm (ed.), *Die Justiz in der Weimarer Republik: Eine Chronik* (Neuwied and Berlin, 1968), 139–40. For a comprehensive analysis of the Jews' legal problems in the Weimar years, see my "Jews and the Courts in Weimar Germany," *Jewish Social Studies,* XXXVII (1975), 99–113. Cf. Ambrose Doskow and Sidney B. Jacoby, "Anti-Semitism and the Law in Pre-Nazi Germany." *Contemporary Jewish Record* (1940), 498–509; Heinrich Hannover and Elisabeth Hannover-Drück, *Politische Justiz 1918–1933* (Frankfurt-am-Main, 1966), 263–73.

members of a right-wing youth group to spit three times while passing a Jewish cemetery. The judge acquitted him, accepting his explanation that he had nothing against Jews as a religious group and opposed them solely on racial grounds.[123]

It would, however, be a mistake to suppose that such travesties of justice were typical of the attitudes of German courts. It was far more common for them to assign appropriately severe penalties to Judeophobes, particularly in cases involving desecrations of Jewish holy places, threats to Jewish lives and property, and boycotts of Jewish businesses. Judicial lenience in other such cases was dictated more often by reluctance to make martyrs out of racists or by their incredibly tender ages than by sympathy with their objectives.[124] The most significant obstacles to the legal defense of Jews were certain lacunae in the German legal code, inherited from the old Kaiserreich and retained throughout the Weimar period. Not only did it lack a sufficiently broad definition of Jewish corporate identity before the law, but it failed to provide adequate provision for class-action suits against anti-Semites. Plans to revise the criminal code were stalled by the political crisis of 1930–33 and were never completed.[125]

The courts were even less hospitable to Jew-haters as plaintiffs than as defendants. Every known case brought to harass Jews or to cripple their self-defense activities was thrown out of court.[126] There was only one case against a Jewish defendant in which Weimar justice came close to miscarrying. In 1926 the murder of a Magdeburg accountant was attributed to his employer, a local Jewish manufacturer named Rudolf Haas. Although the accountant's body had been discovered in a house occupied by an unemployed Nazi, the local criminal inspector and the chief justice of Saxony's state court, neither of whom was a friend of the Jews, were convinced by evidence suggesting that Haas had murdered his employee to keep him from revealing crooked business practices. Only the vigorous intervention of two Social Democrats, Sax-

---

123. Heinemann Stern, *Warum hassen sie uns eigentlich? Jüdisches Leben zwischen den Kriegen* (Düsseldorf, 1970), 168; *Mitteilungen aus dem Verein zur Abwehr des Antisemitismus,* May 9, 1921; *ibid.,* March 24, 1922; Paucker, *Jüdische Abwehrkampf,* 74–84.

124. Löwenfeld, "Memoiren," 289–91, 773–75, 853.

125. Erich Eyck, "Die Stellung der Rechtspflege zu Juden und Judentum," in *Deutsches Judentum und Rechtskrisis* (Berlin, 1927), 37–42; Erich Eyck, "Um die Frage der Kollektivbeleidigung," *Central-Verein Zeitung,* February 26, 1926; Ludwig Foerder, *Antisemitismus und Justiz* (Berlin, 1924), 8–11; Ludwig Foerder, "Zweierlei Mass in der Justiz?" *Israelitisches Familienblatt,* March, 1932; J. Picard, "Die Strafgesetzreform," *ibid.,* July 23, 1926.

126. Niewyk, "Jews and the Courts," 109–10; Leo Gompertz, "Arbeit für die jüdische Jugend in Deutschland: Mein Erlebnis im Dienste des Judentums" (Typescript in Leo Baeck Institute Archives, New York), 3–5.

ony's *Oberpräsident,* Otto Hörsing and the Prussian minister of the interior, Karl Severing, reopened the investigation and prolonged it until further evidence proved the guilt of the jobless Nazi. Subsequently the two judges whose prejudice had stood in the way of Haas's acquittal were demoted to such insignificant posts that both resigned from government service. Not long after Haas's release from prison, Erich Eyck expressed the hope that his case would alert apathetic jurists to the great danger presented by the willingness of some of their colleagues to assume the worst about Jewish defendants.[127] Perhaps it did have some influence, for nothing remotely resembling the Haas case occurred during the subsequent years of the Weimar Republic.

Weimar courts were sufficiently hospitable to Jewish rights to permit their use in at least one important offensive action against a leading anti-Jewish agitator. The intended target was Ludwig Münchmeyer, an Evangelical pastor on the North Sea island of Borkum and the chief attraction at the island's anti-Semitic spa, the largest of its kind in Germany. Bruno Weil, a prominent figure in Centralverein legal defense activities, was outraged that Münchmeyer had succeeded in making Borkum into a kind of a racist preserve where no Jew dared set foot, and he helped draw up plans to destroy the Jew-baiting cleric. These involved the publication of a broadside exposing Münchmeyer's loose morals and scandalous misconduct, a broadside couched in such extravagant terms that the pastor would be virtually obliged to bring legal action against its authors. That was precisely his reaction to the appearance late in 1925 of a pamphlet bearing the provocative title *The False Priest, or the Chief of the Cannibals of the North Sea Islanders.* The Borkum court found its author and publisher guilty of libeling Münchmeyer on two counts and fined each a mere 100 marks, but it also corroborated most of their allegations and expressed the opinion that the pastor had conducted himself in ways "unworthy of a clergyman." Münchmeyer was ruined. Evangelical church authorities, already aware that something was amiss at Borkum, were prompted to defrock him. Thereafter, both Münchmeyer and the racist spa languished for lack of a following, and he was later able to save himself from total oblivion only by throwing in his lot with the victorious Nazi movement.[128]

127. Heinz Braun, *Am Justizmord vorbei: Der Fall Kölling-Haas* (Magdeburg, 1928); *Mitteilungen aus dem Verein zur Abwehr des Antisemitismus,* October 1, 1929; Eyck, "Die Stellung der Rechtspflege," 35–36.
128. Bruno Weil, "Der politische Prozess," in *Deutsches Judentum und Rechtskrisis,* 81; interview with Dr. Eva Reichmann, August 26, 1973; Bruno Weil, "Deutschland Judenrein"

While there were not many Jewish law breakers in the Weimar years, the few who were convicted were treated sternly but fairly by the legal system. Two of Germany's most lurid scandals of governmental corruption involved families of Jews—the Barmats and the Sklareks—which had recently immigrated from Eastern Europe. The brothers Julius, Salomon, and Henri Barmat were accused in 1925 of having obtained loans from the Prussian State Bank by bribing public officials. One of them was subsequently sentenced to prison. In 1929 Max, Leo, and Willi Sklarek did the same thing with Berlin's municipal bank, and two of them received four-year sentences. German Jews alternately applauded stern measures against the malefactors and stressed that no *German* Jew had been involved in either case.[129] In yet another celebrated case, a Jewish cattle dealer in Paderborn, one Kurt Meyer, was sentenced in 1932 to fifteen years imprisonment for the death of his father's non-Jewish maid, pieces of whose body had been found scattered about the nearby countryside by hikers. Meyer confessed to having caused her death by attempting to perform an abortion on her. This lurid affair provided grist for the mills of Nazi ritual murder allegations for years to come.[130]

The German army, unhindered by the judiciary's concepts of justice and influenced by tales of Jewish shirking in the war, numbered more than a few embittered racists among its one hundred thousand officers and men. As early as 1920 some East Prussian army units were wearing the swastika, and anti-Semitic incidents were traced to off-duty soldiers.[131] Such manifestations became increasingly rare after 1923, however, as Reichswehr leaders succeeded in squelching overt demonstrations of antirepublicanism. Only the wretched action of one of Ludendorff's epigones on the general staff, in barring a Jewish field chaplain from speaking at the main ceremonies dedicating the monument to Germany's World War I victory at Tannenberg, marred the

(Typescript in Leo Baeck Institute Archives, New York), 63–64; *Borkumer Beobachter* (Borkum), *Veröffentlichungen zum Münchmeyer Prozess* (Borkum, 1926); Alfred Hirschberg, "Münchmeyer—Prozess auf Borkum," *Central-Verein Zeitung*, May 14, 1926; Hirschberg, "Disziplinverfahren gegen Münchmeyer?" *ibid.*, May 21, 1926; Bruno Weil, "Borkum," *ibid.*, May 28, 1926; A. W., "Nachklänge zum Münchmeyer-Prozess," *Central-Vereins Dienst,* September 1, 1926; *ibid.*, November 17, 1927.

129. Alfred Wiener, "Müssen wir 'abrücken'?" *Central-Verein Zeitung*, February 7, 1925; Otto Nuschke, "Das Untersuchungsergebnis des Barmat- Ausschusses," *ibid.*, October 23, 1925; Werner Rosenberg, "Der Schutzherr der Sklareks," *ibid.*, November 15, 1929.

130. *Frankfurter Zeitung*, September 21, 1932; *Mitteilungen aus dem Verein zur Abwehr des Antisemitismus,* December, 1932.

131. *Mitteilungen aus dem Verein zur Abwehr des Antisemitismus*, November 10, 1920; K. Schmitt, "Antisemitismus in der Armee," *ibid.*, April 16, 1920; Sabatzky, "Meine Erinnerungen," 4–5; Jochmann, "Die Ausbreitung des Antisemitismus," 470–72.

Army's correct behavior.[132] Under the circumstances it is hardly surprising that in 1931 there were only eight Jews who had identified themselves as such in the army. None was an officer. There were probably others who had repudiated the Hebrew faith for religious or tactical reasons, but not many.[133]

The various police forces, in whose ranks war veterans, discharged army men, and other nationalists could be found in great numbers, acquitted themselves surprisingly well. That there were anti-Semites among them is incontestable, and that they harassed and failed to protect Eastern Jews is equally certain.[134] But they could also be every bit as brutal to anti-Semites, particularly when the police forces were in the hands of officers who supported the Republic.[135] In Munich, hardly a hotbed of republican sympathies, Chief of Police Ernst Pöhner was known to be no friend of the Jews. And yet, his adjutant in charge of alien registration opposed the expulsion of Eastern Jews from Bavaria, and members of his regular forces rallied to the protection of Jewish hostages taken by the Nazis during the Beer Hall *Putsch*. Shortly after the *Putsch*, Nazis in Murnau who falsely denounced the Zionist journalist Nahum Goldmann to Munich police as a secret Communist agent were amazed to see them befriend Goldmann and warn the Nazis off.[136]

Police attitudes toward nazism no doubt affected their determination to protect Jews during the last years of the Republic. It is known that some constables regarded the Nazis as allies in efforts to control Communist disorders. In Berlin, for example, there may have been as many as 445 Nazi party members or sympathizers out of between 14,000 and 16,000 uniformed street

132. Sabatzky, "Meine Erinnerungen," 6–8. At the time (1927) it was believed that threats of disruption by anti-Jewish groups may have dictated the decision not to let the Jewish chaplain join his Catholic and Protestant counterparts. That may have been the case, but it seems likely that the organizers of the affair placed even greater importance on assuring Ludendorff's attendance and were willing to slight the Jewish war-dead to do so. Julius Brodnitz, "Tannenberg," *Central-Verein Zeitung*, September 23, 1927.

133. Leo Loewenstein, "Deutschlands Wehrkraft," *Central-Verein Zeitung*, April 17, 1931. According to Loewenstein's reckoning, if Jews had been represented in the army according to their proportion of the population, they would have numbered 34 officers and 864 men.

134. *Jüdische Rundschau*, July 1, 1924; *ibid.*, September 2, 1924; *Allgemeine Zeitung des Judentums*, LXXXV (1921), 2; *Der Schild*, July 3, 1925; Theodor Fritsch's Hammerverlag made a special point of sending its anti-Jewish literature to police officers, and other racist organizations probably did the same. Police report to Reich Commission, January 7, 1922, in Documents of the Reich Commission for the Supervision of Public Order, Bundesarchiv, Koblenz, R 134/16, Folge 75.

135. Sabatzky, "Meine Erinnerungen," 5–6, 11; *Mitteilungen aus dem Verein zur Abwehr des Antisemitismus*, March 24, 1922; *ibid.*, October 31, 1922.

136. Löwenfeld, "Memoiren," 668–71; Ramm, *Die Justiz in der Weimar Republik*, 139–40; Nahum Goldmann, *Memories*, trans. Helen Sebba (London, 1970), 81–82.

police (*Schutzpolizei*), or about 3 percent of the total.[137] The Nazi riots in Berlin on the Jewish New Year, 1931, may provide some clues concerning the effects of that infiltration on police behavior. On the evening of September 12, the first day of Rosh Hashanah, Jews leaving the Fasanen Street synagogue near the Kurfürstendamm were set upon by roving bands of SA men *sans* uniforms or party badges. For more than an hour they employed hit-and-run tactics to rough up anyone who looked Jewish and to wreck a coffeehouse frequented by Jews, all the while chorusing such gems as "Sarah, pack the suitcase, the synagogue's afire!" The police were caught off-guard but eventually made sixty-three arrests and jailed twenty of the rioters. Centralverein officials publicly congratulated the police for their actions, but privately they complained that the magistrates arrived too late and under strength.[138] At their request the Prussian Ministry of the Interior instructed all police units to give special attention to patrolling the areas around synagogues to prevent a recurrence of the riot.[139] Interior Minister Karl Severing himself privately admitted that Nazi sympathies may have kept the police from acting more forcefully.[140] In defense of the police, it may be noted that overt attacks of this kind on Jews were extremely rare and unpredictable, whereas the authorities constantly had their hands full with all sorts of other criminal and political violence.

This selected survey of attitudes toward the Jews on the part of representative German political, educational, administrative, and other groups during the Weimar years reveals that there was a good bit of anti-Semitism, but that it was very unevenly distributed and rarely of the extremist variety sometimes advocated by the Nazis. Aside from the obviously anti-Jewish *völkisch* political parties, only the university students and the army showed any substantial vulnerability to radical anti-Semitism. Elsewhere—in the churches, the left-wing and moderate political parties, the courts, and so on—those who actually wanted to do violence to Jewish rights were exceptional cases. The Nazi

137. Hsi-Huey Liang, *The Berlin Police Force in the Weimar Republic* (Berkeley, 1970), 52, 90–113.
138. *Central-Verein Zeitung*, September 18, 1931; *Der Israelit*, September 24, 1931; Hans Reichmann, "Massnahmen des C. V. aus Anlass der Unruhen am Kurfürstendamm," in Nachlass Moritz Sobernheim, 1288/353001–09; Paucker interview.
139. Wilhelm Abegg to Centralverein, September 17, 1931, in Nachlass Moritz Sobernheim, 1288/353013.
140. Max Reiner, "Mein Leben in Deutschland vor und nach dem Jahre 1930" (Typescript in Leo Baeck Institute Archives, New York), 155–56.

leaders themselves acknowledged the weakness of their racialist appeals by keeping their position on the Jewish question vague and shifting. As case studies of specific groups of Nazis have shown, anti-Semitism rarely played an important part in bringing new converts to National Socialism.[141] On the contrary, Germany's economic and political breakdown after 1929 and exaggerated fears of communism were of vastly greater importance in bringing Hitler a mass following.

The defenders of Jews were perhaps more numerous than their detractors, but they were less well organized simply because they could not regard the Jewish question as a central issue. Acutely aware that anti-Semitism was becoming ever more intensely absorbed in the larger political struggle, they fought it through the Socialist, Catholic, and Democratic parties. A few joined the small Association to Resist Anti-Semitism, which distributed hundreds of thousands of published exposés of racist lies. Both the association and the Centralverein had no trouble in getting the cream of Weimar intellectual and political leaders to sign declarations deploring anti-Semitism. Among the signatories were Thomas and Heinrich Mann, Lujo Brentano, Gerhard Hauptmann, Karl Severing, Veit Valentin, Helmuth von Gerlach, and Hermann Müller.[142] Others denounced Judeophobia on their own.[143]

More common and widespread than outright hatred or sympathy for the Jews was what we have called moderate anti-Semitism, that vague sense of unease about Jews that stopped far short of wanting to harm them but that may have helped to neutralize whatever aversion Germans might otherwise have felt for the Nazis. Marxists who viewed Jews as capitalists, Christians who questioned the Jews' otherworldliness, patriots who feared Jewish ra-

141. Theodore Abel, *The Nazi Movement: Why Hitler Came into Power* (New York, 1966), 154–65; Peter H. Merkl, *Political Violence Under the Swastika: 581 Early Nazis* (Princeton, 1975), 498–517, 687–94; Claudia Koonz, "Nazi Women Before 1933: Rebels Against Emancipation," *Social Science Quarterly*, LVI (1976), 553–63; Jeremy Noakes, *The Nazi Party in Lower Saxony 1921–1933* (London, 1971), 209–10; William Sheridan Allen, *The Nazi Seizure of Power: The Experience of a Single German Town, 1930–1935* (Chicago, 1965), 77, 209–10; Rudolf Heberle, *From Democracy to Nazism* (Baton Rouge, 1945), 46, 88; Pridham, *Hitler's Rise to Power*, 237–44. Merkl and Noakes assign somewhat more importance to anti-Semitism than do the others, but not even they make it a central consideration.

142. *Jüdisch-liberale Zeitung*, May 15, 1932; *Jüdische Rundschau*, September 9, 1930; Arthur Prinz, "Zwei deutsche Krankheiten," *ibid.*, September 20, 1932; *Mitteilungen aus dem Verein zur Abwehr des Antisemitismus*, May 15, 1929; *ibid.*, March, 1931; *ibid.*, June, 1932.

143. See, for example, evidence of Walter von Molo's ringing denunciation of the desecration of Jewish cemeteries in *Der Israelit*, November 1, 1928; a 1932 broadside attacking anti-Semitism, signed by three German nobles, in Arthur Lehmann Collection, Leo Baeck Institute Archives, New York, 888/3246/4; and Friedrich von Oppeln-Bronikowski's call for tolerance and unity, *Gerechtigkeit!*

dicalism, conservatives who saw in Jews the embodiment of modernism—all had in common a certain reluctance to excuse Jews entirely from guilt in the making of their own predicament or to believe that they were in much real danger. While these prejudices were to be found nearly everywhere in the civilized world between the wars, leading to virtually universal indifference to the Jews' fate, in Germany they had the additional and catastrophic consequence of neutralizing anti-Semitism as an issue that might have prevented great numbers of Germans from supporting Hitler. Hence the Nazis were able to attract hard-core anti-Semites with racialist appeals without having to fear that this would drive away an equal or greater number of potential followers. Only in this limited sense should Judeophobia be regarded as a key to Nazi success.

IV

The Jewish Response to Anti-Semitism

German Jews were, by and large, no more successful at appraising their racist opposition than was anyone else. They correctly assessed the subordinate role of anti-Semitism in winning votes for Hitler, but they were uncertain about what he would do should he come to power. Heinemann Stern has noted that when the Nazis did take over early in 1933, Jewish opinion was torn between the pessimists, who expected to lose their citizenship while remaining otherwise unmolested, and the optimists, who anticipated little or no change in their status due to the moderating influence of the non-Nazi right.[1]

Stern's judgment may be applied to the entire period of Hitler's rise to power, and it is likely that the optimists and pessimists were about equally divided. The Centralverein leaned toward pessimism, ridiculing Hitler's bland denial of anti-Jewish intentions, made to an American reporter in 1930, and publishing some of the more nearly blood-curdling Nazi statements about Jews together with the text of the famous "Fighting Song of the SA":

> You Storm Troopers, both young and old
> Put weapons in your hand;
> For the Jews wreak havoc fearfully
> In the German Fatherland.
>
> When the Storm soldier comes under fire
> He feels courageous cheer,
> For when Jews' blood spurts from the knife
> Good times are once more here.[2]

---

1. Stern, *Warum hassen sie uns eigentlich?* 179–80.
2. *Central-Verein Zeitung,* March 7, 1930; *ibid.,* June 24, 1932; *Die Stellung der Nationalsozialistischen Deutschen Arbeiterpartei (NSDAP) zur Judenfrage: Eine Materialsammlung vorgelegt vom Centralverein Deutscher Staatsbürger jüdischen Glaubens* (Berlin, n.d.). Below is the German text of the "Fighting Song":

KAMPFLIED DER SA

Ihr Sturmkolonnen jung und alt,
Nehmt die Waffen in die Hand;
Denn die Juden hausen fürchterlich
Im deutschen Vaterland.

The Orthodox journal *Der Israelit* cannily anticipated that a Nazi regime would be unable to make good on its inflated promises and would need the Jews as continuing scapegoats for a multitude of shortcomings.[3] Fears of economic strangulation through boycott were even more widely and profoundly felt than the threat of estrangement. In Alfred Wiener's words: "Should the Third Reich come, then farewell to justice and prosperity, farewell to public spiritedness and free enterprise."[4]

Evidence of more hopeful assessments of National Socialist policies is equally compelling. Voices within the Centralverein itself called into question the importance of the racial issue to the Nazis. Hans Reichmann, noting Hitler's willingness to bargain with other parties for favorable coalition terms, commented: "the Jewish question, passed off by the Nazis in a thousand ways as the key to world history, plays no decisive role in German politics. In the give-and-take of negotiating for a coalition, it is a question of more substantial matters than the nebulous 'Jewish question.'"[5] Once the Nazis had their ruling coalition, there was hope that President Hindenburg, who had established good relations with the Jews, and the non-Nazi majority on the coalition cabinet would succeed in keeping the Nazis in line. As Ludwig Holländer expressed it: "The new Reich government will soon notice that it has quite different and more difficult problems to solve than the so-called Jewish problem."[6] Moreover, the solid impression that anti-Semitism was not a chief issue to the new Nazi voters probably encouraged the belief that National Socialists would be as loath to alienate them as their right-wing allies with sav-

---

Wenn der Sturmsoldat in's Feuer geht,
Ja, dann hat er frohen Mut.
Denn wenn das Judenblut vom Messer sprizt
Dann geht's noch mal so gut.

3. S. H., "Die Entwicklung des Nationalsozialismus und die politische Funktion des Antisemitismus," *Der Israelit*, July 23, 1931.

4. Alfred Wiener, "Programmerfüllung oder Agitation: Was würde eine Hitler-Mehrheit tun?" *Central-Verein Zeitung*, July 24, 1932; *ibid.*, June 11, 1926; *ibid.*, September 19, 1930; Ludwig Freund, "Die Juden im 'Dritten Reich,'" *Der Schild*, X (1931), 23.

5. Rei [probably Hans R. or Eva Reichmann], "Vor den Entscheidungen," *Central-Verein Zeitung*, May 20, 1932. A similar statement was made earlier by young Centralverein activist Wolfgang Matzdorff: "Anti-Semitism is certainly not the only point in the National Socialist program. It can also remain a completely open question whether it belongs to the most important principles of the NSDAP." "Die politische Lage in Deutschland und der C. V.," *Rundbrief des Reichsjugendausschusses des Centralvereins*, June 13, 1932.

6. Ludwig Holländer, "Die neue Regierung," *Central-Verein Zeitung*, February 2, 1933; Hugo Marx, *Werdegang eines jüdischen Staatsanwalts und Richters in Baden (1892–1933)* (Villingen, 1965), 226; undated biographical statement by Leo Wolff in Leo Wolff Collection, Leo Baeck Institute Archives, New York, 4059/I.2.

age anti-Jewish actions.[7] Only the Zionist *Jüdische Rundschau* perceived that popular attitudes about racism made little difference one way or another; the German people might not be bloodthirsty anti-Semites, but the Nazi leaders were.[8] On the other hand, not even the Zionists anticipated the escalating violence that would culminate in the Holocaust. When the Nazis placarded Jewish shops with the Star of David during the first mass boycott of April 1, 1933, *Jüdische Rundschau* editor Robert Weltsch's advice was to "Wear the yellow badge with pride!"—a statement that made sense only on the assumption that Jewish life in Germany would go on for some time to come.[9]

Throughout the Weimar years, complacency, combined with a sense of helplessness, encouraged some German Jews to adopt a sanguine view of racism. Not a few saw anti-Semitism as a positive boon that alone could keep the Jews from gradual amalgamation with the larger society and ultimate disappearance as a distinctive religious group. Among them was Leipzig Rabbi Felix Goldmann; another was Dr. Kurt Fleischer, the leader of the Liberals in the Berlin Jewish Community Assembly, who in 1929 argued against sending Jewish children to special schools: "We do not fear Judeophobia in the public schools, nor do we fear it for our children, who will have to learn to defend themselves. Anti-Semitism is the scourge that God has sent to us in order to lead us together and weld us together."[10] Similarly, Jewish banker Max Warburg could see in nazism "a necessary reaction" against Germany's foreign enemies and could rejoice "that the German nation, after years of suffering, has brought together so much strength in this [the Nazi] movement."[11] Complacency on the racial issue probably led a few conservative Jews to hope that the Nazis would win sufficient political power to end the Communist threat once and for all.[12]

Perhaps nothing contributed more to the Jews' underestimation of

7. Ludwig Holländer, "Bindet den Helm fester!" *Central-Verein Zeitung,* September 26, 1930; *ibid.,* July 3, 1931.

8. *Jüdische Rundschau,* September 26, 1930. The comment was made in response to a poll of prominent German Jews, made by the Jewish Telegraph Agency, which revealed a widespread belief that anti-Semitism had very little to do with the upsurge in Nazi votes in the 1930 Reichstag elections.

9. *Ibid.,* April 4, 1933.

10. *Gemeindeblatt der Jüdischen Gemeinde zu Berlin,* XIX (1929), 400; interview with Dr. Fred Grubel, July 28, 1975.

11. Max Warburg to Georg Gothein, August 21, 1932, in Nachlass Georg Gothein, 33/134.

12. Fritz Goldberg, "Mein Leben in Deutschland vor und nach dem 30. Januar 1933" (Typescript in Leo Baeck Institute Archives, New York), 35; Kurt Blumenfeld, *Erlebte Judenfrage: Ein Vierteljahrhundert deutscher Zionismus* (Stuttgart, 1962), 182; Hubertus zu Loewenstein, *Conquest of the Past: An Autobiography* (Boston, 1938), 284–85.

Judeophobia before 1933 than the simple fact that few of them ever became victims of direct racist attacks. Certainly there was more anti-Semitic violence in Germany after the First World War than there had been earlier. There were incidents that ranged from name-calling in the streets to beatings of Jews and desecrations of synagogues and Jewish cemeteries. However, a few conspicuous exceptions notwithstanding, there were not many of these cases of actual violence, particularly after the tumultuous early years of the Republic. Those that did occur were usually dealt with by the police and the courts. At least two-thirds of all German Jews lived in sophisticated, upper middle-class districts of the largest cities, where they were disturbed only on the rare occasions when racists actually sought them out. The New Year's riots of 1931 were very much out of the ordinary. So were the few physical attacks on Jews who were active in the prorepublican parties and organizations or in the Centralverein, made during election campaigns in 1930 and 1932.[13] Jewish urbanites, secure in the circle of predominantly Jewish, but also selected non-Jewish friends, knew how to avoid an ugly incident with the odd racist enthusiast. One did not spend his vacation at just any resort; Jewish periodicals regularly ran lists of spas and hotels that excluded Jews and/or catered to a *völkisch* crowd.[14] Nor did one casually reveal his Jewishness to strangers on trains or in other public places. Those obvious rules observed, one could associate anti-Semitic violence primarily with such benighted regions as Poland and Rumania. One could even consider himself fortunate to be spared the demeaning covenants, common in the United States, that barred Jews from living anywhere they wished.[15]

It could be much harder for the few Jews who lived in small towns. Denied the shelter of urban anonymity and a large Jewish community, they were mercilessly harassed wherever local racists could create resentments or exploit existing ones. Boycotts against small-town Jewish doctors and shopkeepers could be especially devastating, and they were virtually impossible to counteract with mere injunctions. In one small town, for example, Nazis robbed a Jewish butcher of most of his business by spreading rumors that Hebrew religious law required him to defile the meat he sold to Gentiles in unspeakable ways.[16] The success of such tactics varied widely with local conditions. In one

13. *Central-Verein Zeitung,* September 19, 1930; *ibid.,* August 5, 1932.
14. In July, 1932, the Centralverein added a special travel service from which information on specific vacation spots could be obtained upon request. *Ibid.,* July 22, 1932.
15. Goldmann, *Memories,* 59.
16. *Central-Verein Zeitung,* May 2, 1930; Julius Moses, "Jüdische Tragödien der Kleinstadt," *Israelitisches Familienblatt,* February 25, 1932. This reprehensible lie must be

locale, the townsfolk rallied to break up a racist gathering by force; in another, they permitted Nazis to drive a Jew out of town.[17]

For the vast majority of German Jews, then, anti-Semitism was an annoying but scarcely terrifying propaganda campaign of charges that ran from the predictable—Jews were traitors, exploiters, and so on—to the preposterous: in a grotesquely twisted anticipation of things to come, Dresden racists accused Jews of stealing the gold fillings from the teeth of corpses in the municipal crematorium.[18] Few Jews had been the targets of personal attacks, but virtually all knew anti-Semites, most of whom they described as punctiliously correct or even friendly in their personal relations with individual Jews.[19] The simple truth is that in most cases anti-Semitism was as abstract to the Jews as Jews were to anti-Semites.

However sanguine German Jews may have been about German racism, they were neither indifferent to their coreligionists who suffered from it nor fatalistic about their civil rights. Most of them supported the self-defense activities of the Centralverein, either directly through membership or, more commonly, indirectly by means of the support given the Centralverein by the clubs and religious communities. Its membership grew steadily from 45,000 at the end of World War I to a high of 72,400 in 1924. On the eve of the Nazi seizure of power it stood at about 64,000. Only the Zionists and a few right-wing Jews rejected Centralverein tactics and ideology.[20]

The Centralverein's work was significant in three respects: overtly, it con-

---

viewed against the background of the great popularity of kosher meat among Germans as a whole and the corresponding envy of non-Jewish butchers. Almost everywhere in Germany the sale of kosher meat outstripped Jewish demand by many times.

17. *Central-Verein Zeitung*, April 3, 1924; *ibid.*, August 22, 1930; Wilhelm Müller, "Kleinstadt Antisemitismus," *ibid.*, December 26, 1930.

18. *Mitteilungen aus dem Verein zur Abwehr des Antisemitismus*, August 20, 1925; *ibid.*, November 20, 1925.

19. Fritz Goldschmidt, "Mein Leben in Deutschland vor und nach dem 30. Januar 1933" (Typescript in Leo Baeck Institute Archives, New York), 6–7; Goldberg, "Mein Leben," 21–22; Kurt Jakob Ball-Kaduri, *Das Leben der Juden in Deutschland im Jahre 1933* (Frankfurt, 1963), 37–38; Walter Heinemann, "Braunschweiger Erinnerungen" (Typescript in Leo Baeck Institute Archives, New York), 67, 71; Oscar Schwarz, "Mein Leben in Deutschland vor und nach dem Jahre 1933" (Typescript in Leo Baeck Institute Archives, New York), 8–10; Friedrich Solon, "Mein Leben in Deutschland vor und nach dem 30. Januar 1933" (Typescript in Leo Baeck Institute Archives, New York), 31–33.

20. Indirectly the Centralverein claimed to represent at least 300,000 German Jews, which was the great majority of the adult Jewish population. Reiner Bernstein, "Zwischen Emanzipation und Antisemitismus: Die Publizistik der deutschen Juden am Beispiel der 'C.V.-Zeitung,'" Organ des Centralvereins deutscher Staatsbürger jüdischen Glaubens, 1924–1933" (Ph.D. dissertation, Free University of Berlin, n.d.), 73; Centralverein to Reich Chancellor Hans Luther, March 1, 1926, in Reich Chancellery Documents on Jewish Affairs, Bundesarchiv, Koblenz, R43 I/2192, L 381847–48.

fronted anti-Semites and their charges with the truth as it saw it; covertly, it aided antiracist political parties and brought pressure on public servants and other influential Germans to counteract the *völkisch* scourge; inwardly, it brought a sense of security and confidence to the Jews themselves. Most of its energy and resources were consumed in public confrontations with Jew-baiting. As early as 1919 it was distributing 50,000 handbills and 10,000 pamphlets daily, a practice that was kept up whenever conditions demanded propaganda to counter racist charges.[21] Until April, 1922, its monthly publication *Im Deutschen Reich,* and thereafter the weekly *Central-Verein Zeitung,* did the same thing. Up to 1926, free copies were sent to all sorts of molders of public opinion, from politicians to clergymen; in that year a special monthly edition was begun especially for this purpose.[22] Only lack of funds prevented this publicity campaign from being widened; the Centralverein repeatedly complained that even its own members were lax in paying dues and funding special projects.[23] Partially as a result of these financial limitations, circulation of the *Central-Verein Zeitung* declined from around 80,000 in 1925 to about 60,000 in 1932.[24] The Jewish defense organization also sent speakers to racist meetings to reply to anti-Jewish allegations during the discussion sessions that usually followed the planned programs. The respondents were not always successful in getting the floor, but in such cases they would demonstratively stalk out, sometimes taking large parts of the crowd with them. Then they could always turn the publicity that had been aroused to good use by staging protest meetings.[25] These and similar tactics earned the Centralverein the nickname "Denunciation League"—a title it bore lightly.

Standing ready to haul anti-Semites before the bar of justice was the Centralverein's legal defense division, an extensive and able branch of an organization led largely by lawyers. It was responsible for the conviction of dozens of racist lawbreakers on a variety of counts ranging from boycott to physical

21. "II. Tätigkeitsbericht," (August 31, 1919), in Centralverin Collection, Leo Baeck Institute Archives, New York, 171/366.

22. The highest publication figures for the *Central-Verein Zeitung* were 80,000 during the years 1923–25. For the *Central-Verein Monatsausgabe* they were 60,000 in 1932. Bernstein, "Zwischen Emanzipation und Antisemitismus," 38–42.

23. Eva Reichmann-Jungmann, "Die Selbstwehr der deutschen Juden," *Central-Verein Zeitung,* July 25, 1930; Ernst Hirsch, "Unsere Zeitung in finanzieller Not," *ibid.,* July 24, 1924; *Im deutschen Reich,* XXVII (1921), 183.

24. Bernstein, "Zwischen Emanzipation und Antisemitismus," 41–42.

25. Ernst Herzfeld, "Lebenserinnerungen" (Typescript in Leo Baeck Institute Archives, New York), 199–201; *Im deutschen Reich,* XXVI (1920), 251–53.

assault, but most commonly for disorderly conduct or slander. The problem of biased judges and prosecuting attorneys notwithstanding, Centralverein lawyers produced a creditable record of success. Among their victims were Julius Streicher, Gregor Strasser, and Pastor Münchmeyer.

Not all Centralverein leaders agreed that public confrontation was the best way to carry on the battle. It had the disadvantage of fighting on defensive ground on terms dictated by the foe. It employed reason to combat an impulse that was at least partially irrational. Its best ammunition could never penetrate the armor of devout Judeophobes, whereas the indifferent multitudes remained largely out of range. These considerations led some German Jews to reject the Centralverein, but for other Jews they called instead for concentration on quiet, behind-the-scenes activities through the self-defense organization.[26] This included furnishing the anti-Nazi parties with money and propaganda, as well as prodding republican politicians to be duly solicitous of Jewish rights. The chief beneficiaries of this aid were the Center and Social Democratic parties and, before 1930, the Democratic party. In Bavaria it was chiefly the Bavarian People's party that stood between the Jews and the Nazis.[27] These actions probably did more to protect the Jews than anything else the Centralverein attempted.

Occasionally these efforts to subsidize antiracist parties could be a source of tension within the Centralverein. Not only did some of its leaders prefer to limit the organization's activities to direct attacks on the enemy, but aid for any given party could easily alienate members who leaned toward the opposite political pole. Although officially neutral on political matters, the Centralverein rejected the Nazis and Nationalists as racists and the Communists as atheists, leaving a wide spectrum, from Social Democrats to People's party, open for approval and support. In June, 1927, the conservative banker Jakob Goldschmidt, incensed over the use of his name in a pamphlet used to raise money for the primarily Social Democratic Reichsbanner paramilitary units, resigned from the Centralverein's board of directors. Although Goldschmidt was subsequently persuaded to return, he and a minority of board members continued to question the wisdom of such tactics.[28] Nevertheless, National Socialism's rapid gains after 1929 virtually obliged the Centralverein to fight

26. Paucker, *Jüdische Abwehrkampf,* 37–38; interview with Dr. Werner J. Cahnmann, July 25, 1975.
27. Paucker, *Jüdische Abwehrkampf,* 87–105.
28. Jakob Goldschmidt to Julius Brodnitz, June 16, 1927, in Alfred Hirschberg Collection, Leo Baeck Institute Archives, New York, 1186/3966/II.26; *Protokoll, C-V Hauptvorstandssitzung,* July 19, 1927, in *ibid.,* 1186/3966/II.27; Brodnitz interview.

it through the surviving prorepublican parties, notably the Catholic and Socialist parties.

Historians have neglected the third aspect of Centralverein activities, its
provision of security to the Jewish psyche. Centralverein leaders repeatedly
acknowledged that theirs was more than a defense organization pure and
simple. Since it was necessary to understand and value whatever one wished
to defend, they underlined the positive fusion of things Jewish and things
German, affirming the legal and moral rights of Jews to live as German citizens. Moreover, the knowledge that Centralverein legal defense teams were
vigilant watchmen over those rights must have added to the sense of well-
being even of those Jews who doubted the effectiveness of the organization's
propaganda against anti-Semitism. In small towns where Jews were having a
particularly hard time with the Nazis, Centralverein interest helped provide
the courage to endure. Werner Cahnmann, a Centralverein syndic in Bavaria,
recalls that his visits to Jews in the smaller south German villages were sometimes greeted with emotional scenes that combined gratitude with relief.[29]

It was perhaps in the nature of its mission that the Centralverein should
have maintained a singularly humorless posture before anyone who dared
trifle with the Jewish image. It publicly protested against and privately re-
monstrated with Jewish artists who employed "Jewish jokes" or Yiddish ac-
cents in movies, the radio, or cabaret skits.[30] Few things annoyed it more than
someone like Willy Prager or Fritz Grünebaum, his "Jewish" features accen-
tuated, arrogantly singing in the Kabaret der Komiker a ditty such as this one:

> How can Sigismund help it,
> that he's so handsome?
> How can Sigismund help it,
> that he's adored?[31]

That there was an element of Jewish "self-hatred" involved in such humor is
undeniable, but the Jews' ability to laugh at themselves more than made up
for it by releasing tensions and lifting spirits.

The second-largest secular Jewish organization, the National League of

29. Cahnmann interview.
30. *Central-Verein Zeitung,* May 26, 1922; Karl Rosenthal, "Leipzig, Brühl Nr. 5," *ibid.,*
May 22, 1924; Carl Pinn, "Gegen das Jüdeln im Radio, *ibid.,* March 13, 1925; *ibid.,* December 31, 1926; Hans Wollenberg, "Der Jude im Film," *ibid.,* September 16, 1927; Ernst G.
Lowenthal, "Misston im Tonfilm," *ibid.,* December 5, 1930.
31. Reichmann and Brodnitz interviews. The "Sigismund Song," a popular hit of the late
1920s, was adapted from the libretto of the operetta "Das weisse Rössel," in which the original
character Sigismund was decidedly not Jewish.

Jewish Frontline Veterans (Reichsbund jüdischer Frontsoldaten), was likewise established for the purpose of defending Jews from their detractors. Founded in Berlin at the end of January, 1919, as the Patriotic League of Jewish Frontline Veterans, it quickly expanded and renamed itself. By 1921 it had recruited 15,000 members, and by 1932 the figure had doubled.[32] It might have attracted a still larger number of Jewish veterans had it not committed itself to dramatizing the Jewish contribution to Germany's recent war effort by limiting membership to Jewish veterans who could prove that they had fought for the Fatherland in the front lines.[33] Under the stolid leadership of Leo Loewenstein, who had developed a sonar device for the German military during the war, it painstakingly documented the numbers of Jewish war dead. Racist figures that were too low by half or more were not allowed to go unchallenged. In 1932 it presented the resulting compilation of nearly 11,000 names to President Hindenburg and representatives of other veterans' groups and the press.[34] But years before it had achieved more notice by taking Munich Judeophobe Dietrich Eckart up on his offer of a thousand marks to anyone who could prove that a Jewish family had provided three sons to the fighting front for a minimum of three weeks. The league found dozens of families that answered the description. Rabbi Freund of Hanover furnished evidence for twenty in his community alone. Eckart paid up, but only after being forced to do so by the courts.[35]

The Jewish frontline veterans took pains to convey their message to the German masses, occasionally, but not usually, in cooperation with the Centralverein. They distributed pamphlets and sent speakers to racist meetings, entering into the discussion only if there were a full house on the theory that they would only make poorly attended meetings more interesting and draw bigger crowds to them in the future. Beginning in 1930 the league's executive director, Ludwig Freund, traveled all over Germany as a full-time speaker and

---

32. *Allgemeine Zeitung des Judentums,* January 31, 1919; *Israelitisches Familienblatt,* September 15, 1921; Heinrich Hamburger, "Der Reichsbund jüdischer Frontsoldaten," *ibid.,* June 2, 1932.

33. This in the face of sporadic attempts to broaden the base of membership. S. London, "Die Förderer Frage," *Der Schild,* IV (1925), 426–27; *ibid.,* IV (1925), 454.

34. Loe[wenstein], "Ran an die Wahrheit!" *ibid.,* VIII (1929), 9; *ibid.,* XI (1932), 169–71; *ibid.,* XII (1933), 26.

35. "1000 Mk. Belohnung!" in Reichsbund jüdischer Frontsoldaten Collection, Wiener Library, London; *Was muss das schaffende Volk vom politischen, wirtschaftlichen, religiösen Juden- und Rassenhass des reaktionären Faschismus wissen? Für Redner und Funktionäre herausgegeben von der Sozialdemokratischen Partei Deutschlands, Ortsverein Hannover* (Hanover, [1924]), 4–5, in Pamphlet Collection, Wiener Library, London.

propagandist. These activities earned it the financial support of several of the larger Jewish religious communities and of Jewish provincial organizations.[36]

The league brought to the fight against anti-Semitism a spartan spirit that befitted a group of frontline veterans. This included emphasizing athletics and land resettlement programs, but still more significant were paramilitary preparations. Early on, league members established clandestine arms caches and formed defensive detachments in Berlin, Munich, Königsberg, Kassel, and Breslau against the possibility of pogroms or of a racist *Putsch*. These they used to good purpose in defending Eastern Jews during the 1923 Berlin riots, during which a veteran shot and mortally wounded one of the racists. To be sure, the veterans had no hope of stopping the riots. Their action was meant principally as a symbolic gesture of defiance and as a means of spurring the police into action. After the courts acquitted them of using their weapons illegally and, in effect, recognized their right to bear arms for defensive purposes, they began openly to patrol the neighborhoods around synagogues.[37] In 1927, following a Nazi attack on Jews in the streets of downtown Berlin, the league joined with the Jewish Boxing Club "Maccabi" and the Zionist Sport Association "Bar Kochba" to found a Jewish Defense Service (Jüdischer Abwehr-Dienst). According to the recollections of one participant, the Defense Service operated under conditions of secrecy but was known to and even armed by the Berlin police (Schutzpolizei). Hence it was in a position to hold the Nazi riots of the Jewish New Year, 1931, within manageable limits until the police appeared.[38] In the following year the league stood arm-in-arm with the republican paramilitary defense organization, the Reichsbanner, to counteract an expected Nazi coup.[39]

By far the most controversial aspect of the league's fight against anti-

36. *Der Schild,* IV (1925), 5, 8–10; Steffan Kann, "Der Reichsbund jüdischer Frontsoldaten," *Der Israelit,* July 19, 1928; various community administrative reports, June 19, 1929, to November 17, 1929, in Jewish Community of Breslau Collection, YIVO Institute for Jewish Research, New York. A more detailed discussion of the veterans' agitation against racist propaganda is found in Dunker, *Der Reichsbund jüdischer Frontsoldaten,* 70–80; and in Rheins, "German Jewish Patriotism," 33–42.
37. Adolph Asch, "Die Inflationjahre 1919–1923" (Typescript in Leo Baeck Institute Archives, New York), 11–12; Walther Kochmann, "Notwehr," *Central-Verein Zeitung,* May 22, 1924; Dunker, *Der Reichsbund jüdischer Frontsoldaten,* 49–61.
38. The participant was the former Zionist functionary Fritz Lewinson, who entered the Jewish Defense Service by way of "Bar Kochba." He attributes the absence of corroborating documents to the need to maintain secrecy. Dunker, *Der Reichsbund jüdischer Frontsoldaten,* 61–66, 262–64. *Cf.* the guarded report concerning the riots in the league's journal, *Der Schild,* X (1931), 149.
39. Paucker, *Jüdische Abwehrkampf,* 35, 250.

Semitism was its emphasis on what it called Jewish "self-discipline," by which it meant keeping Jews from offensive actions that might be exploited by Judeophobes. In 1920 Leo Loewenstein himself took the initiative in founding a special "self-discipline committee" and became its first chairman.[40] Its message: "Out of the inns of gluttony! Away with the mad pursuit of pleasure! Down with vain baubles! *Back to simplicity and serious living!*"[41] It was addressed with special intensity to Jewish women, who were advised to avoid tactless displays of ostentatious clothing and jewelry, and to young Jews, who were admonished to keep their morals from slipping—in public places at the very least.[42] In this it had the ardent support of the most widely read Jewish newspaper, the *Israelitisches Familienblatt,* which offered its readers, at cost, pamphlets exhorting Jews to model behavior, and urged their broad distribution.[43] One league member seriously proposed the creation of extralegal courts where cases involving only Jewish litigants could be tried without displaying dirty linen before the general public.[44]

The veterans' somewhat excessive zeal in pursuing their puritanical view of "self-discipline" aroused both criticism and emulation in the wider Jewish population. The Centralverein was prepared to remind Jewish entrepreneurs that unfair treatment of employees and customers could be a serious source of anti-Jewish sentiments.[45] It would not go further and demand that Jews avoid certain kinds of behavior in which other Germans might indulge with impunity. Not a few Centralverein leaders considered the veterans' extreme efforts to prove Jewish patriotism demeaning, and they privately viewed them with a mixture of mild amusement and condescension.[46] Still, considering the racist harping on the Jews' "destructive" wealth and "un-German" demeanor, the veterans' insistence on "self-discipline" made a good deal of sense, even if it did mean special rules for the Jews. As Centralverein chairman Ludwig Holländer himself put it: "Stepchildren must be doubly good."[47]

---

40. Ernst Schäffer, "Selbstzucht!" *Der Schild,* V (1926), 153.

41. *Kämpft mit uns!* (n.p., n.d., [ca. 1921]), in Reichsbund jüdischer Frontsoldaten Collection. Emphasis in original.

42. *Der Schild,* I (1922), Beilage, 1; Asch, "Die Inflationjahre," 7–8. *Cf.* Dunker, *Der Reichsbund jüdischer Frontsoldaten,* 47–49.

43. *Israelitisches Familienblatt,* August 9, 1923.

44. S. London, "Jüdische Schieds- und Ehrengerichte," *K. C. Blätter,* XVII (1927), 18–20.

45. *Reichstagswahl 1932—Eine Schicksalsstunde des deutschen Judentums,* in Alfred Hirschberg Collection, 1186/3966/II.33; *Central-Verein Zeitung,* November 23, 1922; George Baum, "Jüdische Arbeitgeberpflichten," *ibid.,* March 13, 1924.

46. Brodnitz interview.

47. Gay, "Encounter with Modernism," 59–61.

Outside the Jewish veterans' organization, "self-discipline" gained its greatest support from the Hebrew religious communities, to which the idea appealed on moral grounds. Hence the Jewish High Council in Baden advised its flock in 1919 to improve the Jewish image by abandoning "the exaggerated display of clothing, jewelry, and similar luxury items . . . during this time of widespread want."[48] Similarly, in 1922 the General Alliance of Rabbis in Germany lectured Jews on proper decorum at vacation spots lest Jews as a whole attract criticism.[49] In one case a plaque bearing the names of Jewish war dead was affixed prominently on the exterior of a large urban synagogue, rather than in the customary spot within.[50] Embarrassed over the negative impression left by interminable and often bitter squabbling between various Jewish factions and parties, communal leaders occasionally negotiated moratoria on public election campaigning and the especially hot debates between Zionists and liberals. As the Council of the Prussian Provincial Association of Jewish Communities put it in 1929: "the dignity of the Jewish name and the reputation of the German Jews urgently necessitate the decontamination of the internal Jewish conflict."[51]

The contribution of Jewish religious communities to the struggle against anti-Semitism was by no means limited to the "self-discipline" campaign. On the contrary, some of them established their own self-defense committees to parry racist blows at the end of World War I, before the Centralverein had become well organized outside of Berlin.[52] In addition, several rabbis and community leaders were instrumental in building bridges to their Christian neighbors by inviting groups of them to visit synagogues and there to familiarize themselves with Judaism. Those who did extend such invitations may well have shared Rahel Straus's concern over the lack of ties between Gentiles and Jews. She commented on the distance that separated members of her League of Jewish Women and non-Jewish women who had volunteered to assist them in fighting racism: "we lived among each other, sat together in the same school room, attended university together, met each other at social

---

48. In Reich Chancellery Documents on Jewish Affairs, Bundesarchiv, Koblenz, R43 I/2192, L 381781–2.
49. *Jüdische Rundschau*, June 9, 1922.
50. J. Jacobson, "Mehr Würde!" *Israelitisches Familienblatt*, November 27, 1919.
51. *Ibid.*, November 28, 1929; *Jüdische Rundschau*, January 13, 1925.
52. Marx, *Werdegang eines jüdischen Staatsanwalts*, 128–31; Max Markreich, "Geschichte der Juden in Bremen und Umgegend" (Typescript in Leo Baeck Institute Archives, New York); Elias Straus, "Sigmund Fränkel: Ein Nachruf," *Bayerische Israelitische Gemeindezeitung*, I (1925), 190–94.

events—and were complete strangers. Was it their fault? Ours? Hard to say, but also meaningless. It was a fact, of portentous consequence for the time, that those who wanted to stand up for us knew nothing about us."[53]

Special efforts were made to reach out to Christian church groups and school children. The Essen Jewish Community, with the help of the local Centralverein organization, led the way in 1919, and dozens of synagogues followed suit in subsequent years.[54] Unhappily, some localities built bridges half-heartedly, or not at all. In 1930 the Representative Assembly of the Berlin Jewish Community unanimously adopted a resolution endorsing educational talks in the synagogues for non-Jewish audiences as an effective means of combating prejudice and antagonism, but a year later the idea was still in the planning stage.[55] At least one synagogue canceled the visits of school children because of complaints that they disturbed its peace and quiet.[56] And yet, judging from Nazi protests against such visits, they may have done some good.[57]

According to the minority of German Jews that adhered to Zionism, most of these self-defense efforts did little good at all. They were demeaning in their repetitious apologetics and their double standard of self-discipline. Moreover, they did harm by spreading false hopes and deflecting attention from what the Zionists believed was the one effective antidote to anti-Semitism: Jewish nationalism. Racial prejudice was the inevitable and justifiable response of one people to attempts by another to make it share in the formation of its destiny. It was an instinctive response independent of reason and will, and hence common to all peoples, the Jews included. The one way to fight it was for the races to go their separate ways. For the Jews, that meant self-imposed isolation in Germany as a prelude to emigration to Palestine.

This is not the place to make a detailed exploration of the Zionist viewpoint.[58] Suffice it to say that Zionist measures against anti-Semitism were pitifully inadequate and in no way commensurate with the vitality that they

53. Straus, *Wir lebten in Deutschland*, 266.

54. Eugen Wolbe, "Zum Kapitel 'Aufklärungsarbeit,'" *Central-Verein Zeitung*, February 14, 1924; Hugo Hahn, "Aufklärungsvorträge in jüdischen Gotteshäusern," *ibid*., April 17, 1931; *Israelitisches Familienblatt*, August 19, 1920; *ibid*., August 26, 1926; *Central-Vereins Dienst*, February 15, 1927; *Mitteilungen aus dem Verein zur Abwehr des Antisemitismus*, January, 1930; *Bayerische Israelitische Gemeindezeitung*, VII (1931), 87.

55. *Gemeindeblatt der Jüdischen Gemeinde zu Berlin*, XX (1930), 131–36; *ibid*., XXI (1931), 133; *Der Israelit*, February 26, 1931; interview with Rabbi Dr. Max Grünewald, July 23, 1975.

56. Gustav Cohn, "Synagogenbesuche—Kirchenbesuche," *Israelitisches Familienblatt*, December 1, 1932.

57. *Jüdisch-liberale Zeitung*, XI (1931), Beilage; *Der Israelit*, March 5, 1931.

58. See below, chapter VI.

were capable of mustering for other causes. Hamstrung by a naïve vision of impressing Jew-baiters with Jewish racial consciousness, they became aware of the need to strike back only very late in the day, or else not at all. Whatever they did, the fundamental agreement of Nazis and Zionists that Germans and Jews were incompatible could only embarrass Centralverein attempts to demonstrate the central fact of German Jewish life—that the vast majority of Jews was passionately committed to the well-being of its sole Fatherland, Germany.

And what of the efforts of those larger Jewish groups, the Centralverein, the veterans, and the religious communities? Were they not equally naïve and equally futile? True enough, they relied too much on reason and ended in defeat. But failure was not preordained. The Nazis never polled more than 44 percent of the votes in the free elections that preceded their seizure of power. Hitler became dictator by a combination of backstairs deals and political blackmail, not because most Germans wanted him. We shall never be able precisely to measure the Jews' contribution to stemming the Nazi tide, but it is possible that their own propaganda against nazism and their support for the Social Democrats and the Catholics helped keep Hitler from winning anything like majority support during the Weimar years. Even if their efforts had no influence whatever on the size of the Nazi vote, no one, then or since, could justly fault them for indifference to their own or their country's fate.[59]

59. *Cf.* an open letter from an Alsatian Jew, Gaston Heymann, in which he faulted German Jews for "fatalistic resignation" in the face of the Nazi onslaught. *Deutsche Republik,* IV (1930), 1189–92. For two fairly typical responses from German Jews see *Der Israelit,* July 10, 1930; *Der Morgen,* VI (1930), 300–302.

V

The Jew as German Liberal
The Search for an Assimilationist Identity

That the great majority of German Jews—around three-quarters of them—were liberals hardly comes as a surprise, particularly in the light of their economic, social, and political relationships. Their liberalism corresponded to the ideas of 1789 and 1848 as expressed by Eduard Lasker, Theodor Mommsen, Gabriel Riesser, and Friedrich Naumann: personal freedom, toleration, individualism, representative government, laissez-faire economics. Never mind that the Jews were not always consistent in their liberalism; most of them were most of the time, and their record of loyalty to that cause is at least as good as that of any other group of Germans.

Too much has been made of German liberalism's reluctance to reciprocate with "liberal" attitudes toward the Jews.[1] True enough, German liberals from Dohm to Hellpach urged the Jews to amalgamate and disappear, not out of racial or any other kind of hostility, but out of traditional liberal distrust of "artificial" distinctions growing out of religion and race. Their unattractive secular vision of a human family harmonized in cultural uniformity gave way in practice to unenthusiastic toleration of whatever could not be demolished with reasoned arguments.

Although far from anti-Semitic, these liberal pressures for Jewish amalgamation intensified the effects of conservative intolerance. Both before and after World War I, thousands of Jews quietly changed their names and religion, and frequently intermarried as well. It was all fairly easily accomplished, and it permitted one to escape social anti-Semitism and start anew as a German among Germans. Often such defections only formalized what had long existed de facto. Some prestigious voices could be heard giving intellectual respectability to these moves. The young Walther Rathenau, writing in 1897 under a pseudonym and a few years later under his own name, criticized his fellow Jews for constituting "a half-voluntary, invisible ghetto, not a living member of the nation, but a foreign organism in its body." He admonished

1. Schorsch, *Jewish Reactions to German Anti-Semitism*, 1–12; Tal, *Christians and Jews in Germany*, 81–120.

them that "the state has granted you citizenship in order to educate you to be Germans. You have remained foreigners, and now you demand that it declare full equality of rights? You speak of duties fulfilled: military service and taxes. But there was more than duty to fulfill; namely, trust." Rathenau recommended not conversion to Christianity, but a concerted effort by Jews to replace their "Asiatic" customs and habits with behavior more becoming to Germans.[2] Indeed, Judaism's congeniality to intellectual freedom grew in importance for Rathenau, and in his later years he studied Hasidic mysticism and Hebrew under the influence of Martin Buber, without, however, actively practicing the faith of his fathers.[3]

At very much the same time that Rathenau moderated his amalgamationist expectations, the now largely forgotten Jewish philosopher Constantin Brunner (the pen name of Leo Wertheimer) intensified his demands that Jews become one with Germans. A follower of the rationalist philosophy of Baruch Spinoza, Brunner saw all of history moving inexorably toward unity, a movement that he advised the Jews to join by means of "self-emancipation" from their ingrown sense of otherness. Although before the First World War he had been prepared to wait for the distant future to see amalgamation realized, his patience grew thin after 1918. Brunner then concluded that the Jews' defensive and self-conscious reaction to resurgent anti-Semitism was self-defeating in that it caused them to lose sight of the necessity of self-emancipation from ossified Judaism and its cryptonationalist offspring. Sympathy for Zionism among liberal Jews seemed to him a fundamental misreading of the alternatives before them: ultimate amalgamation, either into Germany or into Jewish nationalism. A close examination of Zionism would expose it to them as a reactionary utopia; their only practical choice was to stop "playing at being Jews."[4]

The theme of partial or complete amalgamation as the unwritten corollary of Jewish emancipation was taken up by a stanch non-Jewish foe of anti-Semitism in the Weimar years, Willy Hellpach. A former minister-president of Baden, this Heidelberg professor had won considerable Jewish support as the

2. Walther Rathenau, "Höre, Israel!" in *Impressionen* (Leipzig, 1902), 3–20. It first appeared in 1897 as an essay by "W. Hartenau" in Maximilian Harden's *Die Zukunft.*
3. Berglar, *Walther Rathenau,* 304–307.
4. Constantin Brunner, *Der Judenhass und die Juden* (Berlin, 1918), 289–344. Written on the eve of World War I, its publication was delayed by the outbreak of hostilities. See also Constantin Brunner, *Höre Israel und Höre Nicht-Israel* (Berlin, 1931), 3–38; Constantin Brunner, *Von der Pflichten der Juden und von den Pflichten des Staates* (Berlin, 1930), 19–62, 159–68. *Cf.* Frederick Ritter, "Constantin Brunner und seine Stellung zur Judenfrage," *Bulletin des Leo Baeck Instituts,* XIV (1975), 40–79.

candidate of the Democratic party in the 1925 presidential election. Three years later he advised Jews to recognize that ethnic amalgamation through intermarriage provided the only practical method of ending Judeophobia.[5] There is reason to believe that many republicans agreed with Hellpach.[6] If one is prepared to accept their claims of good faith, it should not be too difficult to sympathize with their frustration over the persistence of anti-Semitism. Its apparent invulnerability to all kinds of countermeasures seemed to call for drastic action.

Those Jews who heeded the call for amalgamation must be numbered among the "lost Jews" of the Weimar years. No one can say with any certainty how many of them there were, for no census ever inquired beyond one's current religious affiliation. Their anonymity was assured unless public prominence or anti-Semitic detective work called attention to their ethnicity. Felix Theilhaber's estimate that before the World War German Jews lost around one thousand of their coreligionists annually because of apostasy and mixed marriages, if correct, suggests that there were at least 30,000 "non-Jewish Jews" in Germany by the end of the Weimar period.[7] This erosion almost certainly increased during the postwar years, giving cause for fears that German Jews would become thoroughly amalgamated within a generation or two. To consider mixed marriages alone, there was a threefold increase between 1901 and 1927, until by the latter year there was at least one mixed marriage for every two marriages involving only German Jews. Only about one-quarter of the children of mixed marriages were raised as Jews.[8] Hence, if we also include those German Jews who abandoned Judaism before the turn of the century and the children of former Jews who were raised without

5. Willy Hellpach, *Politische Prognose für Deutschland* (Berlin, 1928), 373; Willy Hellpach, "Rasse im deutschen Volkstum," *Mitteilungen aus dem Verein zur Abwehr des Antisemitismus,* XXXVII (1927), 50–54.

6. For example, Ernst Löwenberg, a Jewish teacher in Hamburg, recalled that the members of the republican political club to which he belonged saw no way out of the Jewish question short of the amalgamation of the Jews into the larger society. Ernst Löwenberg, "Mein Leben in Deutschland vor und nach dem 30. Januar 1933" (Typescript in Leo Baeck Institute Archives, New York), 8.

7. Theilhaber, *Der Untergang der deutschen Juden,* 117–18.

8. Ruppin, *Soziologie der Juden,* I, 213, 224–25; Behr, *Der Bevölkerungsrückgang der deutschen Juden,* 111; R. E. May, "Die Entwicklung der jüdischen Mischehen und ihre Wirkung auf die jüdische Gemeinschaft," *Gemeindeblatt der Deutsch-Israelitischen Gemeinde zu Hamburg,* VIII (1932), 1–3. However, as a leader of the League of Jewish Women noted, official figures reflected marriages between Jews and non-Jews in a religious sense only and did not take into consideration the fact that some of them involved baptized Jews whose marriages to religious Jews brought them back to Judaism. Dora Edinger, "Zur Frage der Mischehen," *Gemeindeblatt der Israelitischen Gemeinde Frankfurt a. Main,* III (1925), 3.

Jewish consciousness, there may have been as many as 60,000 ethnic Jews who either strove after amalgamation or else acknowledged their Jewishness in purely secular ways.[9]

The case of Paul Nikolaus Cossmann demonstrated how the amalgamationist impulse, when carried to its extreme conclusion, could culminate in one manifestation of that strange phenomenon, the Jewish anti-Semite. Cossmann, a baptized Jew, had abandoned his liberal affinities in favor of conservative monarchism under the impact of the patriotic hysteria generated by the World War and its aftermath. As editor of the Munich journal *Süddeutsche Monatshefte,* he was among the first to spread the story that Jewish Marxists like Kurt Eisner and Rosa Luxemburg had stabbed an undefeated German army in the back. Later, as formulator of the political comment contained in Germany's largest mass-circulation daily, the *Münchener Neueste Nachrichten,* he kept up a steady barrage aimed at those rootless coffeehouse intellectuals, the Jewish liberals and Socialists. The Nazis would reward Cossmann for his services in undermining German democracy with incarceration and death in Theresienstadt.[10] Fortunately, Cossmann was a unique figure. No other prominent German Jew threw in his lot with the radical right-wing cause.[11] Virtually all amalgamationist Jews were animated by equal parts of liberal nationalism and religious indifference, rather than by reactionary resentments.

Although the numbers of Jews opting for amalgamation continued to grow, most of Germany's Jews persisted in defining their liberalism in less drastic terms. Aware that liberal claims to individualism and tolerance were meaningless in the context of cultural uniformity, they opposed trends towards self-annihilation and spoke instead of their "assimilation" into German society. This rather vague term implied an intimate, mutually satisfying relationship between two distinct entities, a marriage of kindred minds that yet retained their individuality. Its adherents were careful to reject any use of the term that

9. The Nazi census of Jews in Germany, Austria, and the Sudetenland, made on May 17, 1939, found that 84,674 of the 330,539 "racial Jews" were "cross-breeds" having only one or two Jewish grandparents. Whereas 91.5 percent of the "full-blooded Jews" identified themselves as adherents of Judaism, only 6.6 percent of the "cross-breeds" did so. Bruno Blau, "The Jewish Population of Germany 1939–1945," *Jewish Social Studies,* XII (1950), 161–72.

10. Löwenfeld, "Memoiren," 563–68; Hermann Sinsheimer, "Paul Nikolaus Cossmann," in Lamm (ed.), *Von Juden in München,* 295–97.

11. Two cases involving lesser figures that have come to light were those of Kurt Sölling, a Berlin judge and Nazi sympathizer, and Karl Kindermann, a right-wing German student arrested and executed in Russia for plotting to assassinate Trotsky. *Der Israelit,* June 2, 1932; M. W. [Moses Waldmann], "Kindermann," *Jüdische Rundschau,* August 7, 1925.

suggested amalgamation as a proximate or ultimate goal; however integrated into the larger society they might become, Jews would always have a separate identity, and they would be no less good Germans for it. Assimilation was purely and simply what German Jews had received from German culture and buried deep within their souls.[12] It was in this spirit that the Centralverein in 1920 named its new publishing house after Philo Judaeus of Alexandria, who had represented Jewish interests at the court of Caligula and worked to harmonize the Jewish and Hellenistic cultures during the first century A.D.

That there was no need to choose between being a German and being a Jew was the message of the forceful and widely read autobiographical statement by novelist Jakob Wassermann. Although troubled by the persistence of anti-Semitism in Germany—he himself had been fired from a job in his youth for reasons of prejudice—Wassermann asserted that neither his own will nor the hostility of others could rob him of what his nature and his development had made him: "I am a German, and I am a Jew, one as intensely and as completely as the other, inextricably bound together." He professed himself to be so permeated by both ancestral and environmental influences that he was helpless to sort out the two elements in his being.[13]

That Wassermann spoke for the great majority of German Jews is unquestionable. But what constituted the "ancestral" aspect of this intimate relationship? That it was the Hebrew religion had been the belief of the founders of the Centralverein, who had identified the Jews as "German citizens of the Jewish faith." It continued to be a central article of faith to the outstanding leader of Judaism in Weimar Germany, Rabbi Leo Baeck of Berlin. Baeck feared that postemancipation Jews would allow themselves to be seduced by the unrestrained individualism of modern culture. Only the Jewish religion could save them from this "anarchism of the soul." It alone had prevented the Jews from going the way of the ancient Greeks and Romans. It alone would permit that rare "living, creative bond" between Jews and Gentiles that in modern times, he believed, existed solely in the German-speaking lands.[14]

Baeck's assimilationist views, which were shared in varying degrees by the

12. *Central-Verein Zeitung*, July 3, 1925; Paul Meyer, "Zur Frage der Vertiefung der Tendenz," *K. C. Blätter*, IX (1919), 8–10; Rudolf H. Heimansohn, "Sind wir Assimilanten?" *ibid.*, XXI (1931), 11–14.
13. Jakob Wassermann, *Mein Weg als Deutscher und Jude* (Berlin, 1921), 126.
14. Leo Baeck, "Kulturzusammenhänge," *Der Morgen*, I (1925), 72–83; Leo Baeck, "The German Jews," *Leo Baeck Institute Yearbook*, II (1957), 35–36; Siegfried Moses, "The Impact of Leo Baeck's Personality on His Contemporaries," *ibid.*, II (1957) 3–7; Hans Liebeschütz, "Between Past and Future: Leo Baeck's Historical Position," *Leo Baeck Institute Yearbook*, XI (1966), 3–27.

three branches of the Israelite religion—Orthodox, Liberal, and Reform Judaism—were sharpened by the challenge of Zionism. Its secular and nationalistic definition of the Jews threatened to demote the Jewish faith and narrow the Jews' view of the world. Hebrew religious spokesmen responded that Judaism had long ago abandoned its narrow-spirited political and territorial conceits in order to rise to the status of a world religion. Indeed, the great strength of modern Judaism was viewed as its statelessness in an age when religious influences long since had been eclipsed by secular powers. God in His wisdom had dispersed the Jews throughout the world to implant the ideals of justice, love of neighbor, and brotherhood everywhere. The Seder prayer "Next year in Jerusalem!" was interpreted as symbolic of the Jews' ethical and religious idealism, stripped of all nationalistic content. German Jews were admonished to embrace the new Europe as a stage in the realization of the Kingdom of God and His essential unity.[15]

The importance of Judaism to assimilationist thought made a religious revival among Jews more than ordinarily desirable. The fact that such a revival accompanied the Jewish reaction to the World War, anti-Semitism, and the vulgarity of Weimar popular culture has been attested to by several contemporary religious leaders.[16] Apparently it affected Orthodox Jews most profoundly and owed much to contacts with Eastern Jews during and just after the war. In these Eastern coreligionists German Jews discovered a pure, natural Judaism, unsullied by intercourse with Western European civilization.[17] Their example inspired a few young Orthodox rabbinical students to take part of their training at Eastern European yeshivahs.[18] This new interest in the Talmudic tradition and the influx of Eastern Jews helped temporarily to stay the decline of Orthodox Judaism in Weimar Germany.[19]

15. Max Dienemann, *Galuth* (Berlin, 1929), 6–13; Hans Adolf Margolius, "Zionismus und Religiosität," *Israelitisches Familienblatt,* June 21, 1923; Fritz Heinemann, "Das Judentum und das neue Europa," *Gemeindeblatt der Israelitischen Gemeinde Frankfurt a. Main,* IV (1926), 1–3; Bernhard Strauch, "Die Mission des Judentums," *ibid.,* VIII (1930), 305–307.

16. Caesar Seligmann, "Mein Leben: Erinnerungen eines Grossvaters" (Typescript in Leo Baeck Institute Archives, New York), 114–15; Baeck, "Die jüdischen Gemeinden," 444; Grünewald interview.

17. Moses Auerbach, "Zur geistigen Struktur der deutschen Orthodoxie der Gegenwart," in *Festschrift für Jacob Rosenheim* (Frankfurt-am-Main, 1931), 207–208; Zvi Assaria (ed.), *Die Juden in Köln von den ältesten Zeiten bis zur Gegenwart* (Cologne, 1959), 288–89; Carlebach, *Adass Yeshurun of Cologne,* 100–101; Alexander Carlebach, "A German Rabbi Goes East," *Leo Baeck Institute Yearbook,* VI (1961), 60–121.

18. Carlebach, *Adass Yeshurun,* 121–25.

19. In 1924, of thirty-eight students enrolled in the Orthodox Berlin Rabbinical Seminary, twenty-two were Eastern Jews. Isi Jacob Eisner, "Reminiscences of the Berlin Rabbinical Seminary," *Leo Baeck Institute Yearbook,* XII (1967), 41.

Among the great majority of German Jews, however, the signs of religious decline were more numerous than those of revival, and they were not ignored.[20] Apostasy continued to plague Jewish communities everywhere. It was aggravated by an anomaly in the Prussian legal code that permitted a Jew to sever his ties with his congregation and thereby free himself from heavy religious taxes while remaining officially part of the larger Jewish community; a 1931 supreme court decision applied that right to the rest of Germany as well. Increasing numbers of Jews availed themselves of it, placing a growing financial burden on the Jews who stayed on.[21] Apparently those who left did not care enough about Judaism to make the financial sacrifices required to resist its decline.

Worse than apostasy was the widespread religious indifference of those who at least nominally held fast to Judaism. Low attendance at religious services, even on the High Holy Days, was a chronic complaint throughout the Weimar years. The average attendance on High Holy Days during the late 1920s was 58 percent in Breslau, 49 percent in Berlin, and 41 percent in Frankfurt-am-Main.[22] At other times it was very much smaller. In Leipzig only the presence of elderly community members who were paid to be there provided the necessary minimum of ten adult males for weekday services.[23] The practice of closing shops on the Sabbath grew increasingly rare, and Jewish businessmen themselves agitated against any general cessation of business on Jewish holy days.[24] Jews who did attend religious services were some-

---

20. Friedrich Rülf, "Untergang der deutschen Juden?" *Israelitisches Familienblatt*, September 7, 1922; *Jüdisch-liberale Zeitung*, IV (November 7, 1924), 1–3; Rabbi Dr. Norden, "Der Glaube an unsere Sendung," *ibid.*, V (1925), 1; Gustav Löffler, "Religiöse Not," *Der Morgen*, II (1926), 259–71; Th. [Felix Theilhaber?], "Strukturwandlung der Jüdischen Familie," *Central-Verein Zeitung*, November 6, 1931; *Gemeindeblatt der Jüdischen Gemeinde zu Berlin*, XXII (1932), 14–15.

21. Stern, *Warum hassen sie uns eigentlich?* 141–42; Behr, *Der Bevölkerungsrückgang der deutschen Juden*, 99–100; *Jüdische Rundschau*, October 21, 1930; *Israelitisches Familienblatt*, March 17, 1832; *Der Israelit*, January 1, 1931; Ismar Freund, "Welche Rechtsfolgen hat der Austritt aus der Synagogengemeinde?" *Verwaltungsblatt des preussischen Landesverbandes jüdischer Gemeinden*, II (1924), 1.

22. R. E. May, "Der Prozensatz der Teilnahme der Juden Gross-Berlins am Gottesdienst der hohen Feiertage," *Gemeindeblatt der Jüdischen Gemeinde zu Berlin*, XIX (1929), 292–93. For evidence of similar complaints, see "Mahnruf an die Juden der Gemeinde Worms von Rabbiner Dr. Holzer: Mit einem Vorwort Herausgegeben vom Vorstand der Wormser israelitischen Religionsgemeinde," in Landesarchivverwaltung Rheinland-Pfalz (comp.), *Dokumentation zur Geschichte der jüdischen Bevölkerung in Rheinland-Pfalz*, 193–97; Kurt Sabatzky, "Hebung des jüdischen Lebens," *Israelitisches Familienblatt*, December 5, 1929; Zelzer, *Weg und Schicksal der Stuttgarter Juden*, 107–108.

23. Grubel interview.

24. Zelzer, *Weg und Schicksal der Stuttgarter Juden*, 113–14; correspondence between local governments and the Arnsberg district government about closing the cattle markets in the

times faulted for inattentiveness; in Munich so many worshippers left services early that the synagogue fathers took to locking the doors until after the last prayers had been said.[25] Fewer and fewer Jews devoted themselves to collateral activities. Choirs were given up or else maintained by hiring non-Jewish singers; some communities could not muster the required 50 percent of their adult members to attend important business meetings.[26] The numbers of rabbinical students underwent similar decline; in 1928 only 0.1 percent of Jewish students were studying to be rabbis, as compared to the 2.7 percent of Catholic students and 2.6 percent of Protestant students who were preparing for the clergy.[27] The evidence suggests that the number of Jews newly touched by Judaic piety was small, and that, in general, the Weimar Republic's rampant secularism devastated Judaism at least as much as it did the Christian denominations.

And yet, the renewal of Jewish self-consciousness was no illusion. Eva Reichmann has shown that it owed much to the recrudescence of Judeophobia and to the need to find practical means of assisting the homeless Eastern Jews.[28] As such it was an earthly minded impulse dedicated to restoring interest in Jewish tradition, history, and culture. Religion could not be entirely divorced from any of these spheres, but its importance to the consciousness of modern Jews was indistinct and varied widely according to personal opinion. Ludwig Holländer referred decreasingly to the unifying ties of Judaism and increasingly to the Jews' "community of shared destiny" *(Schicksalsgemeinschaft);* that the Centralverein leader personally believed such community to have been formed preeminently by the Jewish religion is certain, which makes it all the more remarkable that he deliberately chose a neutral term that applied equally to the devout and the skeptical.[29] Others affirmed the existence of a uniquely Jewish spirit, exemplified by the question-

---

Rhineland-Westphalia industrial region on the Jewish High Holy Days in September, 1931, in Series "Arnsberg," IG/578, Staatsarchiv, Münster.

25. Bekanntmachung, signed by Eugen Beer, in Leo Baerwald Collection, Leo Baeck Institute Archives, New York, 3680/11.

26. A. H., "Die Chöre in den liberalen Synagogen," *Gemeindeblatt der Israelitischen Gemeinde Frankfurt a. Main,* I (1922), 3; Israel to Oberpräsident Hannover, March 20, 1924, Gustav Noske to Prussian Ministry of Culture, December 23, 1927, both in Series "Hannover," 122a/XVII/374, Niedersächsisches Hauptstaatsarchiv, Hanover.

27. *Israelitisches Familienblatt,* September 6, 1928.

28. Eva G. Reichmann, "Der Bewusstseinswandel der deutschen Juden," in Mosse and Paucker (eds.), *Deutsches Judentum,* 511–612.

29. Ludwig Holländer, *Deutsch-jüdische Probleme der Gegenwart* (Berlin, 1929), 14; Ludwig Holländer, "Warum sind und bleiben wir Juden?" *Central-Verein Zeitung,* December 16, 1932; Georg Götz, "Zur Frage der Entpolitisierung der Religionsgemeinde," *Jüdisch-liberale Zeitung,* XI (November 11, 1931), Beilage, 1.

ing idealism of Jesus, Spinoza, and Else Lasker-Schüler, or of a Jewish intellectual rhythm, faster and more obtrusive than the German.[30] Hence the nonpracticing Jew, Walther Rathenau, could be lauded shortly after his assassination as an inheritor of a specifically Jewish impulse to ethical dedication.[31] Such views left ample room even for such an outspoken critic of organized religion as the aging playwright Ludwig Fulda to remain within the Jewish community for purely secular reasons.[32] For others they acted to restrain Jews from public estrangement from Judaism. Ernst Herzfeld, a prominent corporation lawyer, Centralverein activist, and congregation leader in Essen, convinced one of his sons, who had declared himself an atheist, to go through with his bar mitzvah solely as an affirmation of his bonds with Jewish ethnicity and history.[33] If there were many such testimonies, Judaism's further decline as a religious force was assured.

In practical recognition of these trends, Jewish religious leaders embraced the new emphasis on tradition and culture as the best means of preserving at least a limited role for Judaism to play. Jews might not attend religious services, but significant numbers of them would come to hear lectures or take courses on subjects ranging from the Hebrew language and Yiddish literature to Jewish ethnology and history. In them Judaism might or might not be given prominent attention. Not long after complaints were registered about sparse attendance at the 1932 Jewish New Year services in Berlin, Heinrich Mann packed the Prinzregentenstrasse synagogue there with a Sunday afternoon talk about Jewish culture.[34] Adult education programs involving similar topics were encouraged by Jewish community leaders throughout Germany, and they frequently enlisted the support of the most diverse elements, religious liberals and Orthodox Jews, assimilationists and Zionists.[35]

While liberal Jews increasingly adopted a cultural, rather than a strictly re-

---

30. Lutz Weltmann, "Jüdischer Geist?" *Bayerische Israelitische Gemeindezeitung*, IX (1933), 2; *ibid.*, VI (1929), 140–41.
31. *Central-Verein Zeitung*, June 30, 1922.
32. Ludwig Fulda to Eugen Wolbe, October 19, 1927, in Ludwig Fulda Collection, Leo Baeck Institute Archives, New York, 150/530/II. Fulda was elected president of the Prussian Academy in 1928.
33. Herzfeld, "Lebenserinnerungen," 194–95.
34. Hans Sachs, "Offener Brief an die 7 liberalen Vorsteher der Jüdischen Gemeinde zu Berlin," *Jüdisch-liberale Zeitung*, XII (October 15, 1932), Beilage; *ibid.*, December 1, 1932, Beilage.
35. Richard Koch, "Das Freie Jüdische Lehrhaus im Frankfurt am Main," *Der Jude*, VII (1923), 116-20; Felix Perles, "Mehr Religionsgeschichte!" *Allgemeine Zeitung des Judentums*, LXXXIV (1920), 78–81; *ibid.*, LXXXIII (1919), 63–66; *Der Gemeindebote*, LXXXVI (1921), 2; Zelzer, *Weg und Schicksal der Stuttgarter Juden*, 114–23.

ligious, sense of their Jewishness, some of their rabbis further accommodated the new emphasis by broadening their own Jewish fervor at the expense of theological substance. They began to take greater interest in the social problems of their congregations during the same time that the Jewish communities were spending an increasing percentage of their budgets on cultural and welfare projects (in Berlin those expenditures rose from 25 to 42 percent of the budget between 1919 and 1929).[36] Some might sneer at the "watered-down" Judaism of Germany's lone Reform synagogue, situated in Berlin, but increasingly Liberal Jews adopted its practices of Sunday worship services, seating the sexes together, and placing sermons at the center of attention.[37] Perhaps these were healthy trends that, over the long run and under different circumstances, might have reversed the decline of the Israelite faith.

The partial secularization of the liberal Jews' self-identity opened the way to their dalliance with notions of race. Even before the World War Eugen Fuchs, a cofounder of the Centralverein and its vice-president from 1893 to 1919, had admitted the inadequacy of a purely religious definition of Jewishness and the need to recognize the unique mental and physical characteristics imparted by Jewish descent.[38] Later Ludwig Holländer called favorable attention to Fuchs's statement, flatly asserting that a few racial attributes, much attenuated by the centuries, could still be perceived among German Jews. At the same time he denied that these ethnic remnants in any way justified allegiance to a Jewish nationality; the Jews constituted merely one of the tribal stocks that made up the German people, along with the Saxons, the Bavarians, the Prussians, and all the rest. Nationality was imparted by the German Fatherland alone.[39]

The use of words like *stock (Stamm)* and *descent (Abstammung)* in such statements reflected a broadening of the secular definition of Jewishness to a

36. Grünewald interview; Alfred Jospe, "A Profession in Transition: The German Rabbinate 1910–1939," *Leo Baeck Institute Yearbook*, XIX (1974), 55–56; *Israelitisches Familienblatt*, April 24, 1919; *Der Israelit*, April 24, 1929.

37. *Jüdische Rundschau*, January 25, 1929; *Gemeindeblatt der Jüdischen Gemeinde zu Berlin*, IX (1929), 175–80; *Israelitisches Familienblatt*, September 13, 1928; M. Lipshitz, "Religiöse Feierstunden in den Synagogen am Sonntag Nachmittag," *Jüdisch-liberale Zeitung*, IX (March 29, 1929), 2–3.

38. Jehuda Reinharz, "*Deutschtum* and *Judentum* in the Ideology of the Centralverein Deutscher Staatsbürger Jüdischen Glaubens 1893–1914," *Jewish Social Studies*, XXXVI (1974), 37–38. *Cf.* Schorsch, *Jewish Reactions to German Anti-Semitism*, 147–48; Ruth Pierson, "German Jewish Identity in the Weimar Republic," (Ph.D. dissertation, Yale University, 1970), 60–62.

39. Ludwig Holländer, "Unserem Eugen Fuchs zum Gedenken," *Central-Verein Zeitung*, January 10, 1924; Ludwig Holländer, *Deutsch-jüdische Probleme*, 9–18.

point dangerously close to the *völkisch* position. A romantic conception of Judaism could be equally hospitable to this fateful frame of mind. At some point during the Weimar years, Rabbi Caesar Seligmann of Frankfurt-am-Main delivered a series of sermons refuting rationalist explanations for what was uniquely Jewish in favor of one tracing it to "the dark depths of our hearts": "It is not Jewish conviction, not Jewish doctrine, not the Jewish creed that is the leading, the primary, the inspirational; rather, it is Jewish *sentiment*, the instinctive, call it what you will, call it the community of blood, call it tribal consciousness [*Stammesgefühl*], call it the ethnic soul [*Volksseele*], but best of all call it: the Jewish heart." [40]

By far the most blatant of these statements of racial consciousness came from the Jewish novelists Georg Herrmann and Kurt Münzer. Hermann, the respected observer of and commentator on the Berlin Jewish experience, published in 1919 a statement of disillusionment with Germany's toleration of reborn anti-Semitism. The war and its unhappy outcome had laid bare what he labeled "organic disparities and incompatibilities" (*Wesensverschiedenheiten und Wesensfremdheiten*) between Germans and Jews. As a result, he announced his return to self-conscious Jewishness in a racial rather than a religious sense. Münzer, a novelist of lesser fame and talent, published his *I'm Hungry . . . (Mich hungert . . .)* in 1930 under the pen name of Georg Fink. In it a young half-Jew, raised in the midst of demoralized proletarian conditions without the slightest notion of his ethnic origins, finds himself barred by his "blood" from genuine communion with his surroundings. [41]

Affirmation of membership in the Jewish "race" demonstrated that some Jews had joined with millions of their fellow Germans in flirting with ideas of blood, destiny, and the organic folk community as determining forces in human affairs. Of course, none of them pushed such notions to racialist conclusions by ranking the races, but neither did most Germans. We are more aware than they were of the fundamental contradictions between biological determinism and the liberal spirit of the Enlightenment. The idea of race had not yet fallen into disrepute, and the fledgling disciplines of anthropology and ethnology accepted it with few reservations. Jews as well as non-Jews routinely assumed that race played some role, if not the determining role, in

40. Seligmann, "Mein Leben," 116–17. Emphasis in the original.
41. Georg Hermann, "Zur Frage der Westjuden," *Israelitisches Familienblatt*, September 4, 1919; Georg Fink, *Mich hungert . . .* (Berlin, 1930). See especially Münzer's comment on the novel: Kurt Münzer, "Das unsterbliche Blut," *Bayerische Israelitische Gemeindezeitung*, VI (1930), 34–53.

shaping human behavior.[42] On the other hand, outright denials of the existence of a Jewish race in any biological sense were at least as common as preoccupation with descent.[43] For most liberal Jews, religion and tradition constituted the Jewish component of their being.

Liberal Jews were much less ambiguous about the German component of their assimilated beings. What was Jewish might involve religion, descent, and tradition in various combinations and emphases. What was German was, for the vast majority, fixed in genuine love of country expressed as enthusiasm for its culture, respect for its legitimate policies, and hatred of its foes. Germany was not yet a vital center of European liberalism, but it was becoming one, and it had provided large numbers of Jews with unprecedented opportunities for advancement. Jewish gratitude was both real and abundant. Hermann Cohen's intense German patriotism, fused with an equally intense identification with Judaism, set the example.

That example was followed punctiliously in the World War. Shortly after its outbreak, prominent Jews joined other distinguished German intellectuals, scientists, and artists in signing the "Manifesto of the Ninety-three," which denied charges of German atrocities and violations of Belgian neutrality while affirming united German support for Kaiser and army. Among the signers was the great Jewish chemist, Fritz Haber, who went on to perfect a nitrogen fixation process that permitted the manufacture of explosives in spite of the British blockade, and to develop gas warfare for the War Ministry.[44] German Jews might find their coreligionist Ernst Lissauer a bit extreme in his effusive "Song of Hate Against England," but most probably agreed with Walther Rathenau's prewar statement: "Whoever loves his Fatherland may and should be something of a chauvinist."[45]

These patriotic sentiments were only intensified when anti-Semites challenged their authenticity. They might find expression as prosaic as Richard Willstätter's 1920 letter to a Zurich newspaper protesting an article that described Germany as a sick nation, or as dramatic as a young Jewish veteran's suicide over having been denied membership in a patriotic club.[46] Love of

---

42. Paul Kammerer, "Ist die Rasse veränderlich?" *Der Morgen*, II (1926), 323–38; Friedrich Merkenschlager, "Streifzüge durch die wissenschaftliche und scheinwissenshaftliche Rasseliteratur," *ibid.*, VIII (1932), 163–79.
43. See, for example, Julius Schäffer, "Die Zerstörung des Volksgedankens durch den Rassenwahn," *ibid.*, I (1925), 268–98; Franz Weidenreich, "Das Problem der jüdischen Rasse," *ibid.*, VII (1931), 78–96; Sigmund Feist, *Stammeskunde der Juden* (Leipzig, 1925).
44. Rudolf Stern, "Fritz Haber," *Leo Baeck Institute Yearbook*, VIII (1963), 76–77.
45. Rathenau, "Höre, Israel!" 15.
46. Willstätter, *From My Life*, 323–25; Mann, *Der Antisemitismus*, 16.

country permeated everything, and so it was not surprising when the chairman of the Jewish Community Council in Frankfurt-am-Main, Dr. Richard Merzbach, opened one of its meetings with a statement of joy that a 'round-the-world flight by the *Graf Zeppelin* had raised esteem for Germany everywhere.[47] The Jewish fraternities that flaunted such patriotic names as "Bavaria," "Friburgia," "Thuringia," and "Sprevia" could not have failed to endorse Kurt Alexander's words of 1919: "For us, being German is not a political, but rather a spiritual and emotional concept. For us, being German is an inner experience. In our souls we can no longer distinguish between what is German and what is Jewish. German and Jewish are fused into oneness in our souls, and never can any power on earth tear the German, the love of our homeland, out of our hearts."[48]

Indeed, fraternities of Jewish liberal students were among the most emphatic proponents of the patriotic idea. In 1896 they had federated as the Ring Assembly of the Fraternities of German Students of the Jewish Faith (Kartell-Convent der Verbindungen deutscher Studenten jüdischen Glaubens) for purposes of strengthening their sense of Jewish identity and asserting their German patriotism. From the beginning the emphasis was on the latter as the fraternity members outdid their non-Jewish counterparts in traditional ceremony, flaunting their uniforms, and challenging every disparaging remark with a demand for "satisfaction"—a duel.[49] Denial of satisfaction by rabid anti-Semites frequently led to the Jewish students attacking them with their fists.[50] Only during the depression years did the Ring Assembly lose some of its enthusiasm for proving that its members were good Germans; the wearing of uniforms was made optional, and dueling was de-emphasized in favor of sports. By that time it had become abundantly clear that belligerent displays of patriotism only accelerated the erosion of young Jews to Zionism and Marxism without dissuading German students from following Hitler.[51]

47. *Gemeindeblatt der Israelitischen Gemeinde Frankfurt a. Main,* VIII (1929), 80.
48. Speech on the occasion of the twenty-fifth anniversary of the Sprevia on November 3, 1919, *K. C. Blätter,* IX (1919), 180.
49. For a delightful account of the student days of a Jewish fraternity member at Freiburg-im-Breisgau, see Fred Uhlman, *The Making of an Englishman* (London, 1960), 62–78.
50. In one such case the Jewish fraternity "Ghibellinia" at Freiburg was suspended by university authorities for starting a free-for-all at a local brothel. Hermann Berlak, "Legendenbildung oder Lügennetz?" *K. C. Blätter,* XV (November, 1925), Vertrauliche Beilage, 406.
51. Adolph Asch, *Geschichte des KC im Lichte der deutschen kulturellen und politischen Entwicklung* (London, 1964), 93–119; Kurt Braun, "Reform des K.C.," *K. C. Blätter,* XV (September, 1925), Vertrauliche Beilage, 10–12; "Protokoll der Verhandlungen des Altherrentages zu Hamburg am 27. April 1930," *ibid.,* X (May-June, 1930), Vertrauliche Beilage, 21–25; Fritz Pagel, "Um die Zukunft der K. C. Verbindungen," *ibid.,* X (July, 1930), Vertrauliche Beilage, 61–65; *ibid.,* XI (January, 1931), Vertrauliche Beilage, 1.

At no time in the Weimar period was Jewish patriotic sentiment more abundant than in the first years of peace, when the victorious powers detached from Germany important border areas of mixed populations and handed them over to France and the new state of Poland. In the disputed eastern territories of Posen, Upper Silesia, and West Prussia, the vast majority of Jews aligned themselves with the German cause both out of pro-German sentiment and out of fear of falling under the yoke of the notoriously anti-Semitic Poles. Local Jewish leaders, including Berthold Haase, Saly Ölsner, and Dr. Max Landsberg, were chosen to represent the German point of view to Polish and Entente authorities, a task for which their command of the Polish tongue especially suited them. Other Jews joined the clandestine free-corps units that fought to keep the eastern lands German, or they resisted the Poles in other ways. Not a few of them fell martyrs to the cause, one of them a lad of fifteen.[52] In recognition of these services, all but the most virulent anti-Semites ceased their attacks on Jews; the united front of Germans and Jews was virtually complete on the eastern borders. The Poles, too, recognized this solidarity by including a number of Jews among the 7,000 Germans arrested and held hostage at the former prisoner of war camp at Szczypiorno as a means of forcing Germany to sign the Treaty of Versailles.[53]

United efforts to hold the eastern territories for Germany were only partially successful. The Entente powers, as determined to punish Germany as they were to give Poland access to the sea and an industrial base, transferred hundreds of square miles of German territory to the new state and created a large German minority within it. Jews voted solidly for Germany in plebiscites held under League of Nations' auspices in some of the disputed lands; Jews who had settled elsewhere in Germany but who were still eligible to cast ballots in the plebiscites sometimes traveled great distances to vote for the Fatherland.[54] In areas that could not be saved from the Poles, the vast majority of Jews migrated to German territory, often enriching the communities in which they found new homes. Among them was Dr. Philipp de Haas, who gave up his position as rabbi of the large and influential community at Kattowitz to become district rabbi in Oldenburg.[55] Another emigrant from Kattowitz,

---

52. Wilhelm Lustig, "Erinnerungen aus der Zeit der Volksabstimmung in Oberschlesien" (Typescript in Leo Baeck Institute Archives, New York), 1–8; Stern, *Warum hassen sie uns eigentlich?* 108; *Israelitisches Familienblatt*, August 7, 1924.

53. Berthold Haase, "Mein Leben, was in ihm geschah, und wie ich es erlebte" (Typescript in Leo Baeck Institute Archives, New York), 50–63; Fritz Seifter, "Judentum und Grenzlands deutschtum in Ostoberschlesien," *Central-Verein Zeitung*, June 24, 1932.

54. Arthur Stern, *In bewegter Zeit: Erinnerungen und Gedanken eines jüdischen Nervenarztes* (Jerusalem, 1968), 110–11.

55. Leo Trepp, *Die Landesgemeinde der Juden in Oldenburg* (Oldenburg, 1965), 31.

Heinemann Stern, became principal of a Jewish school in Berlin.[56] Indeed, so many Jewish teachers from the lost eastern territories sought new posts after 1919 that the Jewish communities in Germany were hard pressed to find positions for all of them.

In Alsace-Lorraine there was no comparable Jewish outcry against separation from Germany, although Strassburg's chief rabbi, Dr. Emil Levy, was ousted by French authorities when he publicly refused to hail his city's "liberation."[57] In the occupied Rhineland the Jews demonstratively shunned all ties with the French. Upon this territory's liberation from occupation forces in 1930, Rabbi Max Dienemann delivered a sermon at Offenbach-am-Main comparing the event to the delivery of the Children of Israel from their wanderings in the desert after the escape from Egypt.[58] Another rabbi, Dr. Felix Goldmann of Leipzig, succinctly expressed his coreligionists' feelings about Germany's diminished postwar status:

The notion that Alsace, German to the core, must be lost is something that we both understand and cannot understand. And when we consider that our Polish neighbor has put his hands on Posen and now stretches his covetous fingers toward Upper Silesia and West Prussia, we are seized with righteous rage to think that the fruits of hundreds of years of German culture must be lost so basely. The fact that the impotence of the new Germany obviates any possibility of halting these disgraceful robberies fills us with bitter grief.[59]

Equally strong affection for the best in the German cultural tradition also animated Jewish liberals. Their enthusiastic support for and participation in Weimar culture requires no further elaboration here.[60] In order to assure the most effective transference of these patriotic and cultural values to their children, most Jewish liberals insisted on sending their offspring to public schools together with young non-Jews rather than to separate Jewish schools. They feared that the latter would alienate their young people from Germans and Germany, causing them to retreat into a spiritual and intellectual ghetto. Zionist support for Jewish schools brought these fears to new heights, for it was known that Zionist teachers sometimes devoted themselves to magnifying Palestine and neglecting Germany.[61] The report that Zionist school chil-

---

56. H. Stern, *Warum hassen sie uns eigentlich?* 103–104.
57. *Im Deutschen Reich,* XXV (1919), 167.
58. Sermon text, untitled, July 4, 1930, in Max Dienemann Collection, Leo Baeck Institute Archives, New York.
59. Felix Goldmann, "Umschau," *K. C. Blätter,* IX (1919), 3.
60. See chapter II, above.
61. *Jüdische Rundschau,* March 27, 1928.

dren in Königsberg had refused to write a theme on the subject "How I Can Be a Good German" seemed to prove the divisive and alienating influences of Jewish nationalism.[62] The religious gap, too, would only be widened by segregated education. Far from producing positive results, it would add the appearance of truth to anti-Semitic stories about Jewish secretiveness and immiscibility.[63] Jewish liberals were still by and large confident that Germans and Jews would appreciate and understand each other in direct proportion to their knowledge of each other.

Not only were separate Jewish schools regarded as damaging to the German-Jewish synthesis, but they were also thought of as superfluous by most Jews of the liberal persuasion. Home and synagogue would provide the bulk of the young Jew's appreciation of his religious and cultural traditions; the schools ought properly to concentrate on academic concerns. "After all," one commentator wrote, "there are no such things as Protestant legal studies, one cannot prove the rules of mathematical congruence in a Catholic fashion, and Homeric literature is no Jewish affair."[64] The two hours of school time set aside each week for religious instruction would suffice for Jewish students just as they did for their non-Jewish classmates. Such instruction was available, either during those hours or after school let out, in all but the tiniest communities. Belief in the primacy of secular academic studies also promoted a certain degree of liberal indifference to the decline of the two remaining German Jewish teachers' training colleges at Cologne and Würzburg, especially following the establishment in 1928 of Germany's first nonconfessional teachers' academy at Frankfurt-am-Main, where opportunities existed for Jewish student-teachers to prepare themselves in Judaism and the Hebrew language as well as in traditional academic subjects.[65]

The existence of anti-Semitism among teachers and students in the public schools was not ignored. Jewish liberals were moved by reports of young Jews being subjected to harassment, assaults, and, worst of all, silence by their fellow pupils.[66] Most of them insisted, however, and with some reason, that

62. Felix Goldmann, "Nationaljüdischer Radikalismus," *Im deutschen Reich,* XXV (1919), 50–51.

63. Oscar Cassel, "Die konfessionelle jüdische Schule," *Central-Verein Zeitung,* August 31, 1922; Felix Goldmann, "Jüdische Kultur?" *ibid.,* March 1, 1923; *Gemeindeblatt der Jüdischen Gemeinde zu Berlin,* XVI (1926), 78.

64. Moritz Werner, "Staat und Erziehung," *Der Morgen,* I (1925), 585–93.

65. *Der Israelit,* July 19, July 30, and August 6, 1931; *Verwaltungsblatt des preussischen Landesverbandes jüdischer Gemeinden,* IV (1926), 27–28, 30.

66. Frank Frei, "Aus pommerschen Schulen," *Central-Verein Zeitung,* October 1, 1926; *ibid.,* January 15, 1932; *ibid.,* May 6, 1932; M. Deutschkron, "Erfahrungen eines Ober-

such monstrous conditions were atypical and confined mainly to small communities in parts of eastern and southern Germany. Then, too, they viewed anti-Semitism as a fact of life with which their children should learn to cope sooner rather than later.[67]

A small minority of Jewish liberals raised dissenting voices. They abhorred the prospect of exposing tender youths to possible anti-Semitic abuse, and they feared the further decline of Jewish consciousness outside of Jewish schools.[68] The latter consideration was of special interest to the adherents of Orthodox Judaism, who insisted upon an educational atmosphere fully suffused with religious emphasis.[69] They were equally troubled by occasional official reluctance to excuse Jewish children from attending public school on their holy days. The situation was particularly acute in Saxony, where, until 1929, Jewish pupils could not stay away from classes on certain Jewish holy days without penalty.[70] Jews who shared these concerns normally sent their children to state-run Jewish elementary and secondary schools in the few large cities where they were available. These schools were operated like public schools in every respect except that they recessed only on the Jewish Sabbath and holy days, provided Jewish religious lessons during the two hours set aside each week for such instruction, and had largely Jewish staffs and pupils. The more intransigent Orthodox Jews established small private religious schools for their sons and daughters. The Zionists likewise resorted to private schools, only with emphasis on secular Jewish studies—modern Hebrew, history of the Jews, problems of Palestine—rather than on Judaism.

Had it not been for the challenges of anti-Semitism and Zionism, the majority of Jewish liberals might have been more willing to compromise on the question of integrated or segregated education.[71] As it was, they were resolved

---

lehrers," *ibid.*, January 2, 1925. A moving fictionalized account of the ostracization of a Jewish pupil in a Pomeranian town can be found in Josef Maria Frank, *Volk im Fieber* (Berlin, 1932).

67. M. Kosler, "Mehr Mut!" *Central-Verein Zeitung*, October 31, 1924; *ibid.*, December 25, 1931; *ibid.*, January 1, 1932; *ibid.*, August 31, 1922; *Gemeindeblatt der Israelitischen Gemeinde Frankfurt a. Main*, IV (September/ October, 1925); Clementine Krämer, "Pfadfinder," *Jüdisch-liberale Zeitung*, IV (June 27, 1924), 1.

68. J. Basch, "Ein Beitrag zur Schulfrage," *Allgemeine Zeitung des Judentums*, LXXXV (1921), 156–57; Arthur Galliner, "Die konfessionelle Schule und die religiösen Parteien im Judentum," *Jüdisch-liberale Zeitung*, IX (October 30, 1929), Beilage, 1.

69. *Der Israelit*, January 6, 1921; *ibid.*, December 1, 1921; *ibid.*, October 17, 1930.

70. *Ibid.*, November 26, 1925; *ibid.*, October 18, 1928; Rabbi Dr. Goldmann, "Gleichberechtigung auch der jüdischen Religion," *Central-Verein Zeitung*, November 20, 1925; *ibid.*, September 20, 1929.

71. A contemporary estimate that between 20 and 25 percent of German Jewish youth had been won over to the Zionist camp was probably too high, but it illustrated the deep concern felt by liberal parents over the alienation of their children. *Gemeindeblatt der Israelitischen Gemeinde Frankfurt a. Main*, IX (1931), 213.

to authenticate their commitment to assimilationism and to oppose Zionist efforts to alienate their children from liberal values. Hence they put up strong opposition to coalitions of Zionists, Orthodox Jews, and a few maverick assimilationists that sponsored public and private Jewish schools in many of the German Jewish communities. Liberal majorities on community councils in Berlin, Breslau, and Duisburg—to name but three—denied funds and the use of community buildings to such schools.[72] In Munich even a small subvention for a private Jewish school supported by Zionists and Orthodox Jews prompted stormy debates both before and after the funds were approved in 1928.[73] Two similar schools in Berlin, placed under community control in the late 1920s by a short-lived Zionist-led administration, were denounced by liberals as centers of indoctrination for Jewish nationalism. Once the liberals regained power in Berlin in 1930, they hastened to cut financial aid for the schools and to begin negotiations to have them taken over by the public school system. As a liberal resolution in the community council put it, "the performance of school affairs is not a matter for the [Jewish] community, but rather for the city and state."[74]

Liberal hostility, religious indifference, and economic stress combined to reinforce the decline of Jewish schools that had begun before the World War. Of 195 prewar Jewish elementary schools in Prussia, only 99 were left in 1927. In Bavaria during the same period, only half of 84 schools survived.[75] As early as 1921, three times as many Jewish elementary school children attended public schools as attended Jewish schools.[76] The number of those attending Jewish elementary schools in Munich dropped from 780 to 250 in the decade following 1914, a drop only partially explained by the declining birthrate among Jews.[77] Increasingly during the Weimar years such schools were regarded as institutions to which Eastern Jews and militant Zionists sent their

72. *Jüdische Rundschau*, December 29, 1920; *ibid.*, November 3, 1925; *ibid.*, May 16, 1928; *Israelitisches Familienblatt*, January 21, 1926; M. Steinhardt, "Kampf gegen die jüdische Schule: Antisemitismus im eigenen Lager," *ibid.*, January 21, January 28, and February 4, 1926.

73. *Israelitisches Familienblatt*, June 14, 1928; *Bayerische Israelitische Gemeindezeitung*, V (1929), 144–45, 157–58.

74. *Israelitisches Familienblatt*, December 13, 1928; *Der Israelit*, November 21, 1929; *ibid.*, March 19, 1931; *Gemeindeblatt der Jüdischen Gemeinde zu Berlin*, XX (1930), 22–24; *ibid.*, XXII (1932), 193; Selma Schiratzki, "The Rykestrasse School in Berlin," *Leo Baeck Institute Yearbook*, V (1960), 299–300; *cf.* Walter Breslauer, "Erinnerungen" (Typescript in Leo Baeck Institute Archives, New York), 32.

75. *Der Israelit*, July 26, 1928.

76. Max Grünewald, "The Jewish Teacher," *Leo Baeck Institute Yearbook*, XIX (1974), 67.

77. *Der Israelit*, November 20, 1924.

children. For the liberal majority, attendance at non-Jewish public schools was considered essential to the young Jew's consciousness of being German.

The liberal apotheosis of assimilation that was dramatized by the school controversy encountered a difficult test in the problem of the Eastern Jews. Trapped in Germany after the war by pogroms and revolutions in their old homelands and by the legal and financial difficulties connected with emigration to places like the United States and Palestine, they were a burden both on Germany and the German Jews. As helpless victims of circumstance they inspired pity, but as generators of anti-Semitism and representatives of alien ways and ideas they invited animosity. Which came first, duty to fortuneless foreign coreligionists, or obligations to one's own hard-pressed community and nation?

Jewish liberals sought to honor both commitments. Several of the Jewish communities distinguished themselves by placing their welfare facilities at the refugees' disposal and especially by providing them with temporary food, shelter, and advice. Since it was in the best interest of all concerned to hurry the newcomers on their way to permanent homes outside of Germany, funds were not lacking to buy them tickets to port cities. Concentrating them there, however, could put a strain on local community welfare institutions. In Bremen, 272 Eastern Jews stranded by American immigration restrictions and passport irregularities were well cared for by the city's Jewish charities, which kept the refugees supplied with kosher meals and arranged special classes for their children at local schools. But such generosity was not to be found everywhere, and some communities preferred to minimize aid to the refugees in the hope that they would quickly move on.[78]

In the interest of rationalizing and unifying aid to Eastern Jews, liberals and Zionists joined in founding the Workers' Welfare Office of the Jewish Organizations of Germany (*Arbeiterfürsorgeamt der jüdischen Organisationen Deutschlands*) in January, 1920. Financed in large part by funds from the American Joint Distribution Committee, it provided beds and meals to the destitute refugees, defended their legal rights before government officials, and interceded with East European diplomatic representatives to get them passports. For those who could not or would not leave Germany, it helped to find employment. Prussian officials normally cleared matters involving alien Jews with the Workers' Welfare Office and gave it every opportunity to find employment for individual refugees before taking action against them. By

78. Markreich, "Geschichte der Juden in Bremen," 170–78; Carlebach, *Adass Yeshurun of Cologne*, 78; "Emmy Livneh" (Typescript in Leo Baeck Institute Archives, New York), 6.

1922 it could boast that it had contributed substantially to the total of forty thousand jobs held by Eastern Jews.[79] The successful start at absorbing more than sixty thousand of these refugees into the German economy and society during difficult times was no small accomplishment for Weimar Jewry.

Even as they aided the Eastern Jews, German Jewish liberals were painfully conscious that anti-Semites used the presence of the refugees to score heavily against all the Jews. At a time of widespread unemployment and housing shortages, the racists argued, there was no place in Germany for Eastern Jews, usually neglecting to mention that non-Jewish refugees were even more numerous. Nor could it be denied that desperate Jewish refugees were sometimes reduced to smuggling and other shady business dealings near or beyond the edge of the law. In defending or excusing their coreligionists from exaggerated versions of these charges, German Jews betrayed profound uneasiness over the impression that they left on the masses.[80] If the ties of Jewishness obliged aid, those same ties could play havoc with the popular image of German Jews. The shifty, unwashed, obviously alien Jew of racist caricature was now a common sight in every city in Germany, and it was not unreasonable to fear that many who saw him would conclude that, after all, a Jew was a Jew. In 1925 the Centralverein published a pamphlet by Karlsruhe attorney Jakob Marx, who alleged that a significant minority of Eastern Jews had become "racketeers, swindlers, currency and stock cheaters, and thieves and fences":

I believe that we German Jews have the least cause to treat these kinds of adventurers with indulgence. Not just because . . . Judeophobia derives its most effective arguments against German Jews from the Eastern Jewish question, but above all because so many of our Christian neighbors, who otherwise have made every effort to be objective, have lost confidence in German Jewry as a result of the Eastern Jewish question. It cannot be denied that in the hour of our greatest need many of these people engaged in dealings that were highly dangerous for the national economy.[81]

Under the circumstances, Jewish liberals can perhaps be forgiven for deliberately distancing themselves from the newcomers. When the Bavarian government began to expel Eastern Jews in 1920, the Munich Jewish Community

79. Adler-Rudel, *Ostjuden in Deutschland*, 64–149; Werner Senator, "Zur Ostjudenfrage," *Im deutschen Reich*, XXVII (1921), 214–19; Paul Nathan, "Grenzüberschreitungen, Ostjuden und Antisemiten," *Central-Verein Zeitung*, February 28, 1924; *Jüdische Rundschau*, May 9, 1922.

80. Paul Nathan, "Die Ostjuden in Deutschland und die antisemitische Reaktion," *Central-Verein Zeitung*, July 13, 1922; *Allgemeine Zeitung des Judentums*, LXXXVI (1922), 16; *Jüdische Rundschau*, January 8, 1924.

81. Jakob Marx, *Das deutsche Judentum und seine jüdischen Gegner* (Berlin, 1925), 25.

was afraid to protest openly, preferring instead to do as it was told and send provisions to their internment camp near Ingolstadt and, ultimately, funds for their transportation out of Bavaria.[82] According to one report, the Munich local of the National League of Jewish Frontline Veterans actually wrote a letter to Bavarian officials applauding the removal of unsavory foreign Jewish elements.[83] Among Prussian Jews the internment of Jewish aliens who lacked jobs or papers, although scarcely welcomed, was treated as a matter of no great concern.

Jewish liberals were less callous than these actions suggested. Their attitude rested on the practical realization that tensions produced by alien Jews affected all Germans and therefore ought to be treated as part of the general problem of foreigners in Germany. German interests had to be placed first, but Eastern Jews deserved neither better nor worse treatment than that extended to other aliens. Conditions could be kept from deteriorating still further by sealing the eastern borders and severely punishing illegal immigration.[84] It was a Jew, Walther Rathenau's cousin Fritz Rathenau, who drafted the 1920 edict of the Prussian Ministry of the Interior calling for just that. This action met with widespread Jewish approval. In the words of Rabbi Goldmann:

The question of the Eastern Jews is not only a Jewish problem but also a German problem! Out of self-respect we will see to it that Jews are treated no differently at the border from non-Jews! But if impoverished Germany cuts off immigration from the East for economic and political reasons, that is a decision that has nothing whatever to do with a specifically Jewish viewpoint. It has to do with purely political and economic considerations, and today it is the best Jews who speak out as Germans against immigration into Germany.[85]

That left the question of what to do about the Eastern Jews already in Germany. It was obvious that at least half of them showed no enthusiasm for the rigors of the legal gauntlet that awaited them in the United States or for the

---

82. Löwenfeld, "Memoiren," 668–69; Jakob Reich, "Eine Episode aus der Geschichte der Ostjuden Münchens," in Lamm (ed.), *Von Juden in München*, 321–22.
83. *Jüdische Rundschau*, May 21, 1920.
84. Berthold Haase, "Die Ostjudenfrage," *Central-Verein Zeitung*, May 4, 1922; Haase, "Der gegenwärtige Stand der Ostjudenfrage," *ibid.*, January 25, 1923; H. Stern, "Ein ernstes Wort in ernster Stunde," *Israelitisches Familienblatt*, January 29, 1920; *K. C. Blätter*, May-June, 1921, Vertrauliche Beilage, 26.
85. Felix Goldmann, "Wozu der Lärm? Eine Antwort an Ernst Simon," *Central-Verein Zeitung*, November 26, 1926.

hardships involved in settling in backward places such as Palestine or the Latin American countries. German Jews, lacking the financial resources to help so many refugees buy transportation and land abroad but unwilling to use force to send them on their way, could only acquiesce. Some took comfort from the prospect held out by Jewish journalist Paul Nathan that the Eastern Jews could find new homes in Russian cooperative settlements.[86] Unfortunately, neither the Bolshevik leaders nor the refugees thought much of the idea. Both German and Eastern Jews would have to learn to cope with each other.

In fact, they coped badly. Jewish liberals were prepared to go to great lengths to secure the newcomers' legal rights and economic well-being, but in return they insisted upon the absorption of German Jewish ways with superhuman speed. For their part, Eastern Jews were as determined to preserve the unique features of their traditions as their hosts were to see them go. Although the refugees won applause from some Orthodox Jews for their loyalty to an unreconstructed Judaism,[87] most German Jews swiftly lost patience with them and subjected them to increasingly severe criticism: their school children lacked discipline and their religious teachers were incompetent; they sought to revive antiquated religious practices in the synagogues; they disrupted the communities by voting for Zionists and absorbing most welfare funds while contributing neither time nor money to the ongoing work of the congregations, the communities, or the Centralverein.[88] Their deportment could be execrable. Ernst Herzfeld, a liberal member of the Essen Community Council, recalled finding "heaps of cigarette butts and even herring tails" in rooms provided for them by the community for religious services. "We experienced acute embarrassment when during holy services fist-fights broke out because someone who claimed to be fourth Torah reader was assigned fifth place."[89] Berlin Reform Rabbi Karl Rosenthal raised hackles when he told a Jewish audience in Duisburg that Eastern Jews had injected "a certain atmo-

---

86. Paul Nathan, "Palästinakolonisation/Ostjudenhilfe," *ibid.*, August 14, 1925; Karl Loewenstein, "Pflege des Deutschtum—Zuerst Ostjudenarbeit, *ibid.*, October 5, 1928; Georg Götz, "Emanzipationswerk in Osteuropa," *ibid.*, December 14, 1928.

87. Auerbach, "Zur geistigen Struktur der deutschen Orthodoxie der Gegenwart," 201–202; *Der Israelit,* February 23, 1922.

88. H. Stern, *Warum hassen sie uns eigentlich?* 128–31, 150; Berthold Altmann, "Vor dem Untergang?" *Jüdisch-liberale Zeitung,* November 28, 1924; Alexander Adler, "Der Skandal von Dortmund," *Jüdische Rundschau,* October 28, 1932; Bruno Weil, "Die Landesverbandswahlen," *Central-Verein Zeitung,* February 27, 1925.

89. Herzfeld, "Lebenserinnerungen," 254–55.

sphere of uncleanliness and slovenliness into German Jewry," but it seems likely that a great many Jews agreed with him.[90]

Prostitution among Eastern Jewish women sharpened antagonisms still further. It was the last resort of wives and daughters of Jewish refugees who had emigrated alone, abandoning them to uncertain fates. They were exploited primarily by Jewish white slavers, who normally arranged their transportation to bordellos outside of Europe. Other Jewish prostitutes plied their trade in German cities.[91] Bertha Pappenheim and other leaders of the League of Jewish Women (Jüdischer Frauenbund) took the problem in deadly earnest, providing destitute women with rescue homes and rehabilitation centers and apprising them of the fate that awaited them at the hands of white slave traffickers. Unhappily, in this the league received little support from Jewish religious leaders, most of whom preferred not to call attention to Jewish prostitution. To do so might lend credence to racist assertions that Jews managed all aspects of prostitution and the white slave traffic; Hitler himself had made such a claim in the first volume of *Mein Kampf.*[92] Others agreed with Rabbi Felix Goldmann, who expressed concern over the white slave trade but denied that it constituted a specifically Jewish problem, ignoring the extraordinarily large representation of Jews among traffickers and their victims, and the antiquated Jewish marriage and divorce laws that did not permit abandoned wives to remarry.[93]

Inevitably, such antagonisms poisoned personal relations between German and Eastern Jews. It was well known that neither wealthy German Jews nor refugee Jewish domestics were comfortable together, preferring to serve or be served by non-Jews.[94] Equally apparent was the feeling among many German Jewish parents that the marriage of one of their sons or daughters to an Eastern Jew was even less tolerable than marriage outside the faith. In a celebrated

90. *Jüdische Rundschau,* February 9, 1926; *Gemeindeblatt der Jüdischen Gemeinde zu Berlin,* XVI (1926), 128–30.

91. In 1929 a Jewish women's charitable organization unsuccessfully requested funds from the Breslau Jewish Community to counteract what it described as an "alarming" increase in the number of Jewish prostitutes there. "Soziale Gruppe für erwerbstätige jüdische Frauen und Mädchen" to Breslau Gemeinde, April 16, 1929, in Jewish Community of Breslau Collection.

92. Hitler, *Mein Kampf,* 59.

93. Bertha Pappenheim, *Sisyphus Arbeit* (Leipzig, [1924]); Dora Edinger, *Bertha Pappenheim: Leben und Schriften* (Frankfurt-am-Main, 1963), 17–20; *Der Israelit,* January 1, 1931; *Jüdisch-liberale Zeitung,* July 1, 1927; Marion A. Kaplan, "German-Jewish Feminism in the Twentieth Century," *Jewish Social Studies,* XXXVIII (1976), 44–49.

94. Bella Carlebach-Rosenak, "Lebens Erinnerungen" (Typescript in Leo Baeck Institute Archives, New York), 40.

case of 1921 the daughter of a wealthy Hamburg Jew successfully sued her father for her dowry after she married an Eastern Jew.[95] Community welfare services, often overburdened by the refugees' needs, occasionally discriminated against them. In 1922 the directors of the Jewish Home for the Blind of Germany voted to limit its services to Jews who were citizens of Germany.[96]

Political and social tensions between German Jews and recent Jewish immigrants were sharpened by the latter's unequal distribution among the various communities. Most of them drifted to the industrial cities of Saxony and northwestern Germany and to Berlin. The German capital's large Jewish community could absorb many thousands of Easterners without endangering the hegemony of established elites, but in some cities the number of refugees nearly equaled or actually exceeded those of German Jews. Where that was true, Jewish liberalism defended itself against Zionism and other "alien" ways associated with Eastern Jews by limiting or proscribing their voting rights. One example was Leipzig, where in 1922 four thousand German Jews and eighteen thousand Eastern Jews made their homes.[97] The liberals' denial of community voting rights for aliens in Leipzig aroused furious opposition from Zionists, Orthodox Jews, and Eastern Jews themselves. The community leaders yielded to these pressures for reform in 1923, but only slightly. Eastern Jews were granted suffrage, but for a separate voting list that permitted them to send no more than eight of their fellow aliens to the community council. The other twenty-five seats were reserved for the minority of German Jews. In this way the liberals maintained tight control over the Leipzig community throughout the Weimar years.[98] In Chemnitz, Jewish liberals resorted to the

95. *Israelitisches Familienblatt,* July 28, 1921; *ibid.,* February 16, 1922.
96. *Der Israelit,* January 16, 1930; *Jüdische Rundschau,* May 12, 1922; *ibid.,* November 21, 1922; *ibid.,* May 15, 1923; *ibid.,* June 15, 1928.
97. Jacques Adler, "Brief aus Leipzig," *Jüdische Rundschau,* December 1, 1922. Not all Eastern Jews had entered Germany after 1914. On the contrary, in Leipzig as in every German Jewish community, some of them had lived in Germany for decades or had even been born there. When the Nazis conducted their first census, in June, 1933, they found 98,747 alien Jews, of whom 38,919 had been born in Germany. Many of the well-established Eastern Jews had become highly assimilated by 1914, were enormously patriotic Germans, and fought for their new homeland in the World War. They tended to regard the more recent Jewish immigrants with that special combination of fear and loathing common to those who do not want to be reminded of their own recent origins. Only Germany's extraordinarily involved naturalization procedure, which required ten years of residency and then the approval of all the state governments, kept these Eastern Jews from becoming citizens. On the problem of Jewish naturalization, see *ibid.,* February 6, 1931.
98. *Jüdische Rundschau,* November 6, 1923; *ibid.,* March 4, 1927; *Der Israelit,* April 17, 1924.

same tactics, whereas in Dresden they were content to deny Eastern Jews the right to hold office.[99]

The Prussian state government responded to protests against such tactics by banning them for as far as its authority reached. Jewish liberals in some cities reacted by imposing the payment of taxes to the community as a prerequisite for suffrage in community elections; since many Eastern Jews earned too little to pay such taxes, they were effectively disfranchised.[100] Another liberal tactic was to make the Eastern Jewish vote into a campaign issue. In Recklinghausen, following Prussian state intervention on behalf of voting rights for Eastern Jews, the liberals rallied their forces with denunciations of the "black hordes," the "sons of the steppes of Asia." At the same time they reportedly intimidated refugees with thinly veiled threats to expel them unless they behaved themselves in ways "befitting tolerated persons." Repeated complaints of electoral irregularities perpetrated by liberals against Eastern Jews produced little action from Prussian officialdom, which showed great reluctance to interfere in the internal affairs of the Jewish communities.[101] Outside of Prussia it was common to require alien Jews to wait as long as ten years to establish legal residency for membership in the community.[102] In 1930 Zionists charged that fully twenty-nine liberal-dominated communities denied the vote to Eastern Jews by one means or another; among them were Leipzig, Mainz, Stuttgart, Würzburg, Augsburg, Aachen, and Hanover.[103] In the last-named city the liberals insisted on following the letter of the antique provincial law that banned aliens from membership in German Jewish communities, threatening to resign from and bankrupt the community if the law were reformed. Throughout the Weimar years Hanover remained a deeply divided community. When Eastern Jews slipped into unoccupied pews of the local synagogue to pray, they were handed cards that read: "If you do not leave the synagogue *immediately,* you will be charged with trespassing and *disturbing holy services.*"[104]

99. Harry Epstein, "Nochmals: Das Wahlrecht in den jüdischen Gemeinden Sachsens," *Jüdische Rundschau,* January 18, 1929; *ibid.,* December 20, 1929; *ibid.,* May 15, 1923; *ibid.,* October 26, 1926.

100. *Ibid.,* January 21, 1930; *ibid.,* May 9, 1930. The tax requirement backfired when depression conditions caused liberal Jews to fall into the same condition. *Ibid.,* November 18, 1930.

101. *Ibid.,* April 8, 1930; *ibid.,* March 4, 1924; Max Katz, *et al.,* to Regierungspräsident Münster, March 26, 1927, Regierung Münster, 17153, Staatsarchiv, Münster.

102. *Jüdische Rundschau,* August 21, 1928; *ibid.,* April 18, 1919.

103. *Ibid.,* November 11, 1930.

104. Harry Epstein, "Vor den neuen Judengesetz," *Jüdische Rundschau,* March 1, 1929; *ibid.,* March 15, 1929; *ibid.,* April 24, 1929; *ibid.,* November 26, 1929; correspondence be-

Such apparently illiberal behavior from self-professed liberals should be understood primarily in terms of Zionist attempts at organizing Eastern Jews against the assimilationist synthesis of Germans and Jews. That is what Rabbi Max Dienemann was getting at when he wrote in 1928 that Eastern Jews could not be expected to share the profound sense of love for Germany as "homeland of the soul" felt by German Jews. Hence the newcomers were susceptible to demagogic manipulation by those who wanted to destroy the bonds between German and Jew. With the Jewish communities becoming increasingly cultural as well as religious in character, a decision would have to be made as to whether there was any room there for German-Jewish culture.[105] Far from viewing their stand against Eastern Jewish influence as a betrayal of liberalism, Jewish liberals regarded themselves as defenders of their best ideals against narrow-spirited Jewish nationalism.

More typical of the liberals' point of view was their rapid extension of women's suffrage in community elections. On this issue neither Zionism nor anti-Semitism was an impediment. The League of Jewish Women had agitated for the vote for years, tactfully avoiding any impression of importunity by stressing the desirability of tapping a new source of vigor for the communities and of strengthening women's Jewish consciousness.[106] Prussian officials made no effort to enforce the archaic 1847 law that prohibited women from voting in community elections; on the contrary, they actually encouraged the Jews to treat it as a dead letter, since it was out of tune with the democratic Weimar constitution.[107] Orthodox objections, based on traditional interpretations of Holy Writ, were the chief obstacles to women's suffrage, but they were partially overcome by Frankfurt-am-Main Orthodox Rabbi N. A. Nobel's deduction of women's rights to vote and hold office from the Talmud. Indeed, it was Frankfurt that first granted both of these rights in 1920, and by 1924 four women sat on its community council and one on its executive committee.[108] The outspoken opposition of Rabbi David Hoffmann, head

---

tween Hanover Jewish Community leaders, district officials, and the Prussian Ministry of Culture concerning reform of the community suffrage, June 26, 1922, to May 24, 1932, Hannover, 80/Hann. IIe2, Nr. 127. Niedersächsisches Hauptstaatsarchiv, Hanover.

105. Max Dienemann, "Galuth," *Der Morgen,* IV (1928), 334.

106. *Allgemeine Zeitung des Judentums,* LXXXIII (January 3, 1919), Beilage; *Israelitisches Familienblatt,* February 27, 1919; *ibid.,* March 15, 1923; Kaplan, "German-Jewish Feminism," 50–51.

107. Helene Meyer, "Das Gemeindewahlrecht der jüdischen Frau," *Israelitisches Familienblatt,* December 13, 1923.

108. Ernst Simon, "N. A. Nobel als Prediger," in *Brücken: Gesammelte Aufsätze* (Heidelberg, 1965), 380; interview with Dr. Dora Edinger, by Marion Kaplan, February 17, 1975, typed transcription in Leo Baeck Institute Archives, New York; Rabbi Dr. Klein, "Frauenwahl-

of the Orthodox Berlin seminary, to the holding of communal office by women induced some communities to limit women's rights to those of suffrage. Hence Hamburg granted women's suffrage in 1919 but waited another decade before letting them run for office.[109] Berlin followed the same pattern from 1925 to 1928.[110] Elsewhere, social conservatism combined with sensitivity to Orthodox sentiments to bar women from both suffrage and communal office, particularly in small and medium-size communities. In Saxony, Leipzig alone granted those rights.[111] Still, by the late 1920s about one-half of German Jewish women could vote in the communities' elections on the same basis as men. Of the very large German Jewish communities, only the one in Cologne still denied them suffrage.[112] Hence, although most Jewish men and probably most Jewish women remained conservative in their conception of women's social roles,[113] both increasingly acknowledged the importance of integrating women more intimately into Jewish religious life.

Sensitivity to Orthodox feelings about women's role in community life illustrated a larger trend among German Jews—a determination to overcome doctrinal quarrels that had embittered intra-Jewish relations before the war. In most urban centers unified communities governed all the local Jewish congregations, from the most conservative to the most liberal. The need to preserve unity in the communities challenged the tact and toleration of both Liberal majorities and Orthodox minorities. Community funds had to be spent in scrupulously even-handed ways, and care had to be taken never to outrage other Jews' tenets. On the whole, German Jews succeeded admirably. Typically, when religious issues threatened to tear communities apart, as happened in Breslau and Cologne, separate and autonomous Liberal and Orthodox committees were appointed to supervise all matters touching on their own

recht," *Der Israelit*, February 5, 1925; Eugen Mayer, "Fünf Jahre Gemeindeverwaltung," *Gemeindeblatt der Israelitischen Gemeinde Frankfurt a. Main*, II (June, 1924), 1. Frankfurt remained in the forefront of German Jewish women's liberation by underwriting the education of young women for business and administrative careers. *Jüdische Rundschau*, March 28, 1924; Max Seelig, "Jüdische Frauenbildung und jüdische Frauenschule," *Gemeindeblatt der Israelitischen Gemeinde Frankfurt a. Main*, IV (January, 1926), 5–9.

109. E. Löwenberg, "Mein Leben in Deutschland," 35; *Jüdische Rundschau*, December 30, 1919; Marion A. Kaplan, "German-Jewish Feminism: The Jüdischer Frauenbund, 1904–1938" (Ph.D. dissertation, Columbia University, 1977), 470–72.

110. *Israelitisches Familienblatt*, September 24, 1925.

111. *Der Israelit*, December 5, 1929; Meyer, "Das Gemeindewahlrecht," *Israelitisches Familienblatt*, December 13, 1923.

112. Kaplan, "German-Jewish Feminism" (Ph.D. dissertation), 504–505.

113. See, typically, Max Dienemann, "Lebensgestaltung der jüdischen Frau," *Der Morgen*, VI (1930), 420–30.

worship and educational policies.[114] A few issues remained to disturb community accord. Religious Liberals grumbled about the great cost of maintaining kosher butchers and kosher kitchens for community-run institutions when only the tiny minority of Orthodox Jews held to strict dietary laws.[115] For their part the Orthodox Jews were uneasy about the Liberals' continuing drift away from the letter of Jewish law, and yet they kept their patience in order to minimize that trend and to maintain Orthodox influence in the larger community.[116] This unity, forged in part by more than two decades of cooperation against anti-Semitism in the Centralverein, was successfully translated to the General Alliance of Rabbis in Germany (Allgemeiner Rabbinerverband in Deutschland). Organized in 1896 by Orthodox, Liberal, and Reform rabbis from all over Germany, it retained its unique sense of solidarity by steadfastly avoiding the ventilation of controversial doctrinal issues at its meetings.[117]

In a few German cities, uncompromising Orthodox Jews had formed separatist communities as the best means of upholding strict fidelity to the Torah. Most were small. The separatist community in Berlin numbered only about 250 souls.[118] Its attacks on Liberal Judaism and on unitary communities reached a volume that was quite out of proportion to the size and influence of their source. The Liberals were portrayed as tolerating "godless" elements and trends that undermined the faith. Unitary communities were reported as slighting the needs of Orthodoxy, an inescapable condition when majorities ruled in the place of Holy Writ.[119] The Orthodox separatists insisted that opposition to anti-Semitism through the Centralverein would remain fruitless, since persecution was God's punishment for infidelity; only a return to the Torah would furnish inner support for the present and an end to

---

114. *Jüdische Rundschau,* January 22, 1929; *Der Israelit,* July 10, 1930; *Jüdisch-liberale Zeitung,* VIII (July 6, 1928), Beilage; *ibid.,* IX (September 25, 1929), Beilage.

115. Szanto, "Im Dienste der Gemeinde," 8–9; Felix Makower, "Der liberale Gedanke und die Liberalen," *Jüdisch-liberale Zeitung,* VII (March 11, 1927), 1–3; *Jüdische Rundschau,* July 4, 1930.

116. *Israelitisches Familienblatt,* April 7, 1921; *ibid.,* November 2, 1922; *Jüdische Rundschau,* October 17, 1922; *Jüdisch-liberale Zeitung,* IV (May 23, 1924), Beilage 3; Eugen Wolbe, "Vorstoss der Orthodoxie," *ibid.,* X (April 30, 1930), Beilage; Auerbach, "Zur geistigen Struktur der deutschen Orthodoxie der Gegenwart," 199–201.

117. Alexander Altmann, "The German Rabbi: 1910–1939," *Leo Baeck Institute Yearbook,* XIX (1974), 38–40.

118. The figure refers to adult male members. There was a total of 172,700 Jews in Berlin in 1925. Aron Sandler, "Erinnerungen" (Typescript in Leo Baeck Institute Archives, New York), II, 11.

119. *Der Israelit,* June 26, 1930; *ibid.,* October 17, 1930; *ibid.,* August 21, 1930; *ibid.,* March 12, 1931; *ibid.,* November 26, 1931.

Judeophobia in the future.[120] Perhaps the stridency of these attacks betrayed the separatists' anxiety over future decline. The 1921 decision of Königsberg's separatist community to merge with the larger community must have caused them deep concern.[121] Liberal attitudes of tolerance and mutual respect were growing even among those opposed to Liberal Judaism.

If this discussion of Jewish liberalism has left the impression that it was inconstant and excessively given to compromise with some of the more unsavory aspects of German nationalism, especially on matters related to education and the Eastern Jews, let it be understood that a siege mentality is less than conducive to a full flowering of the idea of freedom. The end of the liberal era was being proclaimed on all sides, and the search for a non-Marxist alternative was the chief passion of the day. Just as the liberal and Social Democratic political parties were fending off a tide of illiberalism with Jewish help, so did most German Jews react defensively against illiberalism in their own ranks. Without an understanding of the Zionist challenge to the liberal creed, the world of Weimar Jewry must remain obscured in shadow.

120. Jakob Tessler, "Ein Weckruf zum Elul-Neumond!" *ibid.*, August 21, 1919; *ibid.*, May 3, 1929. Only the Centralverein's campaign against Zionism elicited separatist support.
121. *Allgemeine Zeitung des Judentums,* LXXXIV (June 24, 1921), Beilage, 2.

The Jew as Jewish Nationalist

The Quest for the Zionist Utopia

Zionists were always a small minority of the German Jews, but that is not good reason to dismiss them as insignificant. It is not just that they posed a real challenge to liberal control of the Jewish communities. They also made positive contributions to the revival of Jewish consciousness during the Weimar years. Perhaps most important of all, their ideology was a whetstone against which the liberal majority sharpened its own identity.

The history of German Zionism before 1919 reveals a progressive abjuration of the idea of Jewish assimilation. The Zionist Federation of Germany (Zionistische Vereinigung für Deutschland) had been founded in 1897 by a handful of German Jews who wished to find a new home for the wretched Jews of Eastern Europe as well as to strengthen their own Jewish consciousness. By 1914 it had attracted nearly 10,000 members, many of whom had long since shaken off the essentially philanthropic Zionism of the founders in favor of militant Jewish nationalism. These Young Turks called themselves "practical Zionists" to underline their involvement in actually settling Jews in Palestine, rather than waiting for the acquisition of a political mandate there or elsewhere as Theodor Herzl and his fellow "political Zionists" had counseled. This second generation of proud young German Zionists, in adopting many of the Palestine-centered views of the Russian Zionist Asher Ginzberg, reacted impatiently to the abiding indignities of German anti-Semitism. It found a determined and articulate leader in Kurt Blumenfeld, who in 1909 was chosen secretary of the Zionist Federation, and in 1924 its president, a post he was to retain until after the Nazis seized power.

The triumph of this new and radicalized Zionist ideology culminated in a resolution adopted at the 1912 Posen convention of the German Zionist Federation calling for every Zionist to plan personally to emigrate to Palestine. Two years later, at its Leipzig convention, the federation declared its conviction that the Jews had no roots whatever in Germany. Both assertions were passed over the passionate objections of the Zionist old guard, which pointed out that such ideological extravagance was certain to cast doubts on German

Zionists' loyalty to Germany, as well as to drive away moderate supporters. The new Zionist majority was prepared to risk such consequences, because it had come to believe that the preservation of Jewishness depended on abolishing all but formal ties with Germany.[1]

Such was the spirit that dominated German Zionism in the Weimar Republic. Assimilation was identified as the chief enemy of the Jews because it bred anti-Semitism and threatened to disfigure and perhaps even smother Jewish life. A young German Zionist, Moritz Goldstein, had outlined the issue shortly before the outbreak of the World War in an essay that caused a minor sensation. He pictured German Jews as dominating virtually every aspect of Germany's literary and artistic life. Their achievements, however admirable, betrayed a lack of genuine rootedness in German culture and inevitably aroused German hatred and antipathy. Among Jews themselves the fatal inner dualism of being both German and Jew excluded all hope of personal harmony and creative greatness. Only by voluntarily withdrawing from German culture did Goldstein believe they could hope to find their Jewish roots once again and, newly nourished by them, cultivate their true identity and find self-respect.[2] His views were partially restated in 1921 by Arnold Zweig, who described the lives of liberal Jews who tried to fit in where they were not wanted and did not belong as "sinking, dissonant, full of conflict, and tragic; sinking as a part of the Jewish people, dissonant to the German nationality, full of conflict in relation to public life, and filled with deep tragedy for those high-minded and valuable individuals who see their place within German culture and as part of the German people."[3]

The Zionist critique of assimilation, then, rested on a certain conviction that all efforts to blend with non-Jews must lead unswervingly to deformed Jewish lives. The new discipline of psychoanalysis was mustered to demonstrate the neurotic effects of divided consciousness. Rootlessness and inferiority complexes were shown to generate everything from revolutionary activity to Jewish anti-Semitism, extreme German nationalism, and suicide.[4]

1. Blumenfeld, *Erlebte Judenfrage,* 59–64, 88–90, 93, 113–16; Schorsch, *Jewish Reactions to German Anti-Semitism,* 179–95; Walter Laqueur, *A History of Zionism* (London, 1972), 156–57; Jehuda Reinharz, *Fatherland or Promised Land: The Dilemma of the German Jew, 1893–1914* (Ann Arbor, 1975), *passim.*
2. The article, which first appeared in the literary journal *Der Kunstwart,* XXV (1912), 281–94, is partially reproduced together with a personal reminiscence by Goldstein in "German Jewry's Dilemma before 1914," *Leo Baeck Institute Yearbook,* II (1957), 236–54.
3. Arnold Zweig, "Der heutige deutsche Antisemitismus," *Der Jude,* V (1920/21), 388.
4. Gerhard Holdheim and Walter Preuss, *Die theoretischen Grundlagen des Zionismus* (Berlin, 1919), 53–54; Gustav Krojanker, "Die Juden in der deutschen Revolution," *Jüdische*

Zionist philosopher Theodor Lessing coined the term "Jewish self-hate" to describe an overreaction to anti-Semitism by attempting to kill the Jew within oneself.[5] Criminality among Jews, such as that of the Barmats and the Sklareks, was likewise declared an excrescence of uprooted assimilationist lives.[6] The view that assimilation would almost inevitably culminate in complete amalgamation, forcefully articulated by the Russian-born Zionist Jakob Klatzkin, found little support in Germany.[7] For the vast majority of German Zionists, assimilation was dangerous precisely because it threatened permanently to suspend German Jews in a state of torment and frustration.

Beyond disfiguring the Jewish character, assimilation intensified anti-Semitism, in the Zionist view. Again Arnold Zweig expanded upon Moritz Goldstein's conception of Judeophobia as the defensive reaction of non-Jews to Jewish intrusion into their culture.

The more intensively the Jew assimilates himself, the more deeply and rapidly he interferes with the nations' spiritual life; his role in poetry, politics, and the arts is widely acknowledged. Since the Jew has fulfilled his obligations to the state, even to the point of sacrificing his life for it, propriety dictates that these tensions remain unstated and, in good times, tolerated. But in times of distress, they come to light on every side. . . . Then only the incitement of hateful agitation is required for these tensions to be converted into rage: and the catastrophic release is found.[8]

Later Zweig recalled Walther Rathenau's tragic end in order to typify the practical conclusion of assimilationist logic.[9]

Not that the end of assimilation would bring about the death of Judeophobia. As German Zionists saw it, anti-Jewish prejudices were deeply implanted in primitive instincts and emotions and hence constituted permanent fixtures of life in the Diaspora. Even a moderate Zionist such as Gustav Krojanker could describe anti-Semitism as the ideological superstructure of "instinctive animal peculiarities" that were natural among groups "divided by

---

Rundschau, August 12, 1919; M. W. [Moses Waldmann], "Kindermann," *ibid.,* August 6, 1925; Ernst Simon, "Rabbiner Dr. B. Jacob: Ein Beitrag zur Psychologie der Assimilation," *ibid.,* February 17, 1928; M. W. [Moses Waldmann], "Nur eine sozialistische Tragödie?" *ibid.,* June 17, 1930.

5. Theodor Lessing, *Der jüdische Selbsthass* (Berlin, 1930), 9–40.

6. *Jüdische Rundschau,* October 18, 1929; *ibid.,* July 1, 1932.

7. Jakob Klatzkin, *Krisis und Entscheidung im Judentum* (Berlin, 1921), especially 9–51; Gustav Krojanker, "Klatzkins Forderungen," *Jüdische Rundschau,* February 3, 1931; Goldmann, *Memories,* 74–80.

8. Zweig, "Der heutige deutsche Antisemitismus," 204.

9. *Jüdische Rundschau,* April 8, 1927.

blood and history." [10] On the subject of unjust judicial verdicts in cases touching on Jewish rights, the Zionist *Jüdische Rundschau* commented: "With logic and facts you cannot refute prejudices that are fixed deep in the blood." [11] That being the case, liberal emancipation could be only a passing phase, a superficial facade hiding eternal hostility. [12] Accordingly, German Zionists took comfort neither in anti-Semitism's temporary decline in the good years of the Weimar Republic nor in non-Jewish voices raised in defense of Jewish rights. For them, Judeophobia was perennial, ubiquitous, and incorrigible; it would go to its grave with the last Jew of the Diaspora. [13]

Zionism was not, however, a philosophy of fatalism; anti-Semitism could not be stamped out, but it could be brought under control, and Zionists believed themselves to be in possession of the only leash—Zionism itself. Its establishment of an independent, self-reliant Jewry separated from the rest of society would win the respect and even the sympathy of non-Jews, the best of whom instinctively sensed that Jews did not belong with them. [14] Recent social and economic trends, not Zionism, had isolated the Jews from other human beings. Zionism proposed to turn that isolation to good advantage by showing the world that Jews could sustain themselves in exile while building a new home in Palestine. [15] *Jüdische Rundschau* editor Robert Weltsch summarized the Zionist faith succinctly, taking a swipe at Centralverein tactics as he did so:

When the Jews have nothing more to hide and actually step forward as Jews, the greater part of anti-Semitism will disappear, especially the abnormal and least supportable part of it. Proclaiming "unswerving cultivation of German sentiment" does nothing to counteract Judeophobia; on the contrary, it only makes non-Jews even more suspicious. A decent non-Jew cannot understand why the Jew, whose specific

10. Gustav Krojanker, "Die antisemitische Idee," *ibid.*, February 24, 1928. For similar comments, see Hugo Schachtel, "Nach 30 Jahren Zionismus," *ibid.*, April 16, 1926; Paul Amann, "Politische Gegenwartsprobleme des deutschen Judentums," *Der Jude*, VIII (1924), 1–8; Holdheim and Preuss, *Die theoretischen Grundlagen*, 52.

11. *Jüdische Rundschau*, April 27, 1928.

12. Sch. Gorelik, "Bekenntnisse eines Zionisten," *ibid.*, May 2, 1930; Kurt Blumenfeld, "Wir werben," *ibid.*, April 1, 1931; Oskar Karbach, "Das Oktroy der jüdischen Emanzipation," *Der Jude*, VII (1923), 72–77.

13. *Jüdische Rundschau*, January 20, 1920; Moses Waldmann, "Fortschritt und Judenhass," *ibid.*, January 6, 1928; *ibid.*, May 4, 1928; M. W. [Moses Waldmann], "Offene Antwort," *ibid.*, July 8, 1930; *ibid.*, September 26, 1930; *ibid.*, August 2, 1932.

14. Gustav Krojanker, "Das Wesen des Antisemitismus," *ibid.*, February 28, 1930; Kurt Willkowski, "Der jüdische Lehrer in Deutschland," *ibid.*, July 4, 1930.

15. Gerhard Holdheim, "Nationaljüdischer Radikalismus?" *ibid.*, March 14, 1919; *ibid.*, January 6, 1925; Kurt Blumenfeld, "Der Zionismus und die Lösung der Judenfrage," *ibid.*, September 12, 1930.

characteristics are obvious to the non-Jew at a glance and are not to be explained away with "scientific arguments," wants to compensate with such loud assertions of his German nationality.[16]

The Centralverein, according to this Zionist analysis, was worse than use-less; its assimilationist doctrines impeded effective countermeasures against anti-Semitism and actually intensified the persecution of Jews. By insisting that Jews were good Germans, it falsely denied their Jewish nationality and tried to force them upon an unwilling Germany. It dishonored the Jewish name with abject apologetics. In its failure effectively to affirm the positive value of Jewishness and the need to nourish it with bonds to Palestine, the Centralverein unwittingly sponsored the "practical suicide" of the Jewish spirit.[17]

At the heart of the Zionist critique of liberal assimilationism lay the convic-tion that Jews constituted a unique race. It was the belief in insurmountable racial differences that made the inevitability of anti-Semitism credible, just as it rationalized the view that every effort to assimilate must go aground on the barrier reef of biological determinism. As Gustav Krojanker put it, the German soul was "determined by the soil and air of this land, determined by the blood and destiny of its people, eternally closed to us. We can grasp it faintly, but our productive stock comes from other provinces, is supplied from different depths, watered from different springs."[18]

The liberal view of Jews as a mere ethnic group was rejected out of hand. That description might apply to African Negroes and to American Indians, but not to a people of culture like the Jews. They were a *Volk*, understood as both race and nation. And they were a *pure* race. Only the Japanese and the Jews had escaped hybridization by successfully discouraging mixed mar-riages.[19] That such marriages might become a more serious problem for the Jews prompted Zionist leaders in the Berlin Jewish Community to authorize a report identifying intermarriage as a threat to the "racial purity of stock."[20]

16. Robert Weltsch, "Worte und Begriffe," *ibid.*, September 14, 1926.

17. *Ibid.*, May 29, 1923; Moritz Bileski, "Jüdischer Geist ohne jüdisches Volk?" *ibid.*, November 2, 1928; *ibid.*, February 20, 1931; Moritz Bileski, "Das Kompromiss des deutschen Judentums," *Der Jude,* V (1920/21), 23.

18. Krojanker, "Die Juden in der deutschen Revolution," *Jüdische Rundschau,* August 12, 1919.

19. *Ibid.*, May 6, 1919; Elias Auerbach, "Rassenkunde," *Der Jude,* V (1920/21), 49–57; Gerhard Holdheim (ed.), *Zionistisches Handbuch* (Berlin, 1923), 3–7.

20. W. Hanauer, "Die Mischehe," in *Jüdisches Jahrbuch 1929* (Berlin, 1929), 37. The re-port appeared at a time when the Berlin Jewish Community was governed by a Zionist-led coali-tion of antiliberal parties.

The maintenance of that "purity" was essential to German Zionism, for it acknowledged the essential prerequisites for nationhood to be "consanguinity of the flesh and solidarity of the soul" together with the "will to establish a closed brotherhood over against all other communities on earth." [21]

The Zionist conviction that racial otherness predetermined German-Jewish incompatibility formed the basis of what can only be described as a Jewish version of *völkisch* ideology, complete with the claim that racial and historical influences had combined to evolve a uniquely Jewish character and typically Jewish behavior. Zionists spoke of a "Jewish spirit" or "Jewish soul" that was notable for its love of knowledge and its ethical idealism. [22] Zionist anthropologist Fritz Kahn identified Moses, Jesus, and Marx as different representatives of the same racially determined drive to serve mankind. [23] A Zionist review of Lion Feuchtwanger's best-selling novel *Success* (*Erfolg*) criticized its optimistic portrayal of a miscarriage of Bavarian justice that was redressed by the dogged persistence of a Jewish attorney and aid from northern Germany. Feuchtwanger's passion for justice, wrote Gustav Krojanker, was a "Jewish affair of the blood" (*Blutsache*), but his definition of justice was incompatible with that of Germans, for whom justice necessarily meant disparate things; different blood, different justice, neither better than the other, perhaps, but irreconcilable. [24]

Other Zionists described Jews as more plastic and sensitive to the need for change than most non-Jews, and hence as pioneers of socialism, capitalism, and of avant-garde cultural movements. [25] On the subject of art, a Zionist writer compared the Jews' fundamental religiosity with Western man's essential positivism: "The temper of all Western creativity is technical, from the St. Matthew Passion to the submarine," whereas "for the Jew, ecstasy, not form, is what matters." [26] Hence a new opera by Kurt Weill was greeted as a work that "only a Jew could have written." [27] True enough, Zionists never explicitly embraced the doctrine of racial superiority and on one occasion

21. Fritz Kahn, *Die Juden als Rasse und Kulturvolk* (Berlin, 1922), 163. *Cf.* E. Auerbach, "Rassenkunde," 383.
22. Elfride Bergel-Gronemann, "Jüdische Wege," *Der Jude,* V (1920/21), 396–403; Fritz Loew, "Judentum und Volkskunst," *ibid.,* VIII (1924), 315–22; Heinrich Berl, "Die Juden in der bildenden Kunst der Gegenwart," *ibid.,* VIII (1924), 323–38.
23. Kahn, *Die Juden als Rasse,* 203–17.
24. *Jüdische Rundschau,* July 28, 1931.
25. Alfred Lemm, "Von der Aufgabe der Juden in Europa," *Der Jude,* II (1917), 310–11; Eugen Höflich, "Jüdischer Volkstum und Staat," *Die Arbeit,* I (1919), 235–38.
26. Friedel Curth, "Abendländische und jüdische Musik," *Jüdische Rundschau,* August 7, 1928.
27. *Ibid.,* March 15, 1932.

specifically damned it, claiming only the right to exist as a race among the races.[28] And yet, as we have seen, assertions of the Jews' alleged moral, intellectual, and emotional advancement were not missing from Zionist propaganda. It had been precisely this "racial arrogance, which was nothing other than the photographic negative of anti-Semitism" that had driven the great sociologist Franz Oppenheimer from Zionism even before the First World War.[29]

No one was more influential in the development of blood-mysticism among German Zionists than the Viennese philosopher Martin Buber, who taught at the University of Frankfurt-am-Main during the Weimar years. Buber's efforts to revive the Hasidic heritage for modern Jews led him to postulate a mystical view of the Jewish people that closely paralleled the development of nonrational *völkisch* ideas among Germans. Shortly before the World War Buber had identified blood as "the deepest, most potent stratum of our being," the collective experience of untold generations of ancestors. Jewish liberals, he claimed, had ignored the power of blood, overcompensating for hostility with a shallow intellectualism, living unhealthy, unbalanced, rootless lives. Self-affirmation required the Jews to understand that "our blood is the creative force in our life."[30] Blood also prevented Jews from being Germans. In a 1918 play dedicated to his son, Rafael, Buber had a young Jew ask a trusted adult advisor why he was different from his Christian playmate. The answer he received went straight to the issue of irrevocably divided national characteristics: "To live as a German means nothing other than truly and completely to live as part of the German community, in communion with the Germans of all ages and with Germandom beyond the ages . . .; that, however, is prohibited for him[the Jew]."[31] It was a tribute to Buber's influence that Zionist publications during the Weimar years were replete with favorable references to "the mysticism of the blood," "racial genius," and the "Jewish people's soul" *(jüdische Volksseele)*.[32]

28. Felix Weltsch, *Nationalismus und Judentum* (Berlin, 1920), 18–23.

29. Franz Oppenheimer, *Erlebtes, Erstrebtes, Erreichtes: Lebenserinnerungen* (Düsseldorf, 1964), 215.

30. Martin Buber, "Judaism and the Jews," in Nahum N. Glatzer (ed.), *On Judaism* (New York, 1967), 17–18. See also Mosse, *Germans and Jews,* 85–92.

31. Martin Buber, *Der Jude und sein Judentum: Gesammelte Aufsätze und Reden* (Cologne, 1963), 693; first published in *Jerubbal, eine Zeitschrift der jüdischen Jugend,* I (1918). There is a certain element of irony in the fact that Buber married a German convert to Judaism. Aubrey Hodes, *Martin Buber: An Intimate Portrait* (New York, 1971), 48.

32. Hans Kohn, "Stimmen," *Der Jude,* VII (1923), 552–56; Nahum Sokolow, "Gesegnet sind die Stillen," *Jüdische Rundschau,* February 1, 1929; *ibid.,* March 10, 1931; Zwi Schweid, "Morris Rosenfeld," *ibid.,* July 6, 1923; *ibid.,* March 13, 1923.

Buber's mysticism also vindicated Jewish claims to Palestine, positing necessary, God-willed bonds of blood and history between land and people. In 1928 Buber told a Zionist fund-raising rally in Munich: "Only this *Volk* can make of this land what this land is destined to be, and only this land can make of the *Volk* what this *Volk* is destined to be."[33] He was insistent, however, that Zionism avoid the chauvinism that had just brought Europe to grief, counseling it instead to view Jewish nationalism as a necessary stepping-stone toward ultimate unity with the whole of humankind.[34]

Instrumental in representing Buber's humanitarian nationalism to German Zionists was Robert Weltsch, a Czech citizen who had moved to Berlin at the end of the World War to become editor-in-chief of the *Jüdische Rundschau*.[35] Again and again Weltsch called attention to the "unique" qualities of Jewish nationalism that separated it from the narrow self-seeking and self-deification of similar movements among other nationalities. Far from consciously afflicting the world with yet another vexatious strain of jingoism, Jewish nationalism freed Jews and enslaved no one. Moreover, it was inevitable, since a communitarian phase was the unavoidable prerequisite for ultimate membership in humanity.[36] With Weltsch stood his colleagues in the German branch of Hapoel Hazair, a faction within the world Zionist movement made up of radicals who were passionately dedicated to Jewish settlement in Palestine and to a non-Marxist socialism. Although not numerous, they included such influential figures as Victor Chaim Arlosoroff and Walter Preuss, in addition to Weltsch and Buber.[37]

The themes of creating a nationalism on a higher moral plane and of employing it solely for the good of mankind found support among other German Zionists, too. Many of them assumed that this "modern, moral, *i.e.*, Jewish nationalism" assured the rights, and hence the friendship, of the Arabs in Palestine. Even if one day, in the very distant future, it took on a Jewish majority, it would be run as a binational state with equality for all. What had been undesirable and perhaps impossible in Europe would become a reality in

33. *Bayerische Israelitische Gemeindezeitung*, IV (1928), 136–38. See also *Jüdische Rundschau*, March 4, 1932; Buber, *Der Jude und sein Judentum*, 330–33.
34. Martin Buber, "Wege und der Weg," *Der Jude*, III (1918/19), 366–67; Mosse, *Germans and Jews*, 89.
35. Moritz Sobernheim to Wohnungsverband Gross-Berlin, December, 1920, in Nachlass Moritz Sobernheim, 1287/349639–40.
36. Robert Weltsch, "Die Judenfrage für den Juden," in Hermann Bahr, *et al.* (eds.), *Der Jud ist Schuld . . . ? Diskussionsbuch über die Judenfrage* (Basel, 1932), 367; Robert Weltsch, "Unsere Nationalismus," *Jüdische Rundschau*, December 11, 1925; Robert Weltsch, "Politische Neujahrsbetrachtung," *ibid.*, September 26, 1924; Robert Weltsch, "Wir und die Araber," *ibid.*, February 24, 1928; R. W., "Zum Neuen Jahre," *ibid.*, October 4, 1929.
37. Preuss, *Ein Ring schliesst sich*, 166–68.

Palestine—amalgamation of the Jews with their "great Arabian brothers" on the basis of common racial ties.[38]

Had the humanitarian nationalism of Buber and Weltsch dominated German Zionism, it might have neutralized the more pernicious ramifications of their racial speculations. Unhappily, there were those among their fellow Zionists who held fast to blood mysticism while rejecting a cosmopolitan outlook in favor of militant anti-Arab chauvinism. This point of view was represented most overtly by members of the Revisionist faction within the German Zionist Federation, although it was by no means limited to them.[39] Followers of the Russian Zionist Vladimir Jabotinsky, the Revisionists were far more aggressive in their pursuit of an early Jewish majority in Palestine than were their fellows. Moreover, they openly advocated the establishment of a Jewish state in Palestine as soon as possible, without regard for the wishes of its Arab population. It could easily hold as many as six million inhabitants, and the wishes of one-half million Arabs would have to bow to the Jews' superior moral claim on the land.[40] Richard Lichtheim, who in 1926 was to become the leading German Revisionist, in 1923 denigrated Arab nationalism as the work of ambitious Arab politicians who cynically manipulated the opinions of a backward and otherwise inert population.[41] The Revisionists were unquestionably more realistic in their anticipation of the fierce resistance to a Jewish takeover of Palestine that could be expected from the Arabs. In their contempt for Arab rights and sensibilities, however, they aligned themselves squarely with some of the less-lovely aspects of previous nationalisms against the humanitarianism of Buber and his followers.

The Revisionist faction was not large; in the 1929 elections for the sixteenth Zionist Congress, it won only about 6 percent of the votes.[42] On the Arab question, however, it spoke for a larger constituency. Anti-Arab com-

---

38. Friedrich Thieberger, "Versuch einer Neubegründung des Nationalismus," *Der Jude*, VIII (1924), 257–66; Bergel-Gronemann, "Jüdische Wege," 402; Theodor Lessing and Jakob Klatzkin, "Internationalismus und Nationalismus," *Jüdische Rundschau*, April 24, 1929; Elias Auerbach, "Judenstaat und binationaler Staat," *Jüdische Rundschau*, January 13, 1931 (quotation); Fritz Schiff, "Zweifel," *ibid.*, May 6, 1919; Isaak Feurring, "Wofür und Wogegen?" *ibid.*, December 6, 1929; Rudolf Seiden, "Joseph Trumpeldor in arabischer Darstellung," *Der Jude*, VIII (1924), 244 (quotation); Arthur Ruppin, "Das Verhältnis der Juden zu den Arabern," *ibid.*, III (1918/19), 456–57.

39. The Revisionists did not constitute themselves as a distinct unit within the German Zionist Federation until 1925. *Israelitisches Familienblatt*, October 1, 1925.

40. Fritz Sternberg, "Fachmänner der Idee," *Der Jude*, IV (1919/20), 90; *Jüdische Rundschau*, January 27, 1928; Schiff, "Zweifel," *ibid.*, May 6, 1919.

41. Richard Lichtheim, "Grundlagen und Ziele der zionistischen Politik," in Holdheim (ed.), *Zionistisches Handbuch*, 156–57. Cf. Richard Lichtheim, *Revision der zionistischen Politik* (Berlin, 1930), 9–16.

42. *Jüdische Rundschau*, June 18 and 28, 1929.

ments occasionally found their way into official German Zionist publications, which usually reflected the "correct" moderate line that soft-pedaled the idea of a Jewish majority and advocated the brotherhood of Jews and Arabs. Such comments characterized the Arabs as uncultured, unwashed, and unfit for participation in self-government.[43] Young Zionists who attended the Blue-White (Blau-Weiss) organization's youth camp at Hilsbach in Baden were regaled with adventure tales of Jews and Arabs that had the distinct American western flavor of courageous settlers battling savage Indians.[44] More commonly, however, anti-Arab sentiments came out less overtly, as in Moritz Sobernheim's private comment of 1919 that the Palestinian Arabs were "totally incapable of achieving anything at all."[45]

The existence of these and similar prejudices among Zionists in Germany and elsewhere was acknowledged by repeated statements condemning them, principally by Martin Buber and Robert Weltsch. Weltsch was particularly concerned to convince his fellow Zionists that the spirit of crass chauvinism would send Jews to Palestine as European conquerors over Oriental natives and establish a permanent colonial relationship between the two peoples.[46] In this he was joined by a Czech colleague, the historian Hans Kohn, who passionately denounced anti-Arab elements in German and world Zionism for their "seigneurial complex" and assumptions of "holy rights of possession" by Jews in Palestine. The outbreak of anti-Jewish riots among the Arabs of Palestine in August, 1929, convinced Kohn of the futility of nurturing a humane, cultural nationalism inside the Zionist movement and led him to break with it once and for all.[47]

Those same riots brought the issue of defining Jewish nationalism dramat-

43. J. H. Castel, "Die Araber in Palästina," *Der Jude,* V (1920/21), 414–18; Helene Hanna Cohn, "Die Erziehung der zweiten Generation," *ibid.,* VI (1921/22), 73–78; Helene Hanna Cohn, "Die zweite Generation in Palästina und die arabische Umwelt," *ibid.,* IX (1925/26), 128–33; Jechiel Haller, "Die Araber und wir," *Jüdische Rundschau,* February 8, 1929.
44. *Blau-Weiss Blätter,* I (1925), 11–15. The Blue-White was the major Zionist youth group in Weimar Germany.
45. Moritz Sobernheim to Adolf Friedemann, October 6, 1919, in Nachlass Moritz Sobernheim, 1288/351033–34. Sobernheim, the German Foreign Office expert on Jewish affairs, was a Zionist in everything but name, his high office rendering formal affiliation with the Zionist Federation unthinkable. His appointment in 1919 was due largely to his superiors' wish to exert the influence of the German contingent within world Zionism.
46. Robert Weltsch, "Worum es geht," in Hans Kohn and Robert Weltsch, *Zionistische Politik* (Mährisch-Ostrau, 1927), 169–82; Buber, *Der Jude und sein Judentum,* 339; R. W., "Politische Aufgaben des Kongresses," *Jüdische Rundschau,* June 19, 1931; Robert Weltsch, "Krieg oder Verständigung?" *Die Arbeit,* III (1921), 67–76.
47. Hans Kohn, "Zur Araberfrage," *Der Jude,* IV (1919/20), 567–69; Hans Kohn, "Zur Araberfrage," *ibid.,* V (1920/21), 737–38; Hans Kohn, "Die Pforte des Ostens," *ibid.,* VII

ically to a head within the Zionist Federation of Germany. Long-standing tensions between Arabs and Jews had erupted into violent attacks on Jewish settlements as a result of conflicting religious and nationalist claims to the Wailing Wall in Jerusalem. They required a week to quell and left 129 Jews, 90 Arabs, and 2 Englishmen dead.[48] In Germany the Revisionists lost no time in using the riots to denounce the leaders of the Zionist Federation for their moderation on the Arab issue.[49] In this they were joined by a group of mavericks from the ruling General Zionist faction led by Max Kollenscher, a Berlin attorney and Zionist (Jewish People's party) representative on the Berlin Jewish Community executive committee. In September, 1929, he resigned from the executive board of the Zionist Federation, attacking Blumenfeld and Weltsch for failing to advocate the meeting of force with force in Palestine. In concert with the Revisionists, Kollenscher and his allies made preparations for an open challenge to the leaders of the German Zionist Federation at its approaching national conference at Jena.[50]

Weltsch and Blumenfeld made few overt concessions to the insurgents. Weltsch had come in for especially vigorous criticism for having blamed the riots on the inflammatory actions of radical Zionists, especially the belligerent marches to the Wailing Wall by flag-carrying units of uniformed Jewish youth organizations. While conceding that the Arabs were "a primitive, easily fanaticized people," he insisted once again that the only way to ease tensions with them was to close the gap determined by language and culture and to overcome distrust and fear with acts of love.[51] He was joined by several leading moderates, including Alfred Berger and Moritz Bileski, in forming the Study Group for Realistic Zionist Policies, dedicated to promoting Jewish-Arab understanding and to combating "the destruction of Zionist morality by

---

(1924), 239–44; Hans Kohn, "Bücher zur zionistischen Ideologie," in Kohn and Weltsch, *Zionistische Politik*, 113–25; Hans Kohn, *Living in a World Revolution: My Encounters with History* (New York, 1964), 143.

48. Alfred Wiener, *Juden und Araber in Palästina* (Berlin, 1929), especially 33–35; Laqueur, *A History of Zionism*, 255–56.

49. *Jüdische Rundschau*, September 13, 17, and 27, 1929; Aron Sandler, "Für oder wider?" *ibid.*, December 3, 1929.

50. Max Kollenscher, "Zur Krisis im deutschen Zionismus," *ibid.*, October 4, 1929; *ibid.*, November 8, 1929; *ibid.*, December 10, 1929; Alfred Katz, "Ortsgruppen-Probleme," *ibid.*, December 13, 1929. In 1921 Kollenscher had helped to found the German Binjan Haarez, a Zionist faction dedicated to building up Palestine with private capital, as opposed to the socialist experiments advocated by Weltsch and the Hapoel Hazair, as well as by other groups of Zionists. *Israelitisches Familienblatt*, August 4, 1921; F. G. [Felix Goldmann], "Neue Strömungen im Zionismus," *K. C. Blätter*, XI (1921), 50.

51. R. W. [Robert Weltsch], "Die blutigen Kämpfe in Palästina," *Jüdische Rundschau*, August 30, 1929; R. W., "Jüdische Solidarität," *ibid.*, September 3, 1929.

means of a kind of war psychosis."[52] Blumenfeld continued his effort to straddle the Zionist factions, publicly endorsing the goal of a Jewish majority in a binational state in Palestine while holding the British responsible for maintaining the guarantees made to both Arabs and Jews in the Balfour Declaration.[53]

The Jena conference at the end of December, 1929, ended in victory for the moderate leadership but also gave evidence of unsuspected radical strength. A motion of no confidence in the editorial staff of the *Jüdische Rundschau*— and hence obviously aimed at the line adopted by Robert Weltsch—failed by a vote of 94 to 47, with 4 abstentions. A more moderate resolution that restated traditional Zionist aims was adopted by a similarly lopsided vote, and the old leaders were reelected by healthy majorities.[54] Still, the crisis brought on by the riots in Palestine had demonstrated that more than the small minority of Revisionist Zionists rejected the humanitarian nationalism espoused by Buber and Weltsch.

Blumenfeld had supported Weltsch against the insurgent attack, placing his own position as leader on the line in defense of his friend and colleague, but in private he is reported to have described the editor's views as irritating and unrepresentative of German Zionist opinion. In Blumenfeld's judgment, German Zionists desired more than a cultural center in Palestine—they demanded self-determination for the Jews there without regard for Arab wishes.[55] Informed of these comments and aware that he was a source of constant friction within the German Zionist movement, Weltsch offered to resign in June, 1930.[56] Blumenfeld declined the offer, for reasons that are not entirely clear. It seems likely that his condemnation of Weltsch was partly a sincere statement of his own views and partly a political effort to shore up his shaky position, whereas his decision to keep Weltsch in his job as *Jüdische Rundschau* editor, in addition to placating the moderates, retained the services of one of the most talented men in Zionist life, a journalist for whom an equally qualified replacement would have been hard to find.[57] Whatever the reason, these postconvention events suggest that not all of the votes cast at

52. Resumé of chapter meeting, September 16, 1929, in Robert Weltsch Collection, Leo Baeck Institute Archives, New York.

53. *Jüdische Rundschau,* September 6, 1929; Kurt Blumenfeld, "Forderungen der Stunde," *ibid.,* October 1, 1929; Blumenfeld, "Delegiertentag und Makkabärtage," *ibid.,* December 24, 1929.

54. *Ibid.,* January 3 and 7, 1930.

55. Weltsch to Moritz Bileski, June 23, 1930, in Weltsch Collection.

56. Weltsch to Kurt Blumenfeld, June 19, 1930, in *ibid.*

57. Blumenfeld, *Erlebte Judenfrage,* 186–87.

Jena in defense of Weltsch came from Zionists who were sympathetic to his views about Jewish nationalism. On this issue, as on that of blood-mysticism, it seems likely that a majority of German Zionists endorsed an aggressively *völkisch* point of view.

The Zionists' alienation from the atomized, industrialized societies of the West also duplicated *völkisch* attitudes. For many, Zionism was principally a repudiation of the ruthless materialism and social striving of their fathers' generation.[58] Oswald Spengler's cultural pessimism was anticipated by Zionist philosopher Theodor Lessing, whose *Decline of the Earth in Spirit* was published in 1916, two years before the first volume of Spengler's *Decline of the West* appeared. Lessing's view of his people was a tragic one. The victims of historical developments that had deprived them of intimate contact with nature and the soil, they had grown overintellectualized and morally and physically decadent under the influence of the Western world's implacable pursuit of Mammon. Their resulting preoccupation with security and material wealth had brought them a half-deserved reputation as exploiters. Their one hope was to reestablish the ties of blood and soil in Palestine.[59] For other Zionists, too, the decay of Western civilization had progressed too far, necessitating a whole new beginning. The imminent collapse of bankrupt liberalism provided new opportunities for a return to what Martin Buber called "the inborn, organic socialism of the people," an escape from the dog-eat-dog world of the isolated and uprooted.[60] It would be easier for the Jews, however, since they would not first have to smash the colossus of the state in order to build a new order; in the "underdeveloped virgin land" of Palestine they could start from scratch.[61]

The longing for community that was common in *völkisch* ideology was re-

---

58. Gerhard Holdheim, "Unser Bruch mit der Tradition," *Jüdische Rundschau,* February 15, 1927. This view of the Jews corresponded to an anti-Semitic stereotype that had deep roots in Germany. Mosse, *Germans and Jews, passim.*

59. Theodor Lessing, *Untergang der Erde am Geist* (3rd ed.; Hanover, 1924), 249–87. Apparently Spengler himself influenced some Zionists. A sketch in a publication commemorating the fiftieth anniversary of the Zionist Blue-White youth group pictures a typical member's library with Spengler's *Decline* conspicuous among volumes by Buber, Ruppin, and Herzl. Fritz Pollack (ed.), *50 Jahre Blau-Weiss* (Naharia, Israel, 1962), 36. According to one Blue-White member, Spengler's work was almost as much discussed as Herzl's *Altneuland.* Herbert Nussbaum, "Weg und Schicksal eines deutschen Juden" (Typescript in Leo Baeck Institute Archives, New York), 8.

60. Martin Buber, "In später Stunde," *Der Jude,* V (1920/21), 1–5. See also R. W. [Robert Weltsch], "In der Zeit der Bedrängnis," *Jüdische Rundschau,* December 4, 1931; Holdheim, "Unser Bruch," *ibid.,* February 15, 1927.

61. Siegfried Lehmann, "Über die Grundlagen eines jüdischen Gemeinwesens," *Der Jude,* IV (1919/20), 11–24.

flected in Zionist determination to found a cooperative, nonmaterialistic basis for Jewish life in Palestine. Zionists of the Buber/Weltsch persuasion preferred to describe the coming society as "socialistic," but it was a vague, moralizing socialism of the heart. Weltsch justified the Zionist marriage of nationalism and socialism as essential to the establishment of a truly humanitarian community: "the fundamental cohesion of human beings is that of the inner, inalienable, natural and spiritual bond, determined by blood and myth... before whose secret the true socialist must reverently humble himself." [62] Within the *Volk* community the mystical virtues of life close to the soil would likewise be nurtured. Eastern Jews, who still retained their ties to the soil, were romanticized, whereas the decay of Western European Jewry was attributed partly to its loss of such contacts. [63]

The special susceptibility of German Zionist youth to *völkisch* influences has not gone unnoticed. The largest Zionist youth movement in Germany, the Blue-White, held in contempt what it considered the complacency of most older Zionists, especially their lack of enthusiasm for resettlement and for socialism. Inspired in the first place by the Wandervogel, a prewar German youth movement, the Blue-White eagerly adopted its spartan discipline and devotion to the leadership principle. Under the charismatic leadership of Walter Moses and the direction of local *"Führers,"* its members steeled themselves for a return to the soil, at first in Germany, but ultimately for Palestine. [64] Blue-White spartanism aspired to heroic standards. One member recalled training hikes in all kinds of weather and once subsisting on earth worms; the girls were expected to undergo the same rigors as the boys. [65] An

62. Robert Weltsch, "Nationalismus und Sozialismus," *ibid.,* 196. See also Eugen Höflich, "Jüdischer Sozialismus," *Die Arbeit,* I (1919), 235–38; Rudolf Samuel, "Nationalismus und Sozialismus," *ibid.,* II (1920), 6–7; Georg Landauer, "Die ewige Forderung des Zionismus," in Max Kreutzberger (ed.), *Der Zionismus im Wandel dreier Jahrzehnte* (Tel Aviv, 1957), 51–55.

63. Ruth Morold, "Jüdische Maler," *Jüdische Rundschau,* February 6, 1925; Samuel Rappaport, "Aus dem religiösen Leben der Ostjuden," *Der Jude,* IV (1919/20), 227–33, 263–74, 306–22, 355–67; *ibid.,* V (1920/21), 147–56, 480–93; *ibid.,* VI (1921/22), 109–21, 159–67, 230–40, 296–99, 346–58, 410–16, 553–59, 615–22, 753–58; *ibid.,* VII (1922/23), 281–92, 335–55, 704–14.

64. Mosse, *Germans and Jews,* 94–102; Walter Gross, "The Zionist Students' Movement," *Leo Baeck Institute Yearbook,* IV (1959), 159; Hermann Meier-Cronemeyer, "Jüdische Jugendbewegung," *Germania Judaica,* VIII (1969), 62–63. The leadership principle seemed to have had Martin Buber's blessing. Significantly, in the play dedicated to his son and described above, the wise, authoritarian advice-giver is referred to as "der Führer." George Mosse has noted that the leadership principle was endorsed by liberal Jewish youth organizations, too. But nowhere was it practiced more systematically and consciously than in the Blue-White. Mosse, *Germans and Jews,* 101.

65. Nussbaum, "Weg und Schicksal eines deutschen Juden," 8.

attempt to discipline the Blue-White, more for its critical independence than for its "Germanic" bearing, was successfully resisted in 1923 when its leaders wriggled out of a merger with the Zionist students' organization arranged by Zionist leaders.[66] Its subsequent absorption by the students' organization in 1927 owed more to the disastrous results of its attempts at settlement in Palestine than to any repudiation of its debt to the German Wandervogel.

Obviously the rejection of liberal assimilationism and adoption of *völkisch* ideology did not induce German Zionists to pursue or justify policies of racial terror and extermination, as it did in the case of the Nazis. Nor is this the place to explore the ramifications of *völkisch* notions for the subsequent history of Zionism. Rather, it is the task of the historian of the German experience to assess the influence of Zionist assumptions on the fate of the German Jews. Did the Zionists' view of deformed Jewish lives outside of Palestine reinforce the anti-Semitic stereotype of the Jews as materialists, exploiters, and traitors? Did their assertions of racial and national otherness and their corrective formula of removing the Jews undermine Jewish claims to citizenship and hasten the day when the Nazis might seek to make Germany *judenrein?*

Liberal Jews answered both questions in the affirmative. They commonly referred to Zionists as "*völkisch* Jews" and accused them of furnishing ammunition to anti-Semites.[67] Their exasperation was unbounded when at one Centralverein meeting Zionist and anti-Semitic hecklers took the same ground.[68] They were certainly correct about what we have called the moderate anti-Semites, such as Wilhelm Stapel and Hans Blüher, who lauded Zionism as the sole practical alternative to otherwise unavoidable friction between Germans and Jews.[69] Moderate racists also welcomed it as a means of drawing ethnic lines more sharply. Max Wundt, although distressed over

66. Georg Landauer, "Zionistische Jugendbewegung in Deutschland," *Die Arbeit*, IV (1922), 13–18; Moritz Bileski, "Post Festum," *Jüdische Rundschau*, February 6, 1923; Martin Plessner, "Zur Diskussion über den Blau-Weiss," *ibid.*, March 2, 1923.

67. *Im deutschen Reich*, XXV (1919), 340–41; H. Stern, "Drei Fragen und drei Antworten," *Israelitisches Familienblatt*, September 15, 1921; Ludwig Holländer, "Warum unsere Wahlparole," *Central-Verein Zeitung*, December 19, 1924; Bruno Weil, "Vor der Entscheidung," *ibid.*, January 29, 1925; *Jüdische Rundschau*, March 20, 1931; *ibid.*, August 5, 1932.

68. *Israelitisches Familienblatt*, June 3, 1920.

69. Hans Blüher, *Deutsches Reich: Judentum und Sozialismus* (Prien, 1920), 19–20; Stapel, *Antisemitismus und Antigermanismus*, 72–75; Otto Hauser, *Geschichte des Judentums* (Weimar, 1921), 524–26; Otto Hauser, *Rassebilder* (Braunschweig, 1925), 236. Significantly, Moritz Goldstein's 1912 essay postulating an unbridgeable cultural gap between Germans and Jews appeared in *Der Kunstwart*, which, although it was not explicitly anti-Jewish, employed Adolf Bartels, a well-known anti-Semite, as literary critic. Goldstein, "German Jewry's Dilemma," 245–46.

140 of WEIMAR GERMANY

what he saw as the Zionists' claims to "chosen people" status, openly embraced their dialectic: "It is only with these *völkisch* Jews that a discussion of the Jewish question is genuinely productive; only with them does the *völkisch* German find the common ground on which discussion is generally possible." [70]

Radical anti-Semites, on the other hand, were far from unanimous on the subject of Zionism. Alfred Roth of the League for Defense and Defiance regularly quoted from Zionist sources to "prove" that Jews did not belong in Germany, and one of the League's pamphlets asserted: "If healthy pride and idealism ... actually still survive among this [the Jewish] people, why did it not long ago seek to acquire a homeland to which it has some right—in the Orient, toward which its blood points." [71] In contrast, Theodor Fritsch reprinted that notorious fraud, the *Protocols of the Elders of Zion,* under the title *The Zionist Protocols,* locating Zionism within a larger Jewish conspiracy to rule the world. [72] The Nazis usually agreed, following the line set down by party philosopher Alfred Rosenberg, who linked Zionism with bolshevism. But in some of their propaganda they perversely endorsed the stated Zionist goal of removing the Jews to Palestine. [73] Evangelical pastor Johann Peperkorn drew the applause of his fellow Nazi deputies in the Prussian Diet in 1932 when he included the following comments in a general tirade against the "corrosive" influence of the Jews on German cultural life:

We are not proposing pogroms, Jewish pogroms of any kind. If you want to know what a pogrom is, open up the Book of Esther. We intend to solve the Jewish problem in quite different fashion. We National Socialists serve a movement that touches the innermost being of the German people. . . . Hence we dare to wish something similar even for the *Volk* that is alien and, at present, hateful to us, the Jews. We wish for them a National Socialist movement in their own ranks. We believe that it ought yet perhaps to be possible for such a great cleansing movement within world Jewry to exhibit other aspects of the Jewish spirit than those that hitherto we have

---

70. Max Wundt, *Deutsche Weltanschauung: Grundzüge völkischen Denkens* (Munich, 1926), 176. See also Hermann Meyer, *Der Deutsche Mensch* (2 vols.; Munich, 1925), II, 47–48.

71. Alfred Roth, *Geheime Fäden im Weltkriege* (Hamburg, 1919), 11–12; Alfred Roth, *Judas Herrschgewalt: Die Deutschvölkischen im Lichte der Behörden und des Staatsgerichtshofes* (Hamburg, 1923), 77; Deutschvölkischer Schutz- und Trutzbund, *Sigfried und Ahasver,* 7 (quotation).

72. *Jüdische Rundschau,* May 23, 1924.

73. Barbara Miller Lane, "Nazi Ideology: Some Unfinished Business," *Central European History,* VII (1974), 13–15; Laqueur, *A History of Zionism,* 384–85; *Central-Verein Zeitung,* February 13, 1925; *ibid.,* February 27, 1931; *Der Israelit,* June 30, 1932.

observed with loathing and disgust. . . . We wish nothing more for the Jewish *Volk* than that they should place leaders at the helm that will bring together this Jewish *Volk* into a great, united Jewish nation, men who will reestablish the Throne of David somewhere on this earth. It is a matter of complete indifference to us whether this great Jewish empire finds its abode in the Crimea or in Palestine. But the Jews must get out of Germany and out of German political, economic, and cultural life. Another solution to the Jewish problem does not exist.[74]

"Get Ready for Palestine," shouted Nazi posters, while storm troopers handed out mock one-way tickets to Jerusalem, to be turned over to any Jew one happened to meet.[75] Insofar as the National Socialists succeeded in persuading Germans that their future plans coincided with those of the most active and vocal Jewish group, the Zionists, their anti-Semitism must have been made to appear essentially harmless. That this had a major impact on the public mind is questionable, however, because the Nazis rarely took Zionism seriously and never drew conclusions from the obvious similarities between their analysis of the Jewish question and that of the Zionists. Nor can there be the slightest doubt that National Socialism's anti-Semitism would not have cooled one degree even if every single German Jew had embraced Zionism.

German Zionism's theoretical rejection of assimilation and its adoption of the *völkisch Weltanschauung* had led unswervingly to the 1912 Posen Resolution calling for every Zionist to plan on emigrating to Palestine. And yet, most of them did not go. Max Kreutzberger has estimated that only 2,000 German Jews had moved to Palestine by 1933.[76] Judging from the fact that many of them were woefully unprepared for the hard life there, it seems unlikely that all of them stayed. Zionist efforts to increase emigration as a means of escaping the depression after 1929 came to nought; where thousands were expected, only a few hundred zealots appeared.[77]

In fact, the Posen Resolution was never taken literally. With Jewish immigration being limited by British authorities in Palestine, first claim belonged to the persecuted Jews of Eastern Europe and to homeless Eastern Jewish refugees elsewhere. Even the most radical Zionists acknowledged that Palestine was physically incapable of absorbing any more than half of the world Jewish

74. *Preussischer Landtag, Sitzungsberichte*, 12. Sitzung, June 24, 1932, p. 938.

75. *Central-Verein Zeitung*, July 8, 1932; Pamphlet Collection, Leo Baeck Institute Archives, New York.

76. Kreutzberger (ed.), *Der Zionismus im Wandel dreier Jahrzehnte*, 15.

77. Fritz Löwenstein, "Der deutsche Zionismus und Palästina," *Jüdische Rundschau*, August 29, 1924; *ibid.*, January 8, 1932; *ibid.*, November 25, 1932; Heinz Boss, "Deutsche Juden in Erez Israel," *ibid.*, February 17, 1933.

population. German Jews, comparatively safe and prosperous, would be among the last to go; some might not go at all. Zionists spoke openly of Palestine as a "cultural center" that would give new strength to Jews in other lands. The idea of emigration was spiritualized into an "eternal ideal" that would give content to the hollow lives of German Jews.[78]

The main and real Zionist aim, then, was to convert the bulk of German Jewry to unassimilated life in Germany. This demanded a sharp division of German and Jewish affairs. Zionists spoke of "Galuth negation" (*Galuth* being their term for the Diaspora)—the process of substituting a primarily Jewish consciousness for a deeply divided one through immersion in such Zionist tasks as fund-raising and proselytizing.[79] They emphatically denied that this involved any repudiation of the Jew's duties as a citizen, since they distinguished between the demands of nationality and those of the state. Hence they welcomed the Weimar Constitution's guarantee of cultural autonomy to foreign language groups in Germany as recognition of the same distinction, lamenting only that it did not go on to acknowledge the special rights of ethnic groups like the Jews. Zionists repeatedly asserted that their division of nationality and state would actually make Jews better and more secure German citizens by enriching their spiritual and cultural life, saving them from political radicalism, and winning them the respect of non-Jews.[80]

The Zionists' obligations to Germany were left undefined, and a variety of opinions on the subject were tolerated within the German Zionist Federation. Militant Zionists acknowledged only the bare minimum of ties to Germany, joining with Robert Weltsch in flatly rejecting all but purely formal obligations: "If I am a Jew, I cannot be a German at the same time."[81] The Zionists' preeminent loyalty was to Jews, wherever they might live. Gerhard Holdheim expressed a typical Zionist sense of amazement that liberal Jews felt "stronger contact with Pomeranian peasants and Bavarian clodhoppers than with the Jews of other lands."[82] While usually avoiding the impression of wanting a

78. *Ibid.*, February 24, 1920; *ibid.*, November 20, 1931; Oskar Baum, "Die jüdische Gefahr," *Der Jude*, VII (1923), 72–77; Fritz Löwenstein, "Grundsätzliches zur zionistischen Gemeindepolitik," *Jüdische Rundschau*, October 20, 1922; M. W. [Moses Waldmann], "Dunam oder Aktie," *ibid.*, February 17, 1928; F. Weltsch, *Nationalismus und Judentum*, 42.

79. Oskar Epstein, "Galuthverneinung?" *Jüdische Rundschau*, September 7, 1928.

80. *Ibid.*, January 31, 1919; *ibid.*, January 26, 1926; Ludwig Strauss, "Zur Frage nach Volkstum und Staat," *Die Arbeit*, I (1919), 42–43; Oscar A. H. Schmitz, "Wünschenswerter und nicht wünschenswerter Juden," *Der Jude*, IX (1925/26), 17–33; *Jüdische Rundschau*, October 3, 1924.

81. Robert Weltsch, "Politik und Bewegung," *Jüdische Rundschau*, February 27, 1920.

82. Gerhard Holdheim, "Nach der Hauptversammlung des C. V.," *ibid.*, February 24, 1928.

special minority status for Jews in Germany, the militants advised total abstinence from German affairs. Zionist Revisionist Nahum Goldmann even went so far as to cover kiosks in Heidelberg with posters urging Jews to boycott elections to the National Assembly in 1919, to the great distress of most local Jews.[83] Even among Zionists who were not as strongly impelled by the need to dramatize their alienation from Germany, normal patriotic feelings could be conspicuously lacking. The *Jüdische Rundschau* commented on the harsh terms of the Treaty of Versailles without a whisper of indignation, and in general the Zionist central organ relegated German affairs to brief and tepid back-page comment.[84] A liberal Jew who was active in the prorepublican paramilitary Reichsbanner organization recalls not a single Zionist among its Jewish members.[85] No doubt many Zionists privately felt what Kurt Blumenfeld later expressed openly—that Germany was "the world of the parvenu and the snob."[86]

That some Zionists demanded rights from a country to which they gave neither sustenance nor ultimate allegiance suggests more than mere naïveté about the political realities of Weimar Germany. It indicates that, for them, Zionism was a neurotic reaction to anti-Semitism or, in the friendlier words of the *Jüdische Rundschau*, "a psychological solution to the Jewish question in that it impels the Jewish people to self-consciousness and renders them immune to the psychic damage of Judeophobia."[87] The myths of present self-sufficiency and future emigration furnished Zionists with an effective survival mentality that rationalized their life in Germany.[88] At the same time, this triumph of passion over reason caused them to abandon the struggle for democracy in Germany and, as we have seen, induced them unwittingly to hand ammunition to the anti-Semites.

Not all Zionists equated "Galuth negation" with aloofness from Germany. The old philanthropic Zionism, officially repudiated in Posen in 1912, lived on, nurtured by the spiritualization of the idea of emigration and the rationalization of continued Jewish life in Germany. It was principally among

83. *Ibid.*, July 8, 1932; Abraham Schwadron, "Der 'Hapoel Hazair' und die Frage nach der Ewigkeit der Galuth," *Die Arbeit*, I (1919), 177–80; Hamburger, "One Hundred Years of Emancipation," 34–35; Marx, *Werdegang eines jüdischen Staatsanwalts*, 132–34.

84. *Jüdische Rundschau*, July 1, 1919.

85. Szanto, "Im Dienste der Gemeinde," 94.

86. Blumenfeld was referring to pre-1914 Germany, but his attitude toward the country of his birth changed little after that time. *Erlebte Judenfrage*, 59.

87. *Jüdische Rundschau*, November 15, 1929.

88. This is a central theme of a recent study by Stephen M. Poppel, *Zionism in Germany 1897–1933* (Philadelphia, 1977), especially pp. 94–101.

these Zionist elements that the rights of citizenship were matched with a sense of positive duty to Germany. Their indignant denials that Zionists had two fatherlands, any more than did German Catholics or Social Democrats, stood blissfully indifferent to the fact that neither had declared themselves unrooted in Germany, as had the Zionists.[89] The most extreme manifestation of this attitude was the holding of public office by such Zionists as Hermann Badt, director of the constitutional department of the Prussian Ministry of the Interior, and Hans Goslar, who headed the press office of the Prussian Ministry of State.[90] Both men were extremely controversial, however, among Zionists and liberals alike, and most German Zionists disapproved of their holding high office. More typical of the Zionist attitude was Kurt Blumenfeld's advice to Jews to distance themselves from the non-Jewish world.[91]

Blumenfeld might insist that Palestine was the Jews' "true national homeland (wahre Volksheimat)."[92] but that did not prevent some of his fellow Zionists from expressing respect, and even affection, for Germany. Ernst Simon, the editor of Martin Buber's journal Der Jude, in the chaotic last months of 1923 criticized Zionist leaders for leaving Germany in the lurch and failing to perceive that anti-Semites did not represent the true Germany.[93] Another writer for the journal excoriated the Russian Jewish historian Simon Dubnow, then living in Berlin, for the anti-German tone of the third volume of his Die neueste Geschichte des jüdischen Volkes.[94] When German Zionist Federation chairman Alfred Landsberg asserted the Zionists' "profound inner bond with German culture," he expressed an opinion that was at least as widely shared among Zionists as indifference or hostility toward Germany.[95]

Despite all the brave talk of German Jewish emigration to Palestine, then, the main thrust of Zionist activity was in other directions, namely raising money and winning new members. The comparatively wealthy Jews of Ger-

89. Jüdische Rundschau, January 26, 1926.
90. For a statement of Goslar's point of view, see his "Zionismus und deutsches Judentum," Jüdisch-liberale Zeitung, V (February 13, 1925), Beilage, 2.
91. Interview with Robert Weltsch, August 20, 1973; Jüdische Rundschau, June 21, 1932; Kurt Blumenfeld, "Die zionistische Haltung," ibid., February 28, 1933. See also Arnold Zweig, "Der Jude in der deutschen Gegenwart," Der Jude, IX (1925/26), 1–8; Alfred Marcus, "Non-Cooperation?" Jüdische Rundschau, July 29, 1932; ibid., February 3, 1933.
92. Jüdische Rundschau, January 10, 1919.
93. Ernst Simon, "Im Chaos," Der Jude, VII (1923), 655–56.
94. Leo Strauss, "Soziologische Geschichtsschreibung?" ibid., VIII (1924), 190–92.
95. Jüdische Rundschau, January 2, 1925. See also Gustav Krojanker, "Der Fall Naumann," ibid., March 31, 1922; Max Kollenscher, "Grundsätzliches zur jüdischen Schulpolitik," ibid., September 13, 1928; Gerhard Holdheim, "Zionistische Organisation und Nicht (organisierter) Zionismus," ibid., April 1, 1931; Gustav Krojanker, "Der Weg zum Deutschtum," Der Jude, IX (1925/26), 59–69.

many were expected to help finance the resettlement of impoverished Eastern Jews in Palestine. German Zionists actually taxed themselves; in 1919, for example, they assessed each member from 60 to 1,000 marks, depending on income, in order to raise 350,000 marks. Suffrage in Zionist Federation elections was made contingent on payment of this "Zionist tax." In addition, some Zionist locals banded together to finance particular settlements in Palestine. Periodic efforts to raise funds from nonmembers as well as members likewise yielded results. In one such drive during the difficult winter of 1923–24, German Zionists raised no less than the equivalent of 102,000 gold marks.[96]

Even more important to German Zionists than fund-raising was the conversion of new members to the cause, for that alone seemed capable of saving their fellow Jews from warped, anxiety-ridden lives. Accordingly, their posture was often quasi-religious and replete with "road to Damascus" conversions and "personal decisions" for Palestine.[97] An official but anonymous Zionist spokesman commented in Calvinistic terms on the "embracing freedom" of the Zionist: "It begins for every individual in the instant when he freely encounters the decision in favor of Zionism, dictated solely by the law born within him. In the name of freedom he marshals himself from that hour on, and he obeys no other power . . . than that which his blood exercises over him."[98] The reward, although distinctly this-worldly, could be expressed as a heavenly vision. For Zionist Georg Landauer the Jews would find in Palestine the kind of harmony that "puts an end to all inhibitions and tensions and engenders the most intimate bonds between human beings."[99]

Armed with this paradisaical vision, German Zionists kept up a ceaseless barrage of propaganda aimed at winning Jews from liberal assimilationism. They sponsored seminars to prepare Zionists for general missionary work, and their leaders attempted to reach prominent Jews on an individual basis. Kurt Blumenfeld, for example, took credit for bringing Albert Einstein into the Zionist fold shortly after the end of the First World War.[100]

96. *Jüdische Rundschau,* June 17, 1919; *ibid.,* May 4, 1923; *ibid.,* April 18, 1924; Robert Weltsch to Chaim Weizmann, February 12, 1924, in Weltsch Collection.

97. M. I. Bodenheimer, *Prelude to Israel,* trans. Israel Cohen (New York, 1963), 60–61; Gerhard Holdheim, "Agency und Zukunft des Zionismus," *Jüdische Rundschau,* August 1, 1924. For a fascinating statement by a former Zionist of his original conversion from "unregenerated" Jewry, see Ernst Ludwig Pinner, "Meine Abkehr vom Zionismus," in Fritz Blankenfeld *et al., Los vom Zionismus* (Frankfurt-am-Main, 1928), 13–16.

98. *Jüdische Rundschau,* March 13, 1923.

99. Landauer, "Die ewige Forderung," 55.

100. *Jüdische Rundschau,* May 8, 1929; Blumenfeld, *Erlebte Judenfrage,* 126–33. Ein-

146 THE JEWS IN WEIMAR GERMANY

The chief target for Zionist propaganda was the Centralverein, because, as we have seen, it was the rallying point for assimilationist ideology as well as the chief Jewish self-defense body. It was accused of neglecting the positive value of the Jews by drawing Jewish self-consciousness from the struggle against anti-Semitism, rather than vice versa. It was denounced as bourgeois, undemocratic, discriminatory against Eastern Jews, and representing an out-dated liberalism.[101] Zionists scored a major coup in 1920 when Albert Ein-stein, in a widely publicized letter, turned down a Centralverein invitation to attend a conference on anti-Semitism in the universities. He asserted that the Jews needed to gain self-respect before they could hope to win the respect of others and criticized the Centralverein for "servility." "Let us leave the Aryans to their anti-Semitism," he wrote, "and confirm our love for our own kind."[102]

Hence the Centralverein's campaign against anti-Semitism, too, found little approval among Zionists, even though they and other Jews were expected to remain in Germany for a long time to come. Zionists inaccurately depicted its educational and political activities as ineffectual because non-Jews allegedly rejected statements from a partisan source. Either they were unaware that the Centralverein usually worked behind the scenes with non-Jewish organiza-tions, or they chose to ignore the fact. Pessimism about the persistence of anti-Semitism and confidence that assimilation bred racial hatred led Zionists to the conclusion that Centralverein efforts were wasteful and coun-terproductive. Nor were the Zionists insensitive to the Centralverein's dogged opposition to their attempts at separating Germans and Jews; that, they in-dignantly charged, made a mockery of the rival organization's claims to neu-trality on all subjects but anti-Semitism.[103] There is some evidence that a few Zionists pragmatically supported the Centralverein for its defensive actions,

---

stein supported Zionism's cultural and charitable activities throughout the remainder of his life, but he consistently repudiated the idea of a Jewish state in Palestine. Hence his attitudes toward Jewish nationalism were always ambivalent, to say the least. Nevertheless, his support was not entirely passive. There is evidence that the great physicist attended a Zionist meeting in 1919. (Moos to Centralverein, December 29, 1919, in Nachlass Moritz Sobernheim, 1287/1349277–78.) Better known are Einstein's 1921 trip to the United States with Chaim Weizmann to raise money for Jerusalem's Hebrew University, and his 1923 visit to Palestine. Ronald W. Clark, *Einstein: The Life and Times* (New York and Cleveland, 1971), 374–403.

101. Bileski, "Das Kompromiss," 20–25; *Israelitisches Familienblatt*, July 17 and 31, 1919; *Jüdische Rundschau*, February 20, 1931.

102. *Jüdische Rundschau*, December 10, 1920.

103. *Ibid.*, January 23, 1920; Schachtel, "Nach 30 Jahren," *ibid.*, April 16, 1926; *ibid.*, May 16, 1928; *ibid.*, October 17, 1930; *ibid.*, May 3, 1932; *ibid.*, January 20, 1925; *ibid.*, February 10, 1928; *ibid.*, March 23, 1928.

particularly in small towns and in southern Germany.[104] Most Zionists, how-ever, worked to undermine the liberal organization. To that end they re-peatedly proposed that truly neutral organizations, such as the local Jewish communities or their provincial federations, take over the Centralverein's self-defense work.[105] It is a measure of their hostility that they were prepared to turn over what they admitted was an essential task to bodies that lacked the disposition and the expertise to do it well.

The first Zionist effort to seduce German Jews away from the as-similationist ideology represented by the Centralverein was made only weeks after the defeat of German arms in the World War. The call went out from the German Zionist Federation for the creation of a Jewish congress to unify the Jews and speak for them on major issues. Invitations were sent to as many Jews as possible to sign and return a card averring: "I declare myself in favor of the convocation of a Congress of Jews living in Germany who, convinced of their membership in the Jewish nation [*Volk*], wish to participate in the development of a living Jewry." [106] The seriousness of this effort may be ques-tioned, for although the prospect of an assimilationist/Zionist dialogue cer-tainly appealed to some liberal Jews, the use of the term "Jewish *Volk*" was certain to antagonize most of them.[107] It was, after all, an article of liberal Jewish faith that German Jews were Jewish in faith and descent, but German in nationality. The Centralverein's response was predictable. A meeting be-tween the top leaders of the two rival organizations on March 6, 1919, ended in a deadlock over the agenda. Nearly three months later the Centralverein's executive board adopted by overwhelming majority a resolution postponing consideration of a Jewish congress until the onset of calmer times and specify-ing that such a congress should comprise "the elected representatives of all German Jews," pointedly omitting reference to a Jewish nationality or to suf-frage for alien Jews resident in Germany. Although the Zionists did not at-tempt to revive the idea, they had drawn a great deal of attention to them-

104. Cahnmann, "The Nazi Threat and the Central Verein," 27–36; [Ludwig] Foerder "Antisemitismus, Zionismus und Centralverein," *Jüdische Rundschau*, June 19, 1923.

105. *Jüdische Rundschau*, July 6, 1923; Max Jacobsohn, "Gemeinden und Or-ganisationen," *ibid.*, September 13, 1928; *ibid.*, February 25, 1930; *Gemeindeblatt der Jüdi-schen Gemeinde zu Berlin*, XXI (1931), 281–82; *Verwaltungsblatt des preussischen Landes-verbandes jüdischer Gemeinden*, IX (1931), 17.

106. Stern, "Zur Frage eines jüdischen Kongresses in Deutschland," *Im deutschen Reich*, XXV (1919), 97–103.

107. *Israelitisches Familienblatt*, January 23, 1919; *Der Israelit*, May 22, 1919; *All-gemeine Zeitung des Judentums*, LXXXIII (June 27, 1919), Beilage; *Jüdische Rundschau*, February 25, 1919.

selves and placed the Centralverein on the defensive for apparently having thwarted the noble purpose of Jewish unity.[108]

Herzl's injunction to his fellow Zionists that they should capture the Jewish communities was followed in Germany with abiding conviction. The vehicle for wresting the communities from assimilationist control was the Jewish People's party (Jüdische Volkspartei), which was founded in May, 1920, to represent Zionist interests on communal bodies. Kurt Blumenfeld elaborated its minimal goal as that of lifting the Jews above exclusive preoccupation with local affairs "so that each community feels responsibility for everything that happens in the Jewish world."[109] That the communities controlled money, schools, and social services suggests that more was involved than mere consciousness-raising, however. The conquest of the communities would place important sources of power and influence in Zionist hands as well as afford an opportunity to change them over into "people's communities" (*Volksgemeinden*), that is, communities where such secular concerns as family subventions to increase the Jewish birth rate and support for Palestine would take on equal stature with purely religious matters.[110] Occasionally Jewish People's party absorption with community affairs caused friction with leaders of the German Zionist Federation, who feared that it might result in a loss of zeal for settling Jews in Palestine, but virtually all Zionists recognized the importance of liberating the communities from the liberals.[111]

The Zionists stood little chance of winning community elections with traditional Jewish nationalist appeals. They insisted upon and frequently won proportional representation on elected community bodies in localities where it was not already adopted. As a result, they were able to have a voice in community affairs even where they constituted small minorities. They also agitated in favor of expanding voting rights for Eastern Jews and young Jews between the ages of eighteen and twenty-five, groups where Zionism found

108. Kurt Blumenfeld, "Der jüdische Kongress in Deutschland," *Jüdische Rundschau,* May 20, 1919; *Die Kongresspolitik der Zionisten und ihre Gefahren* (Berlin, 1919), and *Hauptversammlung des C.V., 28. und 29. Mai, 1919,* both in Centralverein Collection, Wiener Library, London. For an interpretation of this episode that assigns far greater significance to it, see Jacob Toury, "Organizational Problems of German Jewry," *Leo Baeck Institute Yearbook,* XIII (1968), 84–88.

109. *Jüdische Rundschau,* June 1, 1928.

110. R. W. [Robert Weltsch], "Belebung der Gemeinde," *ibid.,* May 18, 1920; Georg Lubinski, "Umbau der Jüdischen Gemeinde," *ibid.,* September 13, 1928; Felix Theilhaber, "Keinen Kaddisch wird man sagen," *ibid.,* February 22, 1929; *ibid.,* February 25, 1930.

111. Sandler, "Erinnerungen," 4; Robert Weltsch, "Zur politischen Lage," *Die Arbeit,* Sonderheft (July, 1928), 12–16.

comparatively strong support. In this they achieved only partial success.[112] As a means of expanding their own ranks of committed Zionists, they skillfully exploited resentment against the liberal establishment among Jews who thought it insensitive to the needs of destitute members of the community, indifferent to Palestine, or insufficiently aggressive in throwing an assertive Jewish identity in the teeth of the anti-Semites.[113] Their championship of women's rights probably won them some support, although reports of male chauvinism among Zionists put limits on the effectiveness of that appeal.[114] In these ways they won community support that was all out of proportion to the membership of the German Zionist Federation. For example, although there were probably no more than 16,000 hard-core Zionists in all of Germany, the Jewish People's party was able to win 25,836 votes in the 1930 elections to the Berlin Jewish Community Council.[115]

These tactics allowed the Jewish People's party to widen its appeal at the community level, but alone they were not enough to launch it into positions of power anywhere in Germany. Occasionally, where Zionists were too weak to hope for substantial electoral success, they chose to forego election campaigns in return for the formation of "unity lists" on which they were guaranteed a few seats and influence or control over welfare and school affairs. That happened in the Dresden community and in Baden's provincial synod.[116] Elsewhere the Zionists allied with other antiliberal parties with the aim of establishing the rule of Zionist-led coalitions. They succeeded twice: in Berlin, in 1926, and in Duisburg two years later.[117]

112. Breslau Zionists to Breslau Jewish Community, August 7, 1930, in Jewish Community of Breslau Collection; *Jüdische Rundschau*, July 11, 1919; *ibid.*, November 27, 1928.

113. S. Wronsky, "Die sozialen Aufgaben der jüdischen Gemeinden," *Jüdische Rundschau*, January 13, 1920; Georg Kareski, "Ein Kapitel aus der Sozialpolitik des Berliner Jüdischen Gemeinde," *ibid.*, August 15, 1922; *ibid.*, May 15, 1923; *ibid.*, January 26, 1926.

114. Helene Hanna Cohn, "Die Frau in der zionistische Bewegung," *Der Jude*, V (1920/21), 533–37; *Jüdische Rundschau*, December 16, 1924; Fritz Weg, "Zur Einheit," *Kameraden*, II (1921), 19–23. As much as the liberals, the Zionists had to take into account Orthodox religious objections to women's suffrage. *Jüdische Rundschau*, January 28, 1930; Oskar Wolfsburg, "Zum Kampf um das Frauenwahlrecht in Hamburg," *ibid.*, March 14, 1930; *Israelitisches Familienblatt*, January 16, 1930; *Bayerische Israelitische Gemeindezeitung*, VI (1930), 221.

115. *Gemeindeblatt der Jüdischen Gemeinde zu Berlin*, XX (December, 1930), 1. In 1925 the Zionist Federation claimed to have 21,450 members. *Jüdische Rundschau*, September 18, 1925. *Cf.* Jacob Hellmann, "Das Problem der Organisation und die Jewish Agency," *Die Arbeit*, IV (1923), 230–39.

116. Otto Simon, "Die Synodalwahlen in Baden," *Jüdische Rundschau*, December 3, 1929; *ibid.*, May 15, 1923.

117. The majority (*i.e.*, winner-take-all) voting system employed by the Duisburg Jewish

The Berlin experience is worth some attention as a case study in a community's response to limited Zionist rule. Elections to the community representative assembly, held on May 26, 1926, had given eight seats to the Jewish People's party, ten to the Liberals, one to the Conservatives, and two to the Religious Center party.[118] For the first time the Liberals had lost their majority, and they had no one to blame but themselves. The Zionists had made a particularly vigorous effort, whereas the Liberals had failed to get out the vote; a mere 40 percent of those eligible to cast ballots did so.[119] Once the initial shock wore off, the Liberals claimed that polling irregularities had invalidated the election, called on the Berlin police to investigate it, and refused to relinquish control of community organs until the police had submitted their report. The police report found that irregularities had indeed occurred, and the Liberals demanded the maintenance of the Liberal majority on the community executive committee and new elections in 1929 as their price for accepting the suspect results. Later they relented, permitting the Zionist-led coalition to take control and subsequently agreeing to new elections in 1930, two years ahead of schedule. For their part the Zionists agreed to share the post of community chairman with their allies. Gerson Simon of the Religious Center party filled the position until January, 1929, when Zionist Georg Kareski took his place. For the first time, Zionists filled some of the other important administrative posts. And yet, neither Liberals nor Zionists were happy with the compromise. The former itched for another opportunity to muster their strength, whereas the latter hoped to free themselves from the encumbrance of their coalition partners.[120]

The nearly four years of limited Zionist rule in Berlin, from 1927 to 1930,

Community meant that the liberals lost all their political influence when they were defeated by a "unity bloc" of opposition parties. Great diplomacy was required to keep them from forming a separatist community. *Ibid.,* June 12, 1928.

118. The Conservative party represented mainly the Orthodox Jews. The Religious Center party, founded in 1910, sought to emphasize the purely confessional character of the communities and to soften all doctrinal and political disputes. Its lack of any real electoral success robbed it of most of its following, especially under the polarized conditions after the 1926 elections. Most of its former supporters joined the liberals. Rabbi S. Weisse, "Ausgleich," *Israelitisches Familienblatt,* July 2, 1925; Gottfried Holländer to Moritz Sobernheim, December 30, 1930, in Nachlass Moritz Sobernheim, 1288/352373.

119. *Gemeindeblatt der Jüdischen Gemeinde zu Berlin,* XVI (1926), 125.

120. *Jüdisch-liberale Zeitung,* VII (February 11, 1927), 1–2; *Der Israelit,* March 28, 1929; *Jüdische Rundschau,* January 11, 1929; *ibid.,* January 29, 1929. A liberal promise to vote funds for a chair at the new Hebrew University in Jerusalem, made as part of the election compromise, later became a source of friction when Zionists claimed that the promise had been for a long-term subsidy and liberals denied it. *Gemeindeblatt der Jüdischen Gemeinde zu Berlin,* XXI (1931), 167–68, 315–16.

was a time of considerable tension in the Jewish community. The parties managed to work together fairly smoothly, with the Conservative and Religious Center party representatives sometimes voting with the Liberals against their Zionist partners. Still, the Liberals complained bitterly of the Jewish People's party insinuating Zionist propaganda into Jewish schools and injecting one-sided material on Palestine into community organs.[121] No doubt they were also dismayed at Zionist spending for the Eastern Jews, including the building of a new polyclinic in the Eastern Jewish quarter of central Berlin.[122] A Zionist proposal that the community make available bags of earth from Palestine for Jews who wished to use them for burials sent the Liberal opposition into apoplexy. Liberal meetings were organized around the theme of "crisis in the community," and at least one prominent Berlin Liberal, Bruno Woyda, spoke ominously of massive resignations from the community and of the formation of a separatist community.[123] Tensions reached their peak late in 1930 as the new elections approached. Each side hypocritically accused the other of sabotaging efforts to postpone the elections and hence avoid dragging a bitter internal struggle out into the open so soon after the first great Nazi electoral success in September of that year. The campaign was extraordinarily hard fought, the Zionists proving the more aggressive by disrupting Liberal rallies and prompting Liberal charges of "Zionist election terror."[124] To Zionist protestations that they had spent money on community social services rather than on purely Zionist goals, the Liberals replied: "In the last three years the Zionist community administration has systematically worked its way toward educating our youth in the spirit of Jewish nationalism and teaching modern Hebrew as their everyday language, so that our children will feel themselves members of a Jewish *Volk* having its home in Palestine."[125]

A new party of conciliation made its appearance during the campaign. Calling itself the Nonpartisan Alliance for the Common Interests and Unity of the Jews, it stressed the damage done by this "fratricidal struggle" to the commu-

121. *Jüdische Rundschau,* March 27, 1928; *Gemeindeblatt der Jüdischen Gemeinde zu Berlin,* XIX (1929), 234–36, 646; *Jüdisch-liberale Zeitung,* X (November 5, 1930), Beilage.
122. Sandler, "Erinnerungen," 25. Sandler, a Zionist, ran hospital affairs for the community during these years of anti-Liberal rule.
123. *Gemeindeblatt der Jüdischen Gemeinde zu Berlin,* XVIII (1928), 75–76; Ernst Emil Schweitzer, "Gewalt und Recht in der Berliner Jüdischen Gemeinde," *Jüdisch-liberale Zeitung,* VIII (February 3, 1928), Beilage; Bruno Woyda, "Einheitsgemeinden oder Bekenntnisgemeinden?" *ibid.,* VII (December 2, 1927), 1; *Jüdische Rundschau,* January 6, 1928.
124. *Jüdische Rundschau,* October 24 and 31, 1930; *Jüdisch-liberale Zeitung,* X (October 29, 1920), 2; *ibid.,* X (November 19, 1930), 1.
125. Undated form letter, in Gemeinde Berlin Collection, Leo Baeck Institute Archives, New York, Z 31/88.

152 THE JEWS IN WEIMAR GERMANY

nity and to the drive against anti-Semitism. Among its candidates were Ismar Freund, a prominent and highly individualistic liberal attorney, and Albert Einstein.[126] It made little headway. In the election, held on November 30, the Liberals achieved the higher turnout on which they had staked their hopes; 55 percent more votes were cast than in 1926. The Liberals regained their absolute majority with more than 53 percent of the vote, the Zionists took about 36 percent, and the remainder was divided among the small parties, of which only the Religious Center party and the Nonpartisan Alliance won enough to gain one seat each on the Representative Council.[127]

By the very nature of its message, Zionist propaganda was certain to arouse the outraged opposition of liberal Jews. They were only too aware of its seductive appeals to young Jews, and they feared that their sons and daughters might slowly become estranged from their Fatherland. What added to the stridency of their responses to Zionism was the insulting character of much Jewish nationalist propaganda. One case in point was the satirical novel, *Tohuwabohu*, published in 1920 by Berlin attorney and active Zionist Sammy Gronemann. In it a young, idealistic Russian Jew comes to the Berlin of Kaiser Wilhelm II to sit at the feet of the most advanced Jewish scholars. Expecting to meet a G. E. Lessing in every third German and a Hermann Cohen in every other German Jew, he finds instead Germans who are mostly anti-Semites and Jews who are sinking ever deeper into self-hatred and moral decay. The rabbi from whom he seeks aid, the deputy chairman of the "General Association of Jewish Vassals in the German Empire," turns out to be a thoroughgoing scoundrel. The Jewish lawyers with whom he comes into contact feverishly divide their time between changing their names, having themselves and their families baptized, and bribing anti-Semites to keep them from publishing their scurrilous attacks. Only the single-minded idealism of the Zionists sheds redeeming light on this sordid world of petty corruption. As Rabbi Felix Goldmann observed at the time, the novel was scarcely a statement designed to improve prospects for Jewish unity.[128]

It would be a mistake to suppose that liberal Jews opposed Zionism because they were without sympathy for establishing a Jewish home in Palestine. Their chief concern was the Zionists' renunciation of German nationality and

126. Various undated election flyers, in Gemeinde Berlin Collection.
127. *Gemeindeblatt der Jüdischen Gemeinde zu Berlin*, XX (December, 1930), 1.
128. Sammy Gronemann, *Tohuwabohu* (Berlin, 1920); Felix Goldmann, "Einheitsfront," *Im deutschen Reich*, XXVI (1920), 329–33.

all that it entailed for the struggle to contain anti-Semitism. As early as 1913, following the Zionist Federation's Posen Resolution, the Centralverein explicitly repudiated the Zionist point of view in a declaration that was reaffirmed by a sixty-seven to six vote of its executive committee in 1924:

> We demand from our members not simply fulfillment of civic duties, but rather German sentiments and the application of those sentiments in civil life.
>
> We do not seek an international solution to the German Jewish question. We intend to contribute to German culture as Germans on the soil of the German Fatherland, and to hold fast to our community, sanctified by our religion and our history.
>
> Insofar as the German Zionist endeavors to establish a secure asylum for the Jews of the East, who have been deprived of their rights, or to lift the Jews' pride in their history and religion, he is welcome as a member [of the Centralverein]. But we must separate ourselves from those Zionists who deny German patriotism consider themselves guests among foreign hosts, and feel a part solely of a Jewish nationality.[129]

Equally anathema to the liberals was the influence of *völkisch* ideology within Zionism. Julius Goldstein, a Darmstadt professor of philosophy, spoke for them when he faulted the Zionists for adopting the materialistic philosophies of race and nation that poisoned the age and threatened it with yet another catastrophe of world-wide dimensions. As late as September, 1932, Centralverein activist Eva Reichmann portrayed Zionism as a neurotic reaction to a passing season of stress. Pathology alone seemed capable of explaining the decision to substitute a biologically determined Jewish nationality for a German Jewish consciousness free from racial overtones. Hence the Centralverein's formal claim to neutrality on Zionism deceived no one.[130] Assimilation was the irreconcilable issue; the liberals thought it indispensable to equality, whereas the Zionists saw in it a mortal threat to the collectivity of Jews.

As destructive as Zionism seemed to be to equality and sanity, liberals often perceived its threat to the Jewish religion as being at least as reprehensible. Ludwig Holländer acknowledged that hostility toward Judaism was not to be found emblazoned on Zionist programs, but he asserted that it was implicit in

129. Sch-r. [Artur Schweriner], "Der Centralverein marschiert!" *Central-Verein Zeitung*, November 7, 1924.

130. Julius Goldstein, "Betrachtungen zum jüdischen Nationalismus," *Im deutschen Reich*, XXVII (1921), 193–201; Eva Reichmann-Jungmann, "Die Judenfrage neugestellt?" *Central-Verein Zeitung*, September 23, 1932; Goldmann, "National-jüdische Radikalismus," 49–62.

Zionism's overweening preoccupation with secular nationalism and that it spilled out in aggressive ways among young Zionist zealots.[131] Nowhere were such fears more common than among Orthodox Jews. Some Orthodox members of the larger communities might work within the Zionist Federation to influence it for the ancient faith; in community politics, Orthodox Jews and Zionists sometimes combined to challenge liberal hegemony.[132] Others, however, agreed with Holländer that Zionism was antireligious, or at best irreligious, and that it placed national before religious considerations. Their fears were confirmed by the secular orientation of most Zionist settlements in Palestine.[133] In contrast, Orthodox Jews who belonged to separatist communities were virtually unanimous in opposing Zionism. Pulling no punches, they labeled nationalism "un-Jewish" and "anti-Torah," and a 1919 statement by their leaders named Orthodox membership in the Zionist Federation "a peril for the unity and inner resolution of Jews who remain faithful to the Torah."[134] The idea of Zion, which rested above every concept of land and politics, promised a rebirth of the Jewish people in all lands, not just in Palestine. Zionism was simply another form of assimilationism, for it would engulf the Jews in the world state system in such a way as to insure their preoccupation with defense against an outraged Arab world for the indefinite future. One of its great attractions to secularized Jews was that it gave them the appearance of becoming "more Jewish" while allowing them to retain their materialistic point of view.[135]

The existence of an expressly Orthodox faction of the German Zionist Federation failed to impress Zionism's Orthodox critics. Known as the Mizrachi, the faction sought to persuade other Orthodox Jews that Zionism was the best means of staying the decline of religious Orthodoxy in a rampantly secu-

131. Holländer, "Warum unsere Wahlparole?" *Central-Verein Zeitung*, December 19, 1924; Holländer, "Klarheit und Wahrheit!" *ibid.*, January 16, 1925.
132. *Der Israelit*, February 10, 1921; *ibid.*, February 5, 1931; *Jüdische Rundschau*, January 13, 1933. The prominent Orthodox Frankfurt rabbi, N. A. Nobel, was an enthusiastic Zionist. Simon, *Brücken: Gesammelte Aufsätze*, 375–80.
133. Aron Barth, *Orthodoxie und Zionismus* (Berlin, 1920), 29; *Central-Verein Zeitung*, July 24, 1925.
134. *Der Israelit*, January 16, 1919; Raphael Levi, "Nationalismus und Israelismus," *ibid.*, April 3, 1919; *ibid.*, January 30, 1919. See also Benzion Beermann, "Zionismus und Misrachismus," *ibid.*, July 27, 1922; *ibid.*, May 13, 1931. Rabbi Joseph Carlebach's cordial reception of Chaim Weizmann in Hamburg shocked other Orthodox Jews and was very atypical of the separatist attitude. Haim H. Cohn, "Joseph Carlebach," *Leo Baeck Institute Yearbook*, V (1960), 58–72.
135. *Der Israelit*, December 18, 1919; *ibid.*, May 26, 1921; *ibid.*, August 18, 1921; *ibid.*, June 22, 1922; Nathan Birnbaum, "Zurück zur eigenen Wunschwelt! Um Erez-Jisroel," *ibid.*, May 4, 1932.

lar age. Its assurances that Orthodox Jews could have a major influence on Zionism had a hollow ring, however, in the light of Mizrachi protests that Zionist Federation leaders ignored its point of view. Pleading for the rights of Zionist minorities, it denounced its fellow Zionists for betraying traditional Judaism to nationalistic hysteria and for downplaying religion and culture both in Germany and in Palestine.[136] Following unsuccessful Mizrachi attempts to divest the Zionist Federation of all control over cultural affairs, which would have placed those affairs in the hands of the various religious and political factions, an open break with Kurt Blumenfeld's leadership occurred at the Twelfth Congress of the German Zionist Federation held in Breslau at the end of May, 1928, with the Mizrachi subsequently deciding to go its own way in Palestine where schools and settlements were concerned.[137] Although it later bowed to internal and external pressure and returned to the larger Zionist fold, it rested uneasily there, rigidly disciplining the younger, more politically oriented Mizrachi and in 1931 breaking with the world Mizrachi organization for its alleged softness on political Zionism.[138]

Zionism might be ideologically reprehensible for liberal Jews, but its unofficial goal of placing a Jewish majority in Palestine drew their disapprobation for practical as well as moral reasons. Berlin Rabbi Alfred Wiener, a known proponent of Zionist-liberal rapprochement, mercilessly catalogued Zionism's utopian qualities as they emerged from his 1926 visit to Palestine. His *Critical Journey through Palestine,* which went through three editions within a few months of its publication in 1927, underlined the economic limitations of the land itself, the political restrictions that the British were legally and morally obliged to impose on Jewish immigration, and the legitimate interests of the Arab majority there.[139] Following the anti-Jewish riots in

136. Friedrich Thieberger, "Abfall im Glauben," *Der Jude,* III (1918/19), 538–40; Friedrich Thieberger, "Lebensform und religiöse Form," *ibid.,* VIII (1924), 58–61; Barth, *Orthodoxie und Zionismus,* 41–46; Alexander Adler, "Für vertrauensvolle Zusammenarbeit," *Jüdische Rundschau,* May 16, 1928; Adler, "Wo liegt der Fehler?" *ibid.,* June 22, 1928; *ibid.,* March 8, 1929; I. Leibowitz, "Grundsätzliches zur innerzionistischen Diskussion," *ibid.,* October 18, 1929; *ibid.,* July 11, 1924.

137. Barth, *Orthodoxie und Zionismus,* 41–46; *Jüdische Rundschau,* June 1, 1928; *ibid.,* November 16, 1928; Bernard Bamberger, "Umgestaltung oder Zerschlagung?" *ibid.,* November 27, 1928.

138. Erich Fromm, "Zum Misrachi Delegiertentag," *Jüdische Rundschau,* May 7, 1920; H. Fränkel, "Die geistigen Strömungen im Misrachi," *ibid.,* June 4, 1920; *ibid.,* March 1, 1929; *ibid.,* October 16, 1931; Oskar Wolfsburg, "Der Austritt des Deutschen Misrachi aus dem Weltmisrachi," *ibid.,* October 16, 1931; *Der Israelit,* May 13, 1931.

139. Alfred Wiener, *Kritische Reise durch Palästina* (3rd ed.; Berlin, 1928), especially 113–18, 145–47. For similar liberal criticism, see *Im deutschen Reich,* XXVI (1920), 270–74; *Central-Verein Zeitung,* January 2, 1925.

Palestine in August, 1929, Wiener condemned the majority within Zionism for discriminating against the Arabs and ignoring their nationalistic sensibilities. Other liberals, less kind, tended to gloat over the Palestinian tragedy. Bruno Weil responded to Zionist attacks on Centralverein defensive tactics at a 1931 meeting of the Prussian Provincial Association of Jewish Communities by noting that, however bad conditions might have become in Germany, Jews were not being murdered there as they were in Palestine and that German Jewish leaders did not require bodyguards, as Chaim Weizmann did in Jerusalem.[140]

The liberal counterattack can only be judged a success. The Centralverein remained the acknowledged Jewish self-defense organization, notwithstanding Zionist efforts to hand its functions over to other bodies. The communities stayed almost solidly in liberal hands, with Zionist inroads limited and localized. The German Jews themselves stubbornly resisted the blandishments of Jewish nationalism. Membership in the Zionist Federation of Germany, far from growing, fell from more than 33,000 in 1923 to 22,000 two years later, reckoned by the number of "shekel payers"—those who made the minimum annual one mark payment into federation coffers. Moreover, as the Zionists themselves admitted, this number included a very great many fellow-travelers and half-hearted philanthropists who lacked any real enthusiasm for Zionist goals.[141] A more realistic figure for the genuinely committed Zionists in Germany may be inferred from the 8,739 "shekel payers" who bothered to vote in the 1929 Zionist Federation elections.[142]

German Zionism's predicament was but part of a larger impasse affecting all of Jewish nationalism. In fact, the movement was in decline and on its way to oblivion when the Third Reich renewed it and presented it with unprecedented possibilities. More than any other single human being, Adolf Hitler made the modern Jewish state.[143]

Zionism's lack of progress raised voices of lamentation and self-examination among its German adherents. Beginning in 1922 and increas-

---

140. Wiener, *Juden und Araber in Palästina*, 17–35; *Verwaltungsblatt des preussischen Landesverbandes jüdischer Gemeinden*, IX (1931), 16. See also J. Stern, "Leid und Sorgen im heiligen Land," *Central-Verein Zeitung*, September 6, 1929.
141. Robert Weiss, "Die Ortsgruppe als Exponent der Gesamtbewegung," *Jüdische Rundschau*, August 15, 1922; *ibid.*, July 3, 1925; *ibid.*, September 18, 1925; Moses Beilinson, "Zionistische Krise und Jüdischer Bund," *Der Jude*, VIII (1924), 267–84; *Central-Verein Zeitung*, September 4, 1925.
142. *Jüdische Rundschau*, June 28, 1929. Two years before the figure had dropped to a low 6,656 votes, prompting a liberal writer to gloat over the "downfall of Zionism." Hugo Spiegler, "Der Niedergang des Zionismus," *Jüdisch-liberale Zeitung*, VI (August 26, 1927), 3.
143. *Cf.* Laqueur, *A History of Zionism*, 406–407, 594–95.

ingly thereafter, they spoke of a "crisis" in their movement and debated the means appropriate to overcoming it. They faulted each other for overconfidence, lack of commitment, and stinginess. Their failure to sweep Jewish youth into the Zionist camp was a particularly bitter pill. Never were Zionist spirits lower than after the 1929 riots in Palestine, when the lack of money, the Arab problem, and the remoteness of Zionism's final goals combined to hang a pall of gloom over the movement.[144]

The internal debate over the causes of stagnation exacerbated existing factionalisms within the federation. The Marxist left, represented by the Poale Zion faction, agitated for a concerted membership drive among newly proletarianized Jews, rather than among the middle class, and sought to carry the class struggle into the Jewish communities. Always a contentious and independent group, the Poale Zion broke with the larger Zionist organizations in 1920 and applied unsuccessfully for membership in the Third International. Thereafter it went its own way, even to the point of running separate lists of candidates in Jewish elections, until it merged with the non-Marxist Hapoel Hazair in 1932.[145] The Mizrachi, of course, argued for greater sensitivity to Orthodox Judaism as a means of finding new converts in its ranks. The Revisionists steadily beat the drums for openly demanding a Jewish state in Palestine and arming Jewish units for purposes of self-protection there; without such politics there would be no rapid settlement of Jews in Palestine, and in the absence of rapid settlement Zionism was doomed to wither on the vine for want of tangible progress.[146] Their boundless contempt for the moderate policies espoused by the *Jüdische Rundschau* came out often, but never so directly as in Richard Lichtheim's comment of 1929: "At one time there was

144. Gerhard Holdheim, "Lösung der zionistische Krise?" *Der Jude,* VIII (1924), 513–23; Karl Glaser, "Fragen des Delegiertentages," *Jüdische Rundschau,* July 28, 1922; Bertram Stern, "Zum Delegiertentag," *ibid.,* August 1, 1922; *ibid.,* June 1, 1928; *ibid.,* June 22, 1928; Chajim Arlosoroff, "Etappen," *Die Arbeit,* IV (1924), 274–81; *Blau-Weiss Blätter,* I (1924), 60–62; Hans Kaufmann, "Zionistische Organisation und zionistische Jugend," *Jüdische Rundschau,* February 13, 1931; Harry Bein, "Eine Schicksalsfrage des deutschen Zionismus?" *ibid.,* October 27, 1931; R. W. [Robert Weltsch], "Ein sorgenvoller Kongress," *ibid.,* June 26, 1931.

145. *Ibid.,* October 19, 1920; Kurt Blumenfeld, "Neue Arbeit," *ibid.,* September 13, 1928; Kurt Löwenstein, "Zionistische Organisation und Poale Zion," *ibid.,* January 29, 1929; *ibid.,* October 7, 1932; *Verwaltungsblatt des preussischen Landesverbandes jüdischer Gemeinden,* X (1932), 17; Fritz Fränkel, "Religiöser Sozialismus und die Poale-Zion," *Der Morgen,* VI (1930), 303–305; "Aufzeichnung," February, 1921, in Nachlass Moritz Sobernheim, 1287/349519–20.

146. For a summary of the Revisionist viewpoint following the 1929 Arab riots, see Lichtheim, *Revision der zionistischen Politik,* 43–54. *Cf.* Nachum Goldmann, "Die Radikalen Zionisten vor dem Kongress," *Jüdische Rundschau,* May 29, 1931.

politics in the *J. R.;* now it has been replaced by articles on music." [147] A small group of Zionist intellectuals calling themselves Radical Zionists, led in Germany by Nahum Goldmann, stood close to the Revisionists, differing with them principally on the issue of the mass party. The Radicals urged the Zionist Federation to give up all pretense of mass organization and make itself over into an elite of utterly committed revolutionaries. They joined with the Revisionists and like-minded militants in ousting the moderate leadership of Chaim Weizmann at the seventeenth World Zionist Congress in Basel in July, 1931. [148] That these elements were unable to topple Blumenfeld and Weltsch in Germany suggests that Zionism there was somewhat more conservative than it was elsewhere. There the amorphous General Zionists, who rejected the extreme reforms advocated by the radical factions, maintained their leadership even in the face of stagnation and demoralization. [149]

Liberal intransigence and Zionist inertia were the preconditions for the start of rapprochement between the two camps. The moderate leaders of German Zionism, having spurned the radical solution to the Zionist crisis, could not fail to acknowledge that some measure of flexibility and diplomacy was needed if they were to raise money and exert influence among liberal Jews. The latter, reassured of the continuing efficacy of their *Weltanschauung,* could afford to be generous on the issue of charity for Palestine. Even the most outspoken anti-Zionists, with few exceptions, had consistently claimed sympathy for the idea of Palestine as a refuge for homeless Jews. They had limited their objections to Zionism's assertion of a separate Jewish nationality and its rejection of ties of sentiment to Germany.

A brief historical survey of majority responses to Zionist drives to raise money for Palestine provides a useful measure of changing liberal attitudes. The creation of a neutral fund-raising agency, the Keren Hayesod, in 1920 was at first a source of some embarrassment to the liberals. To support it could only strengthen Zionism economically while weakening resistance to

147. *Jüdische Rundschau,* April 24, 1929.
148. Nahum Goldmann, "Prinzipielles zur Organisationsreform," *ibid.,* December 19, 1924; Goldmann, "Die Radikalen Zionisten vor dem Kongress," *ibid.,* May 29, 1931; Goldmann, *Memories,* 104–18.
149. But not by themselves. The General Zionists lost ground in Germany, just as they did in the world Zionist movement, requiring Blumenfeld to rely on Mizrachi and Hapoel Hazair support for his policies. The results of the 1931 elections in Germany for delegates to the seventeenth Zionist Congress provide some clues to the sentiments of German Zionists: General Zionists, 2,321 votes and 2 delegates; United Zionist-Socialist party (a fusion of the Poale Zion and Hapoel Hazair), 2,410 votes and 3 delegates; Revisionists, 1,189 votes and 1 delegate; Mizrachi, 2,028 votes and 2 delegates; Radicals, 546 votes and 1 delegate. *Jüdische Rundschau,* June 12, 1931.

the siren song of Jewish nationalism; to oppose it would open the liberals to charges of hypocrisy and leave many persecuted Eastern Jews to their fate. In fact, initial liberal responses were mixed. A group of liberal rabbis, Leo Baeck of Berlin and Felix Goldmann of Leipzig prominent among them, signed on early and urged the widest possible support for the Keren Hayesod.[150] The General Alliance of Rabbis in Germany, at its first meeting after World War I, held on May 18, 1921, unanimously passed a resolution declaring it a "holy duty" to assist in building a Jewish home in Palestine.[151] The widely read liberal *Israelitisches Familienblatt* began a regular column sympathetic to the fund early in 1922, and several Jewish communities contributed money, including those of Hamburg, Königsberg, and Leipzig. Others, however, specifically rejected proposals for such subventions.[152] Rabbi Hugo Fuchs of Chemnitz named every penny given to the fund a "sin."[153] The Centralverein called attention to the great need for charity at home and reproached the Keren Hayesod as a Zionist Trojan horse. This resistance helped keep contributions in Germany low compared to those in other countries.[154] By the late 1920s, however, liberal attitudes were changing. Under the skillful chairmanship of Berlin banker Oskar Wassermann, the Keren Hayesod was proving itself scrupulously independent of Zionist control. Rabbi Fuchs was among the first to change his mind, and by 1926 he was writing to his fellow rabbis soliciting their support for the fund.[155] Two years later Ludwig Holländer restated the Centralverein's opposition to it, but he bowed to growing dissatisfaction with that policy by declaring it a subsidiary issue on which everyone should form his own opinions. By that time, too, the German Keren Hayesod had improved its fund-raising record somewhat.[156]

The moderation of liberal thinking became dramatically apparent in March, 1927, when the Conference of Liberal Rabbis of Germany adopted a resolution making each Jew's attitude toward Zionism a purely personal one.

150. *Ibid.*, May 5 and 9, 1922.

151. *Allgemeine Zeitung des Judentums*, LXXXV (1921), 138.

152. Lynkeus, "Die andere Seite," *Jüdische Rundschau*, April 4, 1922; *ibid.*, October 20, 1922; *ibid.*, November 17, 1922; *ibid.*, April 8, 1925; *Israelitisches Familienblatt*, March 1, 1928.

153. Fuchs, "Keren Hajessod," *Israelitisches Familienblatt*, December 23, 1920.

154. *Central-Verein Zeitung*, May 4, 1922; Ludwig Holländer, "Nach der Hauptversammlung," *ibid.*, March 19, 1926; *ibid.*, March 26, 1926; Ruppin, *Soziologie der Juden*, II, 262.

155. Various correspondence, January and February, 1926, in Hugo Fuchs Collection, Leo Baeck Institute Archives, New York, 411/1169/1–18.

156. *Central-Verein Zeitung*, February 17, 1928; *Jüdische Rundschau*, November 16, 1928.

During the debate on the resolution, which dominated the conference meeting, Leo Baeck argued that the youthful spirit of Zionism ought to be harnessed in order to rescue Judaism from galloping complacency. To their approval of individual liberal support for Zionism, however, the rabbis set strict limits, stipulating the primacy of religion in all resettlement programs and emphatically renouncing any conception of the Jews as a nationality.[157]

This formula of individual choice shortly became the saving prescription for the Centralverein as well. For years a minority of its members had worked to conciliate liberals and Zionists and especially to nullify opposition to the Keren Hayesod and other forms of charitable aid for Palestine. They included, in addition to Rabbis Baeck and Goldmann, Friedrich Brodnitz, the son of Centralverein chairman Julius Brodnitz, and liberal youth leader Ludwig Tietz.[158] The Centralverein syndic in Breslau, Ludwig Foerder, had made himself a center of controversy by vigorously advocating policy changes that would have facilitated liberal-Zionist rapprochement.[159] Among some of the Centralverein rank-and-file, and especially among its young members, the hard-core opposition to Zionism of the older generation seemed passé in light of Zionist practice in Germany. They admired the Zionists' spirit and idealism, and without actually endorsing Jewish nationalism, they advocated limited cooperation in cultural, charitable, and self-defense matters.[160]

The new attitude made its first official breakthrough on the issue of supporting the "enlarged" Jewish Agency. The Jewish Agency, an official advisory body to the British mandatory government in Palestine, had been identical with the World Zionist Organization until 1928, when it was decided to reconstitute it with equal numbers of Zionist and non-Zionist Jews in order to broaden support for Zionist work in Palestine. Liberal advocates of rapprochement jumped at the opportunity to save the work of resettling Jews from Zionist extremism.[161] The Centralverein's executive committee, at the end of a two-day debate over whether or not to send representatives to the

157. Seligmann, "Mein Leben," 115; *Jüdische Rundschau*, April 1, 1927; *Israelitisches Familienblatt*, April 7, 1927.

158. Reichmann and Brodnitz interviews.

159. Foerder, "Antisemitismus, Zionismus und Centralverein," *Jüdische Rundschau*, June 19, 1923; *ibid.*, May 15, 1925.

160. Ernst L. Loewenberg, "Jakob Loewenberg: Excerpts from His Diaries and Letters," *Leo Baeck Institute Yearbook*, XV (1970), 208–209; *Israelitisches Familienblatt*, October 30, 1924; *Jüdische Rundschau*, March 21, 1922; *ibid.*, July 20, 1928.

161. Alfred Wiener, "Die Jewish Agency," *Central-Verein Zeitung*, October 7, 1927; Friedrich Brodnitz, "Zionismus oder jüdische Gemeinschaft?" *ibid.*, June 15, 1928; Brodnitz, "Wahlen zur Jewish Agency," *ibid.*, July 5, 1929; *Gemeindeblatt der Jüdischen Gemeinde zu*

Jewish Agency, decided in the negative but significantly left each member free to choose for himself whether or not to join or support the new body.[162]

The Zionists, too, contributed to rapprochement, although for reasons more of tactics than of conviction. Virtually from the time of the founding of the Keren Hayesod in 1920, they assumed that efforts to involve non-Zionist Jews in fund-raising activities required that they moderate their ideological attacks on assimilationism somewhat, a concession that radical Zionists bitterly resented.[163] The Zionist majority, however, reluctantly accepted it as the price of extending Zionist influence in Germany.[164]

That both groups placed sharp limits on cooperation with the other side became swiftly apparent, especially from the liberals, who, after all, had made more concessions in the first place. The Centralverein reiterated its rejection of Zionist ideology while Ludwig Tietz, one of its most conciliatory leaders, warned the Zionists that the organization was united and adamant in its opposition to Jewish nationalism.[165] A group of about one hundred outspoken anti-Zionist Jewish liberals of all religious and political persuasions met in Berlin's Kaiserhof Hotel on September 19, 1929, in order to found the Action Committee of German Jews. After spurning appeals by representatives of the extreme right and left, it adopted a resolution urging the Jews to resist Zionist and Jewish Agency attempts at garnering sympathy from the recent riots in Palestine. Those unhappy events, it went on, should instead be laid at the Zionists' own door, and it ended with the words:

We profess ourselves to be part of Jewry, but we reject every Jewish nationalism. We, together with the overwhelming majority of German Jews, consider ourselves to be part of the *German,* not the Jewish, *Volk.* We see in the establishment of a Jewish national homeland a misstep that cannot fail to endanger the emancipatory work of the pioneers of German Jewry and the religious and moral tasks of Judaism.[166]

Berlin, XIX (1929), 468–73; *Gemeindeblatt der Israelitischen Gemeinde Frankfurt a. Main,* VIII (1929), 138–41.

162. *Central-Verein Zeitung,* March 29, 1929.

163. Fritz Löwenstein, "Ideal und Realität," *Jüdische Rundschau,* May 16, 1922; Lichtheim, *Revision der zionistischen Politik,* 30–33; Bodenheimer, *Prelude to Israel,* 307–309; Goldmann, *Memories,* 96–103.

164. Holdheim, "Agency und Zukunft," *Jüdische Rundschau,* August 1, 1924; Holdheim, "Zionistische Organisation," *ibid.,* April 1, 1931.

165. Ludwig Tietz, "C. V.—Zionismus—Jewish Agency," *Central-Verein Zeitung,* February 28, 1930.

166. Unsigned anti-Jewish Agency appeal addressed to Centralverein leaders, January 11, 1930, in Leo Wolff Collection, 1616/4059 IV, 1.

Within a short time the committee had secured signatures from a large minority of the Centralverein executive committee, including Dr. Bruno Glaserfeld, chairman of the Berlin Centralverein, and Leo Wolff; others who signed were Hugo Ostberg, the moving spirit of the Action Committee; Rabbis Julius Galliner and Joseph Lehmann; and Alfred Peyser, former head of the right-wing League of German Nationalist Jews.[167] For their part, the Zionists lost no time in informing the liberals that there would be no let-up in the ideological struggle, however welcome the softening of their attitude might be. Nor were the liberals reassured when Zionists sardonically dubbed the two groups making up the Jewish Agency "Zionists" and "not-quite-Zionists."[168]

Mutual reluctance to carry rapprochement too far was mirrored in the fate of the Reichstag Election Committee in 1930. Formed by representatives of various liberal Jewish organizations, most notably the Centralverein, and the German Zionist Federation at the initiative of the Berlin Jewish Community Executive Council, it aimed at securing cooperative anti-Nazi action in the campaign for the September Reichstag election. The Nazis had already secured an ominous electoral breakthrough in the Thuringian provincial elections held the year before, and, on the surface at least, a common sense of urgency held the parties together. The committee, which contributed money and propaganda to the democratic parties, succeeded in spreading to virtually every major city in Germany; only the hard-core anti-Zionist, anti-Eastern Jewish Centralverein local in Chemnitz refused to go along.[169] It dissolved itself immediately following the election, however, and nothing of the kind was ever attempted again. Zionists accused the Centralverein of dominating the committee, whereas the liberal organization responded that the Zionists had contributed scarcely any time or money to it.[170] In fact, the Zionists had not altered their view of anti-Semitism as inevitable and ubiquitous, capable

167. Two invitations to anti-Zionist meetings, September 12 and December 7, 1929, and [Felix?] Makower to Leo Wolff, February 9, 1930, all in *ibid.*, *454/1212/34–36*; Szanto, "Im Dienste der Gemeinde," 70–74. On the League of German Nationalist Jews, see below, chapter VII.

168. *Jüdische Rundschau*, July 17, 1928; Rudolf Samuel, "Zum Thema 'Innere Befriedigung,'" *ibid.*, July 17, 1928; *ibid.*, April 5, 1929; *Central-Verein Zeitung*, August 23, 1929.

169. Also on the committee were representatives from the B'nai B'rith, the National League of Jewish Frontline Veterans, and the Berlin Jewish Community. It was chaired by the deputy chairman of the Centralverein, Bruno Weil. *Israelitisches Familienblatt*, July 31, 1930; M. N. [Max Naumann], "Der Koscher-Zettel," *Der nationaldeutsche Jude*, September, 1930; *Jüdische Rundschau*, August 22, 1930.

170. *Jüdisch-liberale Zeitung*, XI (January 14, 1931), Beilage; *Jüdische Rundschau*, January 9, 1931; Georg Kareski, "Der C. V. auf dem Kriegspfade," *ibid.*, January 23, 1931; Paucker, *Der jüdische Abwehrkampf*, 42–44.

of being controlled only by pulling away from other people's politics, not by trying to convince them, falsely, that Jews could be or were good Germans. Thereafter the two groups went their separate ways, the Centralverein tirelessly assisting the prorepublican parties against the Hitlerites, the Zionist Federation holding itself aloof from the political fray. The latter's one official concession to the need for active self-defense was to publish, starting early in 1932, a monthly edition of the *Jüdische Rundschau* for non-Jews; its stated objectives were to show that Zionists were doing something to counteract divided German-Jewish existence and to refute anti-Zionist statements from liberal sources.[171]

And yet the decline in bitterness between liberals and Zionists was real and palpable. During the declining years of the Weimar Republic it was possible for the first time for gentlemanly debates to take place between the two sides, while at the same time their direct attacks on each other became fewer and gentler.[172] Zionist Georg Kareski's 1931 attack on Jewish liberal policies as those of "marauders and looters of corpses" became the exception rather than the rule.[173] The election of a Zionist as chairman of the League of Jewish Women in a major German city, unthinkable only a few years before, became reality in 1932.[174] Whether or not to appropriate community funds for Zionist charities could still produce bitter and demonstrative debates, as it did in Berlin in 1932, but, typically, as in that case, a small contribution minimally acceptable to both sides could be agreed upon.[175] Franchise reform, on the other hand, remained a deeply divisive subject in several communities, including Dortmund, Dresden, Leipzig, and Chemnitz.[176] That issue aside, liberals and Zionists, while far from united, were usually prepared to observe a benevolent truce, at least while the Nazi tide flowed high.

By the end of the Weimar period, Kurt Blumenfeld and his colleagues could take some pride in the progress of Zionism since 1918. The German Zionist Federation had sent few German Jews to Palestine, but it had aided many Jews from less tolerant regions to settle there. By illuminating the plight of the

171. Kurt Blumenfeld, "Ein Wort an Nichtjuden," *Jüdische Rundschau*, January 22, 1932.
172. *Ibid.*, February 20, 1931.
173. *Gemeindeblatt der Jüdischen Gemeinde zu Berlin*, XXI (1931), 363–66.
174. The woman in question was Rahel Straus of Munich. Straus, *Wir lebten in Deutschland*, 259.
175. *Jüdische Rundschau*, April 12, 1932; *ibid.*, May 20, 1932; *Jüdisch-liberale Zeitung*, XII (April 15, 1932), Beilage.
186. *Jüdische Rundschau*, June 17, 1930; J. Adler, "Das Wahlunrecht in Leipzig," *ibid.*, December 12, 1930; J. Adler, "Die Chemnitzer Gefahr," *ibid.*, January 30, 1931; *ibid.*, October 9, 1931; Alexander Adler, "Der Skandal von Dortmund," *ibid.*, October 28, 1932.

Eastern Jews and the promise of the Balfour Declaration, it had won the philanthropy and the sympathy of a growing minority of liberal Jews. It had provided its own membership with the myth of a transfigured future that made the trials of the present easier to bear. Its challenge to the liberals for community control had forced them to broaden their concerns to include less affluent Jews. No less than the anti-Semites, the Zionists had kept their liberal opponents on the defensive almost without respite, sharpening the latter's Jewish self-consciousness and driving thoughts of amalgamation beyond the pale. Robert Weltsch used only mild hyperbole when he commented in 1928 that "the whole of Jewish life orients itself around Zionism." [177]

As impressive as these gains were, they still could not obscure Zionism's failure to make significant inroads into the assimilationist commitments of most German Jews. By the end of the Weimar years the Jewish nationalists could claim increased contributions for Zionism, but not more souls. Their fundamental error was to assert a present psychological estrangement and future physical alienation that few of them really felt or planned and that few Jews outside their own ranks could tolerate. How much more sympathy and support they might have won had they refrained from such excesses! The Zionists' claim to a separate *völkisch* identity, although scarcely decisive in determining the approaching Jewish tragedy, further disrupted the life of the Jewish community and denied the liberal and republican groups much-needed aid in defense of German democracy. There remain grave doubts that German Zionism, for all its services to the cause of Jewish self-esteem and charity, benefited German Jewry more than it damaged it.

---

177. R. W. [Robert Weltsch], "Schawuoth und Delegiertentag," *ibid.*, May 23, 1928.

The Jew as German Chauvinist
The Psychological Fruits of Rejection

German Zionists were not alone in attributing anti-Semitism principally to the liberal notion that one could be both a German and a Jew, one as much as the other. A small group of right-wing Jews, although passionately opposed to the Zionist alternative, professed to see major flaws in the behavior of the Jewish majority that partially justified Germanic hostility and called for major mending action. It contended that the Jews, far from immersing themselves too deeply in things Teutonic, had unwisely held themselves back from full commitment to Germany out of exaggerated fears of amalgamation; failure to embrace their Fatherland wholeheartedly would leave them dangerously isolated and tragically rootless.

Organizer of this right-wing reaction was Dr. Max Naumann, a Berlin lawyer, member of Berlin's Reform congregation and of the Centralverein, and former captain in the Bavarian Reserve. In the summer of 1920, Naumann and three associates visited the Berlin headquarters of the Centralverein to complain to Ludwig Holländer that the organization induced Jews to make political decisions from a Jewish, rather than a German, point of view. They said that the Centralverein was remiss in fostering a patriotic attitude among German Jews, that it was inconsistent in addressing itself to matters touching on the most sensitive foreign policy issues, and that it consciously or unconsciously discouraged Jews from supporting the German People's party and other right-of-center political groups. A Jew, they concluded, ought to be free to join any party that corresponded with his personal philosophy, and he should fight any anti-Semitism he might find there from within. Holländer responded by repeating the Centralverein's well-known policy of neutrality on all but overtly anti-Jewish parties and protested that he himself had been critical of anti-People's party sentiment within the Centralverein. In an effort to disarm Naumann, he tried to interest him in the Centralverein's efforts to combat Zionism, and he invited Naumann to contribute an article to *Im deutschen Reich* on the subject of the People's party and its stand on anti-Semitism. Naumann agreed to write the article, but when Holländer read it he concluded that it directly urged Centralverein members to support the People's party and that to publish it would constitute outright endorsement of a party that was somewhat ambivalent on the Jewish question.

Naumann interpreted this refusal as proof of Centralverein partiality for the Democratic party and set out to expose the organization to his coreligionists.[1] Late that year he published in the People's party's chief Rhineland newspaper, the *Kölnische Zeitung,* an article entitled "Concerning German Nationalist Jews," and soon thereafter had it published in pamphlet form. In it Naumann professed to discern three groups among German Jews. The first consisted of the Zionists, whose impatient, unrequited love for Germany had soured into radical Jewish nationalism. Although resting solidly and solely on their Jewishness, their proselytizing raids among young Jews demoralized the Jewish community, while their international organization fed anti-Semitic claims of a Jewish world conspiracy.

Naumann's second group, far larger than the first, was the great mass of German nationalist Jews for whom there was only a German, never a Jewish, standpoint on politics. They proudly acknowledged their Jewish origins, but they perceived that nations are formed out of common consciousness, not ethnic derivation. They combated Judeophobia, not with craven apologetics, but with self-respect and patriotism. In the Eastern Jews they saw a pitiable band of foreigners to which Germany was in no shape to extend aid. Lamentably, the reserve of these German nationalists obscured their true importance compared to other Jewish groups.

Between these two groups of equally self-conscious and determined Jews Naumann identified an amorphous collection of Jews whose loyalties were divided between things German and things Jewish. Within them an interminable battle raged, denying them a clear sense of identity and impelling them to assert militantly their worth as human beings. The resulting behavior—pushiness, underhandedness, ostentatious displays of wealth, knowledge, and negative criticism—identified by racists as emanating from the "Jewish spirit," was in fact typical of the parvenu of any race. Naumann labelled these insecure souls "in-betweeners" (*Zwischenschichtler*)[2] or, occasionally,

1. Ludwig Holländer, "Denkschrift über die Bestrebungen des Rechtsanwalts Dr. Max Naumann in Berlin auf Begründung eines Verbandes nationaldeutscher Juden" (Berlin, 1921), and Max Naumann, "Denkschrift über die Treibereien des Syndikus Dr. Ludwig Holländer in Berlin betreffend den Verband nationaldeutscher Juden" (Berlin, 1921), both in Centralverein Collection, Wiener Library.
2. The English language scarcely does justice to this word, which suggests individuals wan-

"fifty-percenters." He implied that the Centralverein spoke for them by commenting on their oversensitivity to anti-Semitism, which, he said, they saw in all criticism of Jews, no matter how justified.[3]

If Naumann's outburst was designed to pressure the Centralverein into an attitude more sympathetic to the political right, he must have been dismayed by the brief response in the organization's journal insisting that, after all, the Centralverein spoke for the "German nationalist Jews" too and rejecting only his negative comments about Eastern Jews.[4] Naumann fired back a reply attacking the Centralverein for its lack of success after twenty-seven years of effort. Its failure to end anti-Semitism and to achieve a united Jewish front he attributed to the Centralverein's emphasis on religion and citizenship, neither of which sufficed. Stress on ethnicity, on the other hand, would come dangerously close to Zionism. Unity between Jews and Jews, and Germans and Jews, could be achieved only by fostering a German nationalist point of view, the touchstone for which was the attitude taken toward that "dangerous guest," the Eastern Jew.[5]

A hardening of the Centralverein's position on Naumann was now scarcely avoidable, for his criticisms had gone well beyond the original complaint of Centralverein prejudice against the People's party and now included charges that the organization lacked patriotism and misapprehended the causes of anti-Semitism. In February, 1921, Ludwig Holländer distributed a secret memorandum to Centralverein leaders relating his version of the previous year's discussions with Naumann. A copy fell into Naumann's hands, and he composed a blistering reply, impudently marked "Not Secret," accusing Holländer of falsifying the record. But before doing that he and eighty-eight like-minded Jews founded the League of German Nationalist Jews in Berlin on March 20, 1921.[6] The decision to do so followed hard upon the appearance of an article by Holländer that criticized the People's party for tolerating anti-Semitism in some of its local branches.[7]

From then until its dissolution by the Nazis, the League of German Nationalist Jews (Verband nationaldeutscher Juden) was dominated by its

---

dering in a no-man's-land between two well-established groups, lacking firm roots in either. For a more detailed examination of Naumann's ideology, see Rheins, "German Jewish Patriotism," 58–101.

3. Max Naumann, *Vom nationaldeutschen Juden* (Berlin, 1920), 3–22.
4. K. A. [Kurt Alexander], "Zeitschau," *Im deutschen Reich*, XXVI (1920), 372–78.
5. Max Naumann, "Vom nationaldeutschen Juden," *ibid.*, XXVII (1921), 26–30.
6. Holländer, "Denkschrift"; Naumann, "Denkschrift."
7. L. H., "Wahlen," *Im deutschen Reich*, XXVII (1921), 91.

founder to such an extent that it was commonly referred to as the "Naumann League" and its members as "Naumannites." Even after Naumann passed the league's chairmanship to the less-volatile Berlin physician Alfred Peyser in April, 1926, he remained its best-known member and chief spokesman, retaining the title of "honorary chairman." Peyser, in turn, resigned because of overwork and was succeeded by Georg Siegmann in September, 1926.[8] Naumann returned to his old post following the Nazi takeover in 1933, this time naming himself "League *Führer*." From fragmentary information that is available about league adherents, they appear to have been solid members of the urban middle class, attorneys, bankers, and doctors, but, with rare exceptions, scarcely leaders in their communities.[9] Aside from Naumann and Peyser, the most prominent member was Dr. Siegfried Breslauer, chief political editor of the *Berliner Lokalanzeiger,* a newspaper that stood close to the right wing of the People's party.[10]

From the inception of the league, Naumann and his associates worked feverishly to awaken reticent Jews of patriotic sentiments as well as to win over as many "in-betweeners" as possible. Although severely hamstrung by lack of funds, they did manage in 1921 to publish a handful of propaganda pamphlets and, in the following year, to found a newspaper that appeared irregularly until 1931. They also spread the word by sending speakers to as many Jewish groups as would have them. These efforts were financed, in part, by contributions from league members and sympathizers in the business and financial community, the most prominent of whom was the Berlin banker Martin Schiff, who died in 1929.[11]

The main target of the propaganda of the League of German Nationalist Jews was the "in-betweeners," who, although they were the most problematical of German Jews, were also the ones most in need of enlightenment. The Zionists, on the other hand, were regarded as beyond saving, having lost all feeling for Germany. Naumann argued that the three groups he had identified were the results of diverse responses to emancipation. Some Jews reacted negatively, cherishing the old allegiances, holding fast to Orthodoxy

8. *Der nationaldeutsche Jude* (September, 1926), 11.

9. Klaus J. Herrmann, *Das dritte Reich und die deutsch-jüdischen Organisationen 1933– 1934* (Cologne, 1969), 36–37.

10. Max Naumann, "Nachwort," *Mitteilungsblatt des Verbandes nationaldeutscher Juden,* No. 2 (1922), 3–4; *Jüdische Rundschau,* December 16, 1924.

11. Klaus J. Herrmann, personal letter, January 31, 1976. The name of the newspaper was *Mitteilungsblatt des Verbandes nationaldeutscher Juden* from 1922 to 1925, when its name was changed to *Der nationaldeutsche Jude.*

and to the Jews of all lands, and forming only half-hearted formal ties to Germany. Theodor Herzl secularized this impulse and ended the self-deception of ostensible love for Germany. Other Jews greeted emancipation with seemly gratitude and quickly cast down deep roots into German soil. Their spiritual progeny were the German nationalist Jews of Weimar Germany. The "in-betweeners" thought they could have it both ways, isolating things Jewish under the heading of "religion" and expecting to be Germans in every other way. Doubts about the compatibility of the two, and half-perceived consciousness of harboring un-German impulses, were dismissed as inconsistent with the privacy of religious matters. They were fond of comparing themselves to Roman Catholics, whose international organization had ceased to be a source of embarrassment with the end of the *Kulturkampf,* forgetting as they did so that Catholics have no identification with a rival homeland like Palestine. For those insufficiently narcotized by this use of religion to obscure their own divided allegiances, there were always stronger pills in the form of special courses of study to deepen the Jewish consciousness, perhaps supplemented by talk of a Jewish mission to improve world morals.[12]

Naumann and his followers repeatedly hammered home their conviction that religion really had nothing to do with the modern Jewish question. Neither Jews nor their detractors took religion very seriously any more. The time had come to view the Jewish question as a sociological problem, since a Jew in the modern context was anyone of Jewish descent who still thought of himself as a Jew. Accordingly, any member of the Jewish cultural community (as distinct from the religious community) could join the League of German Nationalist Jews.[13] Although the league claimed neutrality on Jewish religious questions, some of its spokesmen advocated ending such specific Jewish religious practices as Saturday Sabbaths and pilgrimage festivals in favor of observing Sunday as the Sabbath and Christmas as a German holiday. Naumann in a moment of excitement was capable of exclaiming: "We reject Yahweh, the old tribal god of an Asiatic nomadic horde. We have a German god!"[14] And when a Zionist-led coalition took over the Berlin Jewish Community in the late 1920s, he threatened to lead patriotic Jews in withdrawing from it.[15]

The divided loyalties of the "in-betweeners" were reprehensible in and of

---

12. Max Naumann, *Vom mosaischen und nicht-mosaischen Juden* (Berlin, 1921), 21–35.
13. *Ibid.*, 13, 15–20; Max Naumann, *Brennende Fragen für den deutschen Juden,* in Verband nationaldeutscher Juden Collection, Wiener Library, London.
14. *Jüdische Rundschau,* February 1, 1924; Rheins, "German Jewish Patriotism," 63–68.
15. *Jüdische Rundschau,* February 3, 1928.

themselves, but they became downright dangerous when they fostered anti-Semitic responses, as Naumann and his supporters were certain they did. German Jews of uncertain commitment were only too easily turned into shirkers and leftist revolutionaries, as events during and after the World War had demonstrated. Half-hearted Germans with their pacifist plays, discordant music, and leftist tirades degraded everything sacred to the German soul. In the words of Naumann's newspaper: "A single Tucholsky breeds millions of anti-Semites."[16]

Solidarity with the Eastern Jews was identified as the most conspicuous sin of the "fifty-percenters," whose split allegiances desensitized them to the damage the newcomers did to Germany and to the German Jews. The Eastern Jews gravitated to "communist, syndicalist, Jewish-nationalist, or other organizations that stand in opposition to everything German."[17] Using underhanded tactics, they took advantage of runaway inflation to buy property and bonds from desperate owners for a fraction of their real value. Such practices precipitated the November, 1923, riots in Berlin, and insofar as foreign Jews were their victims, they had it coming to them. But since rioters seldom made fine distinctions, German Jews were duty-bound to protect their own best interests by striking out at the foreign interlopers whenever the police were not present to do so themselves.[18] Bavaria's laudable expulsions of Eastern Jews put the matter in sharpest relief; only prejudice in favor of foreign coreligionists could justify excluding these shady elements from the general ban on immigration at a time when Germans could scarcely provide for their own needs.[19] Only if German Jews rejected the newcomers as decisively as did the rest of the nation would they be worthy to be called Germans.

Next to the Eastern Jews on Naumann's index was Zionism. It, too, produced Judeophobia by promoting the idea of German-Jewish racial incompatibility, but its sins were minor compared to those of the "in-betweeners" who effectively endorsed Zionism by cooperating with such agencies as the Keren Hayesod and the enlarged Jewish Agency and by working to achieve a united front with the Zionists.[20] Worse still, their lukewarmness alienated Jewish youth and left it fair game for eager Zionist recruiters. The hard line on

16. Max Naumann, "Dennoch!" *Mitteilungsblatt des Verbandes nationaldeutscher Juden,* No. 5 (1923), 1–3; *ibid.,* No. 2 (1922), 3 (quotation).
17. *Ibid.,* No. 2 (1922), 2.
18. *Ibid.,* No. 5 (1923), Beilage; *Jüdische Rundschau,* December 22, 1922.
19. *Jüdische Rundschau,* January 18, 1924.
20. Max Naumann, "Zionismus und Alljudentum," *Deutsche Allgemeine Zeitung,* August 7, 1923. When leaders of the Berlin Jewish Community officially received Chaim Weitzmann during his visit to the capital in 1925, Naumann excoriated their action as "a slap in the face of

Zionism that Naumann advocated was taken up by his followers in Breslau, who in 1924 reserved space in local newspapers next to Keren Hayesod advertisements for a film about Palestine, which they urged everyone to boycott because it was Zionist propaganda. They further succeeded in persuading the owner of the movie house to cancel a second showing of the film on patriotic grounds by arguing that the money it would raise was destined to leave Germany and enrich an English-held land.[21] Two years later the Naumannites sponsored lectures by an ex-Zionist from Austria, Robert Peiper, who toured Germany to tell "The Truth about Palestine."[22]

Naumann professed a grudging respect for genuine Zionists who practiced what they preached and went to live in Palestine. After all, if they wanted to march backward into the ghetto, that was their business. But they were a minority. The greatest part of the so-called Zionists were mere Jewish nationalists who used the immense practical difficulties of emigration to excuse their remaining in Germany. They performed their national duties, however unenthusiastically, and thought this earned them the rights of citizenship. A few had the audacity to accept high offices in the German government, handing more free ammunition to the racists, who regularly held forth on the theme of "foreign domination of Germany." Naumann advised the Zionists voluntarily to apply for the status of a national minority, under which they would perform the duties of citizens but refrain from planning for Germany's future. Failure to do so, he warned, would almost certainly lead to its being imposed upon them from hostile sources or, worse yet, to pogroms.[23]

Partiality, then, to Eastern Jews and Zionists was to be avoided, as was any other act that might be interpreted as the promotion of their own special interests by the Jews. Hence Naumann underlined the importance of supporting political parties without regard for their stand on anti-Semitism. Of course, no Jew would associate with a group that did not want him, but the mere presence of Judeophobes was no reason to boycott a party that otherwise corresponded to one's political philosophy. To fight courageously for Germany and against anti-Semitism in such a party would achieve more than all the Centralverein-style apologetics imaginable. Nor was a party's opposition to racism alone sufficient reason to merit support. Accordingly, the

---

the German people." *Verwaltungsblatt des preussischen Landesverbandes jüdischer Gemeinden,* IV (March 10, 1926), 23.

21. J. Marx, *Das deutsche Judentum und seine jüdischen Gegner,* 52; *Jüdische Rundschau,* January 25, 1924.

22. *Jüdische Rundschau,* March 26, 1926.

23. Max Naumann, *Von Zionisten und Jüdisch-nationalen* (Berlin, 1921), 26–48.

League of German Nationalist Jews professed political neutrality and advised its members to vote on German, not on Jewish grounds.[24]

Naumann claimed to have attracted members from parties ranging from the Nationalist party to the Social Democratic party. That was probably true, but the anti-Semitism of the former and the icy hostility toward the Naumannites of the latter put the overwhelming majority of league members in the Democratic and People's parties.[25] Only the youth section of the league's Munich branch gave direct evidence of far-right sentiments when it rushed to defend arch-anti-Semite General Ludendorff from a Centralverein attack in 1923, much to the surprise and embarrassment of league leaders.[26] Naumann himself was a member of the People's party, and league publications occasionally reflected that bias. One unconfirmed report had party leader Gustav Stresemann himself taking part in a league meeting late in 1921.[27] Naumann was certainly not unaware of the anti-Semitism that lurked in various corners of the People's party; in 1925 an official league inquiry was addressed to the party's central committee demanding to know what it intended to do to weed out anti-Semites. The reply was evasive, but it did reaffirm the party's official opposition to Judeophobia.[28]

For Naumann, then, anti-Semitism was no mere tool of reactionary politicians, but rather a residue of ancient prejudices, aggravated by Jews formulating policies from uniquely Jewish standpoints and giving aid and comfort to radicals, Zionists, and Eastern Jews. It was a fundamental error to think that it could be fought successfully just by countering fiction with fact. That was the Centralverein's great mistake. Alfred Peyser praised both it and the Association to Resist Anti-Semitism for their useful services in exposing racist fallacies, but he joined Naumann in underlining the need for fostering patriotic sentiments to build bridges of unity between Germans and Jews. That would have to be accomplished outside of the two organizations, given their "in-betweener" mentality.[29] And yet, both Peyser and Naumann—and

24. *Mitteilungsblatt des Verbandes nationaldeutscher Juden,* No. 1A (1924), 2.

25. Two self-professed Social Democratic Naumannites were Hermann Samter and Erich Köhrer. Samter, "Ist der Verband nationaldeutsche Juden eine rechtsstehend Organisation?" *Der nationaldeutsche Jude,* No. 2 (1930), 7; S. Rudel, "Noch einmal Naumann," *Jüdische Rundschau,* December 5, 1924, p. 697. But for the official stand of the Social Democratic party, see *Vorwärts,* July 7, 1921, March 1, 1922, September 28, 1926; Carl Eisfeld, *Jüdischer Antisemitismus und Arbeiterschaft* (Hagen, 1922), 3–30.

26. *Mitteilungsblatt des Verbandes nationaldeutscher Juden,* No. 4 (1923), Beilage.

27. *Mitteilungen des Syndikus des Centralvereins deutscher Staatsbürger jüdischen Glaubens,* III (1921), 166–67; cf. *Der nationaldeutsche Jude,* No. 5 (1925), 7.

28. *Israelitisches Familienblatt,* May 14, 1925.

29. Alfred Peyser, *Der Begriff "nationaldeutsch" in unserer Erziehungsarbeit* (Berlin, n.d.), 2; Max Naumann, *Ganz-Deutsche oder Halb-Deutsche?* (Berlin, 1921), 1–3.

presumably an undetermined number of lesser Naumannites—remained nominal Centralverein members throughout the Weimar years, and at least two members of the Centralverein's executive committee were members of the League of German Nationalist Jews.[30]

Backhanded expressions of Naumannite support notwithstanding, the Centralverein could not regard the founding of the league as anything but an affront. It swiftly warned Jews that the league was superfluous and dangerous because it sought partially to duplicate and wholly to undermine the work of the Centralverein. Its very existence cast doubts on the patriotism of the Centralverein's thousands of members, who automatically became suspect of being "fifty-percenters." The Naumannites' refusal to define Jews in a religious sense had forced them to fall back on descent, making them as *völkisch* as the Zionists. They were wrong about Centralverein softness on Zionism and downright cruel in their willingness to leave the Eastern Jews friendless and hopeless. Most important, the practical result of always putting things German before things Jewish would be to let anti-Semites dictate how Jews should think and act, since it was the racists whom Naumann wanted to appease.[31] The liberal Jewish press in Germany was virtually unanimous in concluding that the Naumannites were "Jewish anti-Semites."[32] This response no doubt betrayed the fear that any appearance of intimacy between Jews and the political right would alienate the Socialist workers, who were the most formidable bulwark against pogroms in Germany.[33]

The Centralverein must have feared that Naumann would find substantial support among German Jews, or that he would tarnish the Jewish image, or both; for it gave considerable attention to refuting his arguments, sent speakers to reply whenever he spoke, and in at least one case used its influence to prevent him from making his case before a Jewish audience.[34] The Naumannites fought back with determined propaganda, a spate of law suits brought by Naumann against a variety of Centralverein personalities, and epithets—

30. *Jüdische Rundschau,* April 24, June 12, 1925. Presumably the Naumannites on the Centralverein executive committee were Alfred Peyser and Dr. Hugo Strassmann. Klaus J. Herrmann, personal letters, December 31, 1975, and January 22, 1976.

31. *Im deutschen Reich,* XXVII (1921), 110; Ludwig Holländer, "Verband national-deutscher Juden und Central-Verein deutscher Staatsbürger jüdischen Glaubens," *ibid.,* 111–22.

32. Julius Brodnitz, "Eine Erwiderung und eine Warnung," *Israelitisches Familienblatt,* January 12, 1922; Hugo Sonnenfeld, "Naumanns Lehre," *ibid.,* February 2, 1922.

33. Fabias Schach, "Nationaldeutsche Juden," *Allgemeine Zeitung des Judentums,* LXXXVI (1922), 13–15.

34. The case involved a meeting of the National League of Jewish Frontline Veterans. Paul Nathan, "Eine Antwort an Herrn Dr. Max Naumann," *Central-Verein Zeitung,* May 18, 1922; *ibid.,* June 15, 1922.

the "Central Association of the Friends of the Ghetto" was made up of "sniffers after anti-Semites."[35] The Zionists, not content to malign Naumann in print as a "mental case," occasionally visited league meetings in force to monopolize the discussion periods and to assure that they ended either in screaming free-for-alls, or, at the very least, in hearty renditions of the "Hatikvah."[36] For their part, the anti-Semites, far from being impressed by the patriotism of the League of German Nationalist Jews, alternated between using league propaganda to reinforce their own attacks upon Eastern Jews and commenting snidely on the Naumannites' Jewish talent for play-acting.[37]

Alone among the groups opposed to Naumann, the liberal Jews were prepared to make concessions to his league. In drawing up their list of candidates for the first elections to choose delegates to the Chamber of Deputies of the Prussian Provincial Association of Jewish Communities in 1925, the liberals agreed to include the names of two league members, Alfred Peyser and Arthur Eisenhardt, in return for which the league consented to support that list on the basis of a common aversion to Zionism.[38] The liberals must have known that this action was certain to arouse dissension in their own ranks, as indeed it did, with the Breslau Centralverein local being particularly vociferous in its complaints.[39] And yet, the liabilities seemed to be far outweighed by the advantages: the Naumannites were kept from putting up their own rival list of candidates while whatever votes they commanded went to the liberals; the liberals' patriotic and anti-Zionist credentials were given added weight; and the public spectacle of further intra-Jewish squabbling was partially averted. Peyser was elected outright, whereas Eisenhardt had to settle for alternate delegate status. Upon the death of another liberal deputy in September, 1925, he took a place in the chamber in his own right.[40]

The combination of fierce counterpropaganda and judicious concessions succeeded in containing the League of German Nationalist Jews. Although small bands of militant Naumannites operated in several of the larger com-

---

35. *Jüdische Rundschau,* June 12, 1925; *Central-Verein Zeitung,* February 8, 1923; *ibid.,* October 24, 1930; *Der nationaldeutsche Jude,* No. 11/12 (1926), 2.
36. *Jüdische Rundschau,* February 1, 1924; *ibid.,* November 28, 1924; *Israelitisches Familienblatt,* February 7, 1924.
37. *Mitteilungen des Syndikus des Centralvereins deutscher Staatsbürger jüdischen Glaubens,* III (1921), 164–68; *Jüdische Rundschau,* April 3, 1925; *Israelitisches Familienblatt,* June 22, 1922.
38. *Jüdische Rundschau,* October 31, 1924; *ibid.,* March 10, 1925; *ibid.,* March 27, 1925.
39. *Ibid.,* April 24, 1925; *ibid.,* November 28, 1924. See also *ibid.,* May 22, 1925; *Israelitisches Familienblatt,* April 28, 1921.
40. *Jüdische Rundschau,* September 18, 1925.

munities, especially in cities like Breslau and Munich with significant conservative and/or Eastern Jewish populations, some major Jewish communities had no league chapter at all, or only a nominal one. When Naumann came to Hamburg in 1922, for example, the fierce opposition of Centralverein and religious leaders prevented him from founding a local branch of the league there. Indeed, there never was such a branch in Hamburg.[41] The league's "German List" of candidates for the Berlin Jewish Community's representative assembly elections in 1930 drew fewer than 1,400 votes, less than 2 percent of the total votes cast and too few to elect even a single representative.[42] Nor did the league newsletter ever exceed a circulation of about 6,000. Before the end of 1925 the Centralverein was able to publish one last systematic criticism of league policies and to declare that it would waste no more energy to refute them.[43]

Naumann and his league were all but forgotten during the second half of the twenties, only to gain renewed notoriety during the years of National Socialism's rise to power. In 1932 Naumann published a series of newspaper and pamphlet essays that were addressed directly to the issues of Nazi anti-Semitism and the proper Jewish response to it. He minimized the importance of Hitler's Judeophobia and maximized the great services that the Nazis, and perhaps only the Nazis, could perform. Hitler was portrayed as a political genius who had outgrown the anti-Semitism that a few of his followers continued to push. Their racialist comments were but "background noise" that must not obscure the idealistic essence of National Socialism. Failure to perceive that essence exacerbated mutual hatreds and made it hard for Hitler to keep his followers in line. Patriotic Jews should join non-Nazi nationalist organizations that might help strengthen Hitler's moderate hand and seek thereby to establish common ground on which ultimately both Nazis and Jews might stand. For the first time Naumann dwelt on the un-German evils of Social Democratic Marxism, which he identified as an increasingly popular creed among "in-betweeners," contrasting it with true German socialism, which brought all Germans together for cooperative, patriotic work. Only the absence of precise economic and political proposals in the Nazi program came in for serious, but passing, criticism in Naumann's analysis.[44] It is virtually

41. Löwenberg, "Mein Leben," 49; *Israelitisches Familienblatt,* June 15, 1922.
42. Max Naumann, "Keine Leichenrede," *Der nationaldeutsche Jude,* No. 12 (1930), 1–2.
43. J. Marx, *Das deutsche Judentum und seine jüdischen Gegner,* 1–59; *Central-Verein Zeitung,* October 2, 1925.
44. Max Naumann, *Sozialismus, Nationalsozialismus und nationaldeutsches Judentum* (n.p., 1932), 5–14; *Jüdische Rundschau,* August 5, 1932.

certain that he and his disciples were kept from following the rest of Germany's middle-class conservatives into outright support for National Socialism only by its persistent anti-Semitism. Shortly before Weimar Germany's last free elections, held on March 5, 1933, Naumann endorsed the German Nationalist People's party, then allied with the Nazis.[45] No doubt he assumed that the National Socialist wave was unstoppable and that the Nationalists alone would be in a position to moderate its impact.

It is doubtful that many Jews took Naumann's advice seriously in those last months of the Weimar Republic. Among those who did were right-wing members of the German Jewish youth organization Kameraden. Alarmed by the growth of Marxist sentiments in that organization, they contributed to its trifurcation in May, 1932, into two rival leftist groups and the small (400-member) conservative nationalist "Black Squad" (Schwarzes Fähnlein), which sought to reaffirm Jewish membership in German society with a romantic glorification of medieval Teutonic military values. A similar path was taken by the young Jewish theologian Hans-Joachim Schoeps, who worked with the State party until it was outlawed by the Nazis early in 1933, when he established the 150-member "German Vanguard—German Jewish Followers" (Deutscher Vortrupp, Gefolgschaft deutscher Juden) to gather up those young Jews who recognized the fallacies of liberalism and were willing to adopt soldierly virtues. Early in April, 1933, these two youth groups joined with the League of German Nationalist Jews and the National League of Jewish Frontline Veterans to form a short-lived "Action Committee of Jewish Germans" that, it was hoped, would present a credible negotiating partner to the Nazis in formulating a new political and social status for the Jews. Their attempts to find an honorable place for Jews in the Third Reich must appear pathetic now, but at the time it did not seem unreasonable to suppose that the only practical hope for them lay in cooperation with the Nazi state, especially when National Socialist statements that culminated in the Nuremberg Laws of 1935 implied a secure place for German Jews as tolerated aliens. But by the end of 1935 their organizations had been banned and their leaders were being pitilessly badgered. Most of their members were to be exterminated by the Nazis during World War II. Naumann, after being mishandled by Nazi thugs, died of cancer in Berlin in May, 1939, and so was spared the ultimate disillusionment of the Final Solution.[46]

45. *Jewish Daily Bulletin*, February 24, 1933.

46. Hans-Joachim Schoeps, *Wir deutschen Juden* (Berlin, 1934), 28–33; Hans-Joachim Schoeps, *Die letzten dreissig Jahre* (Stuttgart, 1956), 86–101; Dunker, *Der Reichsbund*

Neither its small following nor its tragic end should obscure the significance of the League of German Nationalist Jews. Its very existence increased liberal reluctance to make concessions to Zionism. It did not require an aversion to Jewish nationalism to suspect that such concessions might alienate enough Jews to weaken the broad liberal coalition. Such was the reasoning that led to the coopting of Naumannite candidates in the 1924 Jewish elections in Prussia. And it is hard to escape the impression that few liberals needed much urging; the liberal cheers that greeted Alfred Peyser's nationalistic speeches before the Prussian Provincial Association of Jewish Communities were not feigned.[47] Less tangible was the influence, direct and indirect, that the Naumannites exerted on their coreligionists after the Nazis seized power. What is certain is that thousands of German Jews were prepared to leave Germany only as a last resort and that, given the realities of the Third Reich in its early years, Naumann's analysis seemed to offer some hope of eventual Nazi-Jewish understanding. His tragic failure to achieve a compromise with the Nazis took on added dimension as it became clear that chauvinism had blinded thousands of Jews to any alternative to life as Germans in Germany.

---

jüdischer Frontsoldaten, 131–31a; Herrmann, *Das dritte Reich*, 25–27, 74–80. An excellent history of the two right-wing Jewish youth groups is provided in Rheins, "German Jewish Patriotism," 102–90.

47. *Verwaltungsblatt des preussischen Landesverbandes jüdischer Gemeinden*, X (September 28, 1932), 22.

The Divisive Landscape of German Jewry

The essential liberalism of most German Jews caused them to shun the rival radicalisms of Zionism and Germanic superpatriotism. Together the two extremist nationalisms held the loyalty of no more than 10 percent of the Jews. That this widespread liberal consensus could not be translated into a unified organization that would have represented the interests of all the German Jews suggests that religious differences and regional particularisms were at least as potent issues as the liberal-Zionist controversy. Orthodox Jews feared the domination of Liberal Judaism, whereas Jews of all persuasions in the smaller German states dreaded the rule of Prussian Jews, who outnumbered all of them put together. Their concerns about majority rule, coupled with Zionist efforts to shift Jewish communal life from a religious to a national basis, blocked repeated efforts at establishing Jewish organizational unity in Weimar Germany.

These efforts were not innovations of the Weimar years. As Professor Toury has shown, they had important antecedents in the decades before the World War.[1] At the turn of the century, leaders of the Centralverein and of the Alliance of German Jewish Communities (Deutsch-Israelitischer Gemeindebund), a body of notables appointed by the governing boards of the Jewish communities, attempted to elevate the alliance to the status of a central organization of German Jews that would secure their public legal status by gaining the rights of a "legal person." The alliance won that legal status in 1898, but fears of injecting disruptive religious and political debates into peaceful alliance relationships prompted it to assign the task of unifying German Jewry to a new organization, the Federation of German Jews (Verband der deutschen Juden). The federation, founded in 1904, differed from the alliance in that it was made up of representatives of large Jewish organizations (including the Centralverein and the alliance) and of individual Jewish dignitaries, in

---

1. Jacob Toury, "Organizational Problems of German Jewry: Steps towards the Establishment of a Central Organization (1893–1920)," *Leo Baeck Institute Yearbook*, XIII (1968), 57–79.

addition to the usual communal deputations. It performed valuable services in supplementing the Centralverein's struggle against official and unofficial anti-Semitism, but it never managed to secure the unqualified recognition of its intended constituency. Separatist Orthodox Jews could not be won over to federation membership at all, whereas Jewish groups that did belong regularly approached government officials directly without any regard for the federation's claims to act as official spokesman in all Jewish affairs.[2] Only in the administration of charity was genuine unity established, and that under the impact of the First World War. The Central Welfare Office of the German Jews (Zentralwohlfahrtsstelle der deutschen Juden) was founded in 1917 to coordinate the activities of all Jewish charities in Germany. It performed its tasks creditably throughout the Weimar years, and in 1926 the German government formally recognized it as the official agency for Jewish charitable activities.[3] Welfare work excepted, German Jews were no closer to organizational unity at the beginning of the Weimar period than they had been twenty years before.

Germany's difficult postwar situation gave new cogency to the old arguments for a unified organization of all the Jews. More than ever before, small Jewish communities stood on the brink of financial ruin as the result of inflation and the migration of wage-earning, tax-paying members to the large urban centers. Some regularized scheme of subventions, raised by an institution with the authority to draw funds from the wealthier communities, was essential to sustain Judaism in the villages and small towns of Germany. Moreover, article 137 of the new Weimar Constitution granted full equal rights of association to all religious communities for purposes of securing official recognition and badly needed state aid.[4] Finally, the largely propagandistic Zionist call for a "Jewish congress," although it had been successfully resisted by the liberal majority, had dramatized a certain ground swell of popular sentiment for organizational unity and placed the onus for delaying it on the anti-Zionist establishment.[5] With all of these considerations in mind, the

2. Schorsch, *Jewish Reactions to German Anti-Semitism*, 149–77. On the Federation of German Jews, see Marjorie Lamberti, *Jewish Activism in Imperial Germany: The Struggle for Civil Equality* (New Haven and London, 1978), 53–54, 87, 141–43; Marjorie Lamberti, "The Attempt to Form a Jewish Bloc: Jewish Notables and Politics in Wilhelmian Germany," *Central European History*, III (1970), 73–93.

3. Giora Lotan, "The Zentralwohlfahrtsstelle," *Leo Baeck Institute Yearbook*, IV (1959), 185–207.

4. Max Kollenscher, "Der Preussische Landesverband Jüdischer Gemeinden," *Jüdische Rundschau*, November 21, 1924; Herzfeld, "Lebenserinnerungen," 258; Toury, "Organizational Problems of German Jewry," 88–90.

5. See above, pp. 147–48.

Alliance of German Jewish Communities for the first time moved decisively to seize the initiative for Jewish unity. In doing so it brushed aside attempts by the Federation of German Jews to fill the need for Jewish unity with yet a third organization, constructed, like the federation, out of both religious and secular Jewish bodies. The federation's failure to secure the support of the Jewish communities prompted it to step aside early in 1921 and to dissolve itself a year later.[6]

The alliance assigned the task of altering its statutes so as to reconstitute itself as a body representing all German Jews to the Berlin legal historian, Ismar Freund, instructing him to submit the document to the next alliance convention on February 29, 1920. Freund's draft instrument attempted to satisfy both democratic and oligarchical expectations by proposing the creation of a representative assembly elected by the direct and equal suffrage of all adult German Jews, and a council consisting of appointed representatives of the Jewish communities and of organizations of Hebrew religious leaders.[7] In fact, it satisfied only the small communities that desperately yearned for subventions. The large Jewish communities hesitated to endorse Freund's plan, fearing that the democratically elected assembly might appropriate excessive sums of money that would have to be supplied by the more nearly solvent urban Jews.[8] Orthodox Jews, and especially those who belonged to separatist congregations, expressed concern that the democratic rule of liberal majorities would cause "religious convictions to become superficial, certain religious principles to be disavowed, and the independent conduct of affairs to be impaired." They expressed horror that funds drawn from Orthodox sources might be used by a pan-Jewish organization to help support Liberal and Reform institutions. The election of representatives by women as well as men likewise went against the Orthodox grain.[9] Separatist Orthodoxy's response was to establish in 1920 its own national confederation, the Union of Orthodox Jewish Communities of Germany (Bund gesetztreuer jüdischer Gemeinden Deutschlands), seated in Halberstadt.

For the Zionists, in contrast, Freund's draft was not nearly democratic enough. They swiftly rejected it as a sellout to reactionary communal leaders.[10] Shortly thereafter the Jewish nationalists submitted a rival version that

6. *Jüdische Rundschau,* May 26, 1922.
7. Ismar Freund, "Gesamtorganisation des deutschen Judentums," *Allgemeine Zeitung des Judentums,* LXXXIV (1920), 85–88, 97–100. The draft proposal is reproduced on pp. 99–100.
8. *Israelitisches Familienblatt,* July 22, 1920; *ibid.,* December 14, 1920.
9. *Der Israelit,* May 19, 1921 (quotation); *ibid.,* March 3, 1921.
10. *Jüdische Rundschau,* February 27, 1920.

did away with the "undemocratic" council, provided for proportional representation of the parties running candidates for election to the representative assembly, and required the elimination of undemocratic procedures (such as suffrage restrictions on alien Jews and winner-take-all elections) in all Jewish communities aspiring to membership in the new body.[11] Freund replied, quite logically, that the changes in communal statutes demanded by the Zionists would require the alteration of various state laws, a process that would take years to complete. There was no practical alternative to constituting the unified organization out of the existing religious communities. Although he did not say so, he implied that Zionism's demands for elimination of the council, where the power of the Jewish religious communities was centered, betrayed its objective of transforming the Jews from a confessional body into a nationalistic clan.[12] By taking an intransigent attitude on the adoption of democratic principles where they were not entirely appropriate and at a time when they could not be immediately realized, the Zionists dealt a staggering blow to Freund's plan for a pan-Jewish organization. The big Jewish communities might have been appeased with grants of special fiscal powers in the council. Orthodox Jews who belonged to unitary Jewish communities probably could have been pacified by carefully isolating affairs of worship and doctrine into separate Orthodox and Liberal committees, as had been done by some of the larger communities. But the Zionist demands were, by their very nature, nonnegotiable; because they could not be accepted, they constituted a virtual veto of a unified Jewish organization built on the religious communities.[13] Separatist Orthodoxy was equally intransigent, but a central organization that would have included all but this small and declining sect was by no means out of the question.

Every bit as devastating to the fate of Freund's blueprint for a united Jewish organization as the Zionist response was the attitude of the south German Jews, and especially those of Bavaria, where the majority of them lived. The Bavarian Jews, traditionally jealous of their local identity and suspicious of their north German coreligionists, whom they regarded as excessively disputatious and dogmatic, reacted sensitively to the prospect of "Prussian domination." (More than 70 percent of all German Jews lived in Prussia; only about 9 percent of them made their homes in Bavaria.) On April 20, 1920,

11. Siegbert Stein, "Die Entwürfe für die Gesamtorganisation des deutschen Judentums," *ibid.*, April 23, 1920.
12. Ismar Freund, "Der Stand der Gesamtorganisation," *Israelitisches Familienblatt*, May 13, 1920.
13. *Cf.* Toury, "Organizational Problems of German Jewry," 89.

only a few weeks after Freund unveiled his plan to convert the Alliance of German Jewish Communities into a unified Jewish organization, representatives of the Bavarian Hebrew communities met in Nuremberg to establish their own provincial organization, the Association of Bavarian Jewish Communities (Verband Bayerischer Israelitischer Gemeinden).[14] Whether this action was inspired primarily by impatience to arrange aid for struggling Bavarian Jewish communities, by pessimism over the chances of establishing a national organization, or by determination to frustrate Freund's version of such an organization is not certain. It may, however, be significant that article 8 of the proposed constitution for the association called for the "promotion of a German general organization with regard to the provincial organizations," and that even that endorsement of an approach very different from Freund's was demoted to an appendix in the final version of the document.[15] Clearly the sentiment in Bavaria favored a national federation of provincial Jewish associations insofar as it contemplated any organizational unity at all.[16] The establishment of the Bavarian provincial association at the very moment when Freund's draft constitution for a national organization was being discussed and debated could only have had a chilling effect on the chances for its adoption.

Hence, although the Alliance of German Jewish Communities gamely adopted the substance of Freund's proposals and declared itself the national organization of German Jews at a meeting held in Berlin on January 23, 1921, the combined opposition of Zionists, south German Jews, and some Orthodox factions rendered it a stillbirth.[17] By the end of that year it was clear that the alliance would never win governmental recognition in the face of their disapprobation. The alliance, its stature greatly diminished, lingered on for years with little more to do than administer a few Jewish charitable and educational institutions.[18]

There was little choice left for Prussian Jews but to follow Bavaria's lead and form their own provincial association. The predicament of their small,

14. Provincial Jewish associations already existed by law in several of the German states, including Baden, Württemberg, Oldenburg, and Mecklenburg-Schwerin. *Israelitisches Familienblatt*, June 22, 1922.

15. Neumeyer, "Erinnerungen," 137–51. Neumeyer, a Munich attorney and chairman of his Jewish community, was the author of the draft constitution and was chosen first president of the association.

16. Hermann Badt, "Demokratie gegen 'liberale' Reaktion," *Jüdische Rundschau*, January 28, 1925.

17. *Israelitisches Familienblatt*, January 27, 1921.

18. Heinz Caspari, "Der Deutsch-Israelitische Gemeindebund," *ibid.*, May 19, 1932.

impecunious communities was acute and growing. Ismar Freund himself acknowledged the need for a provincial body to help them and, perhaps, to provide a new approach to the problem of unity.[19] At the instance of the Berlin Jewish Community, a meeting of community representatives from all over Prussia, held on June 25, 1922, created the Prussian Provincial Association of Jewish Communities (Preussischer Landesverband jüdischer Gemeinden). Its constitution closely resembled Freund's draft instrument for the abortive national organization.[20] This time the Zionists put up only minimal opposition. They, too, were not insensitive to the financial plight of the small communities, and they apparently chose to work for the democratization of the association from within, rationalizing their inconsistency by noting that the new organization made no pretense of representing all the German Jews.[21] Separatist Orthodoxy, intransigent as ever, founded its own Prussian Provincial Association of Orthodox Congregations (Preussischer Landesverband gesetztreuer Synagogengemeinden) on June 21, 1922, in order to compete for state aid on an equal footing with its rivals.[22] Its membership came to number approximately 130 communities, compared to the 722 communities that had joined the larger association by 1929.[23]

The establishment of provincial associations of Jews in virtually all the German states was not necessarily meant to wreck every prospect for organizational unity. And yet, the existence of the state bodies could not help but remove much of the immediacy from arguments for pan-Jewish union. The Weimar Constitution assigned religious affairs to the individual states, which allowed the provincial Jewish organizations to obtain government subsidies directly from their state administrations. When Ismar Freund, still working nominally under the auspices of the Alliance of German Jewish Communities, attempted to revive interest in his earlier plan for a national organization, he

19. Ismar Freund, "Organisation des preussischen Judentums," *ibid.*, June 15, 1922.
20. H. Stern, *Warum hassen sie uns eigentlich?* 135–37; Kurt Wilhelm, "The Jewish Community in the Post-Emancipation Period," *Leo Baeck Institute Yearbook*, II (1957), 66–67. A recently completed history of the Prussian Provincial Association of Jewish Communities by its last secretary, Max Birnbaum, was not available for my perusal. It is tentatively scheduled for publication by J. C. B. Mohr (Tübingen) in the series "Schriftenreihe wissenschaftlicher Arbeiten des Leo Baeck Instituts" under the title *Staat und Synagoge: Eine Geschichte des Preussischen Landesverbandes jüdischer Gemeinden*.
21. Sandler, "Erinnerungen," II, 36; Kollenscher, "Der Preussische Landesverband," *Jüdische Rundschau*, November 21, 1924.
22. *Der Israelit*, June 22, 1922.
23. Rabbi E. Munk to Moritz Sobernheim, November 13, 1929, in Nachlass Moritz Sobernheim, 1287/350128; "Stenographischer Bericht der vierten Verbandstagung des Preussischen Landesverbandes jüdischer Gemeinden," *Verwaltungsblatt des preussischen Landesverbandes jüdischer Gemeinden*, VII (February 15, 1929), 6.

quickly ran headlong into a united front of the south German associations (Bavaria, Baden, and Württemberg) demanding a federation of the provincial organizations rather than a unitary association of Jewish individuals or communities. The southerners also insisted upon limiting Prussia's role in such a way as to prevent its dictating policies for the whole of German Jewry. A draft constitution reflecting these demands, to which Freund resigned himself, was rejected by the Prussian Provincial Association late in 1926. Both the Zionist minority and most of the liberal majority in its representative assembly objected to the limits placed on Prussia's voting power in the proposed organization, denouncing them as undemocratic.[24] Throughout all of the negotiations leading up to this vote, the separatist Orthodoxy maintained its distance, sending no active plenipotentiaries but rather mere observers who, according to one report, carped endlessly on religious practices that deviated from the ultra-Orthodox point of view.[25]

Although a failure, this 1926 effort represented a turning point in the movement toward Jewish union. The Prussian negotiators had acquiesced in the federative approach to unity, and their association had earnestly debated a draft proposal based on the federal principle. No one seriously attempted to substitute another approach, however much he may have wanted to. From this point on, any further hopes for a national organization rested on the willingness of one or both sides to compromise on the issue of granting representation to the provincial associations according to their size alone or according to some formula that would greatly mitigate Prussia's power. Early in 1927 the south German provincial associations—Bavaria, Baden, and Württemberg—joined with that of Hesse to form a working group to present a common front in future negotiations for a national union.[26] At two major negotiation sessions held in Nuremberg in March, 1928, and in Cologne three months later, for the purpose of drawing up yet another draft constitution, the south Germans allied with other small provincial associations to demand that real power be centered in a council on which every association would have at least one representative. The Prussians noted that some of the associations represented only a few thousand Jews and advocated their collective representation by only one delegate. The south Germans attempted to dilute

24. *Bayerische Israelitische Gemeindezeitung*, II (1926), 97–100, 310.

25. *Ibid.*, III (1927), 195–98; Szanto, "Im Dienste der Gemeinde," 28–29.

26. Fritz Silber, "Die Tagung des Bayerischen Landesverbandes," *Israelitisches Familienblatt*, March 24, 1927. The extent of south German Jewish unity was most impressive. Even the Bavarian Zionists broke with their north German colleagues to endorse the federative principle. *Bayerische Israelitische Gemeindezeitung*, III (1927), 198.

Prussian influence still further by incorporating into the council a number of so-called "upholders of culture" (*Kulturträger*), including rabbis, teachers, and representatives of Jewish welfare and religious institutions.

Their efforts paid off handsomely. Not only did they get their way on the council when the final draft was drawn up at the Cologne conference, but they also managed to keep the legislative body of the proposed organization, the "national convention," from playing a significant role. It was to meet only once every three years and to consist only partly of representatives of the democratically chosen provincial assemblies; in states without democratically elected assemblies, there were to be direct elections to the national convention according to proportional representation. The rest of the delegates were to be *Kulturträger* appointed by the council. The National Federation of German Jews (Reichsverband der deutschen Juden), as the organization was to be called, was to come into being on or after the first day of 1929, provided that both the Prussian and Bavarian provincial associations had approved its constitution.[27]

Reflecting as it did primarily the particularistic concerns of the south German Jews, the constitution's fate depended entirely on the action of the Prussian Association of German Jewish Communities. At the meeting of its representative assembly in Berlin on February 3–4, 1929, Zionist delegates were not alone in raking the draft constitution over the coals for its undemocratic features. Liberal leaders made no attempt to defend those aspects of the document but instead argued that this was the best that could be done and probably represented the last opportunity to secure a national Jewish organization for the foreseeable future. In the end the constitution was defeated by a vote of forty-six to forty-five, with seven abstentions. The cause of German Jewish unity went down for the last time in the Weimar Republic by the margin of one vote.[28]

The talks that led up to this abortive attempt were not entirely fruitless, however. At the Cologne meeting of June, 1928, the negotiators agreed to es-

27. "Niederschrift über die Sitzung der Vertreter der Landesverbände und des D.I.G.B. zur Beratung über die Gründung einer Reichsorganisation in Nürnberg am 4. März 1928," 9–12, and "Niederschrift über die Sitzung der Vertreter der Landesverbände und des D.I.G.B. zur Beratung über die Gründung einer Reichsorganisation in Köln/Rh. am 3. Juni 1928," 2–5, both in Preussischer Landesverband Jüdischer Gemeinden Collection, Wiener Library.

28. "Stenographischer Bericht der fünften Verbandstagung des Preussischen Landesverbandes jüdischer Gemeinden," *Verwaltungsblatt des preussischen Landesverbandes jüdischer Gemeinden*, VII (May 30, 1929), 32–44; Max Kollenscher, "Der Reichsverband der deutschen Juden," *Gemeindeblatt der Jüdischen Gemeinde zu Berlin*, XIX (1929), 103–104; Heinrich Stern, "Zur Frage des Reichsverbandes der deutschen Juden," *ibid.*, 105–106.

tablish a Working Group of the Jewish Provincial Associations (Arbeitsgemeinschaft der jüdischen Landesverbände) that was to take on some of the functions of a formal national organization until one was finally approved. The Working Group, which met for the first time in Berlin on September 2, 1928, acted as an all-Jewish council on such matters as education, kosher slaughter, and support for various Jewish institutions.[29] In January, 1932, it adopted the name National Representation of the German Jews (Reichsvertretung der deutschen Juden) as one more suited to a body having the additional task of representing Jewish interests to the national government.[30] This was the direct forerunner of the more broadly based organization of the same name that was founded in September, 1933, as the official national Jewish organization in Nazi Germany. It had required the full force of the totalitarian state to overcome the outward manifestations of German Jewry's internal differences.

Both mutual recriminations and renewed efforts at compromise followed the 1929 collapse of plans for a federation of Jewish provincial bodies. The south Germans complained of Prussian unreliability and disunity, whereas the north Germans castigated the southerners for their antidemocratic particularism. And yet, before the end of the following year the Prussian Association had called together a mixed discussion commission of fifteen members that produced a new draft proposal in February, 1932. Three months later representatives of the various provincial bodies met once again, this time in Frankfurt-am-Main, to debate the proposal's bicameral solution to the differences between Prussia and the smaller states. Neither this meeting nor a subsequent one in Baden-Baden later that month produced any progress.[31]

The provincial Jewish associations, in which some had seen the building blocks of Jewish organizational unity, had been made into its chief impediment. They did, however, serve more limited purposes. They had been called into being primarily to help the smaller Jewish communities survive their economic crises. Hence they acted as official conduits for state aid granted to recognized religious bodies by the state governments of Germany. For example, the Prussian Provincial Association secured an average yearly appropriation

---

29. "Niederschrift über die Sitzung der Arbeitsgemeinschaft der jüdischen Landesverbände des deutschen Reiches am Sonntag, den 2. September 1928," in Preussischer Landesverband Jüdischer Gemeinden Collection.

30. *Jüdisch-liberale Zeitung,* XII (March 1, 1933), 1.

31. Mimeographed reports from Liberal deputies to the Prussian Provincial Association of Jewish Communities, June–August, 1932, in Preussischer Landesverband Jüdischer Gemeinden Collection; *Israelitisches Familienblatt,* May 26, 1932.

of 286,000 marks from the Prussian Diet between 1926 and 1932, which it distributed to approximately 250 of its neediest communities.[32] The rival separatist Orthodox association likewise received government financial assistance, although in lesser quantities commensurate with its smaller membership. A vexing problem for both was the double membership held by sixty or so communities that hoped to draw subventions from each of the associations, but neither dared expel the offenders for fear of jeopardizing its recognition by the Prussian Ministry of Culture.[33] The dramatic cut in these Prussian subventions (from 330,000 to 150,000 marks) in the austerity budget of 1932 came as a devastating blow to all concerned.[34] Similar subventions were provided by the other German states, except in Braunschweig and Thuringia, where there were no Jewish provincial associations,[35] and in Hesse, where radical Social Democrats, voting against subventions for all religious groups, and the Catholic Center party cast the decisive votes against appropriations for the Jews.[36]

Bavarian authorities were somewhat less generous than the Prussians. State aid to the Association of Bavarian Jewish Communities averaged 60,000 marks after 1923, or 1.22 marks per Jewish inhabitant.[37] In Prussia the figure averaged 1.41 marks. The Bavarian Jews grumbled that their appropriations amounted to less than one-third of the government's subvention to Roman

32. Erich Spinaza, "Der Preussische Landesverband jüdischer Gemeinden," *Israelitisches Familienblatt*, July 28, 1932. Subventions were delayed by austerity measures taken during the inflationary crisis and, in 1924, by the premature dissolution of the Prussian Diet. The first subvention was approved late in 1925 after some vacillation on the part of the Social Democrats and controversy over the size of the allotment. Prussian Provincial Association of Jewish Communities to Prussian Diet, August 27, 1925, and Prussian Provincial Association of Jewish Communities to SPD delegation in the Prussian Diet, December 1, 1925, both in Ismar Freund Collection, Leo Baeck Institute Archives, New York, 1258/4169; *Israelitisches Familienblatt*, December 24, 1925.

33. "Stenographischer Bericht der sechsten Verbandstagung des Preussischen Landesverbandes jüdischer Gemeinden," *Verwaltungsblatt des preussischen Landesverbandes jüdischer Gemeinden*, VIII (July 1, 1930), 8.

34. "Stenographischer Bericht der Verbandstagung des Preussischen Landesverbandes jüdischer Gemeinden," *ibid.*, X (1932), 2–9.

35. *Jüdische Rundschau*, August 21, 1928. In Thuringia, interminable bickering between the old Jewish corporate bodies, and especially between the largest community, Eisenach, and the rest of the Thuringian Jews over the scope of action and competence of a provincial association lay at the bottom of the situation. Fritz Noak, "Gemeindeverbände," *ibid.*, November 17, 1922; *ibid.*, August 26, 1932.

36. Ludwig Kronenberger, "Gleiches Recht für Alle!" *Israelitisches Familienblatt*, March 28, 1929; *Der Israelit*, January 26, 1928; *ibid.*, March 21, 1929; *ibid.*, May 8, 1930.

37. Subventions amounting to 50,000 marks were appropriated in 1924. The figure was increased to 60,000 marks for each year from 1925 to 1928, when it was set at 70,000 marks. *Israelitisches Familienblatt*, July 16, 1925; *Jüdische Rundschau*, June 22, 1928; *Der Israelit*, July 4, 1929.

Catholics, and they were only partly mollified by association president Alfred Neumeyer's reminder that the Bavarian State had taken on the burden of financing the Church at the time of its secularization in the nineteenth century, an experience foreign to that of the Jews.[38] Similar complaints were made by Prussia's Jews, although the disparity between subventions for Jewish and Christian organizations was not as great there. Ismar Freund had a point when he noted that Prussian Jews paid around 4.5 percent of the state taxes but received less than 0.5 percent of the funds annually appropriated for all state aid to religious groups.[39]

In addition to providing subventions to needy Hebrew communities by way of the Jewish provincial associations, the states also contributed money directly to the communities to support the salaries of rabbis and teachers of Judaism in the public schools. In Prussia this aid amounted to 450,000 marks annually.[40] During the inflation year of 1923, Ismar Freund persuaded the German Reichstag to approve emergency grants for the communities, as well as loans that could be repaid at face value (which, given the rate of inflation, amounted to gifts).[41]

Some idea of how important this aid was to the Jewish communities was given by Ismar Freund in an address to the first regular meeting of the Prussian Provincial Association of Jewish Communities on June 21, 1925. He observed that of the slightly more than 900 Jewish communities in Prussia, only 63 had so much as a single rabbi, whereas more than 800 were without regular spiritual ministration:

Not even a single teacher will be found in 285 communities, [whereas] 219 communities have not one religious functionary of any kind. One hundred nine Prussian Jewish communities are without religious instruction, and more than 400 of them have no cemetery, house of worship, or other institution required of Jewish communities by tradition or religious law. These numbers plainly tell us not only that we are close to debacle, but that *Prussian Jewry stands in the midst of debacle.*

Freund noted that some of the small Jewish communities taxed their members to the hilt in order to finance needed religious services, and still it was often

38. *Bayerische Israelitische Gemeindezeitung,* IV (1928), 203.

39. "Stenographischer Bericht der dritten Verbandstagung des Preussischen Landesverbandes jüdischer Gemeinden," *Verwaltungsblatt des preussischen Landesverbandes jüdischer Gemeinden,* V (June 15, 1927), 5; "Stenographischer Bericht der sechsten Verbandstagung," *ibid.,* VIII (July 1, 1930), 7; "Stenographischer Bericht der Verbandstagung," *ibid.,* X (September 28, 1932), 16.

40. *Ibid.,* IV (September 20, 1926), 5.

41. Ismar [Freund], "Die Rettung der jüdischen Gemeinden," *Central-Verein Zeitung,* June 29, 1923; Ismar Freund, "November-Reichshilfe für die Gemeinden," *ibid.,* November 2, 1923.

not nearly enough.[42] It was not unusual for the small communities to assess taxation of 100 percent or more of the national income tax, which was at least ten times the average level in most of the large urban communities.[43] In 1931, when the tax on members of the Berlin Jewish Community was set at 11 percent of their income taxes, at least forty-eight small Prussian communities set the tax rate at 100 to 150 percent, and thirty-eight communities taxed above 150 percent.[44] In small communities such as these, government aid could make up a not inconsiderable portion of their income. For example, in seventeen small Westphalian Jewish communities having tax rates ranging from 33 to 160 percent, state subventions funneled through the Prussian Provincial Association provided for 21 percent of their total budgets and, in one case, 65 percent of the budget of a particularly hard-pressed community.[45]

In view of the financial agony of some of the small Jewish communities, and considering the limited government funds that were made available to aid them, it is all the more remarkable that the provincial associations mined so few resources among their own prosperous members. The fairly typical 1929 budget for the Prussian Provincial Association derived only 640,000 marks from its member communities, less than twice the 325,000-mark state subvention for that year and less than 2 marks for each Prussian Jew. Slightly less than half that year's budget was allotted to the impecunious communities; the rest went to educational and welfare institutions and to pay the administrative costs of the association.[46] Occasionally member communities withheld their dues to protest association policies with which they disagreed or else because they put pet projects of their own first.[47] Nor did the Bavarian association outdo itself in generosity. It had the right to tax individual Jews directly, but

42. "Stenographischer Bericht der ersten Verbandstagung des Preussischen Landesverbandes jüdischer Gemeinden," *Verwaltungsblatt des preussischen Landesverbandes jüdischer Gemeinden,* IV (March 10, 1926), 6.

43. Religious taxes were normally established by local church and synagogue authorities as a percentage of the national income tax. They were collected by government officials, who passed them on to the proper religious bodies.

44. *Gemeindeblatt der Jüdischen Gemeinde zu Berlin,* XXI (1931), 249–52; Max Birnbaum, "Die Not der jüdischen Klein- und Mittelgemeinden," *ibid.,* 337–39.

45. "Übersicht über die vorgeschlagenen Beihilfen für Synagogengemeinden: Provinz Westfalen, Regierungsbezirk Arnsberg," n.d. [*ca.* 1926] Kreis Wittgenstein, L. A. 587, Staatsarchiv, Münster.

46. *Verwaltungsblatt des preussischen Landesverbandes jüdischer Gemeinden,* VI (September 1, 1928), 7–8.

47. "Stenographischer Bericht der vierten Verbandstagung," *ibid.,* VII (February 15, 1929), 19; "Stenographischer Bericht der sechsten Verbandstagung," *ibid.,* VIII (July 1, 1930), 5–6; Stern, *Warum hassen sie uns eigentlich?,* 137–38. In 1929 unpaid dues owed to the association amounted to 100,000 marks. *Verwaltungsblatt des preussischen Landesverbandes jüdischer Gemeinden,* VII (February 15, 1929), 55.

most of the time it did so at a rate of only 3 percent.[48] No doubt this financial conservatism was dictated in large part by fears of driving Jews to resign from their communities in order to avoid paying high taxes.[49]

The provincial Jewish associations likewise represented the legal interests of their constituents before their respective state governments, and the largest of them, that in Prussia, took up the task of modernizing the antiquated laws that governed Jewish affairs there. The old law of 1847, still in force, recognized only the individual Jewish communities as legal entities and hence had discouraged the growth of any ecclesiastical concept of Jewish unity. Small wonder, then, that the Prussian state government insisted upon its revision or replacement as a prerequisite for offical recognition of the two Prussian associations of Jewish communities.[50] Moreover, other "Jewish laws" were still very much operative in areas of Prussia that had been annexed since 1847, including Hanover, Schleswig, Holstein, Hesse, Frankfurt-am-Main, and six other former states, making a total of twelve different legal systems.[51] Prussian officials frequently made it easier for the Jews by failing to enforce the letter of these anachronisms; for example, in Kassel, where ancient Hessian statutes prescribed that state officials appoint Jewish community elders, the elders were, in fact, popularly elected to responsible posts, with state approval given as a matter of formality.[52] The fact that the Prussian Association of Jewish Communities never gained full recognition from the state government did not prevent Prussian officialdom from treating it as though it did. And yet, even though de facto Jewish self-administration was widespread in Prussia, the modernization and rationalization of the laws on Jewish affairs was desirable at the very least because Jews frequently appealed to government officials to settle internal community disputes relating to the Jews' legal status. Those appeals were most numerous in matters of suffrage and disputed elections, where the old religious and political taboos clashed head-on with the new democratic spirit.

The draft of a new law governing Jewish affairs, one that represented the minimum Zionist demands and the maximum liberal concessions, was ap-

48. *Israelitisches Familienblatt,* July 14, 1921; *Bayerische Israelitische Gemeindezeitung,* VIII (1932), 118.

49. Harry Epstein, "Achtzig Jahre," *Jüdische Rundschau,* April 1, 1927.

50. Baeck, "Die jüdischen Gemeinden," 442–44; Ahron Sandler, "The Struggle for Unification," *Leo Baeck Institute Yearbook,* II (1957), 83–84.

51. Ismar Freund, "Die Revision des preussischen Judenrechts," *Gemeindeblatt der Jüdischen Gemeinde zu Berlin,* XV (1925), 122–24.

52. *Jüdische Rundschau,* September 13, 1928.

proved by the Prussian Association in June, 1928, and sent on to the Prussian Ministry of Culture. Zionist insistence on strict adherence to democratic principles showed in its clauses prohibiting tax payments, citizenship, or residency of more than two years as preconditions for suffrage in any Jewish election. It also produced the stipulation that proportional representation would be adopted upon the request of 10 percent of the voters in any Jewish community. The draft made it easy for Jews to resign from their communities in order to join separatist communities or to form their own; without such a stipulation there would have been no hope of attracting the support of separatist Orthodoxy for the document. At the same time it made heavy-handed attempts at halting the erosion of the Jewish tax base by holding each community to membership in an officially recognized Jewish provincial association and requiring a Jew who left his congregation without joining another to continue paying taxes directly to one of the Jewish provincial bodies.[53]

The separatists among Prussia's Orthodox Jews were only partially reassured by the attention given to the right of individuals to leave the majority communities. The possibility of being forced to join the large Prussian Provincial Association of Jewish Communities carried with it the prospect of having to submit to majority rule on such matters as women's suffrage and support for Zionist projects. Although it is true that the draft law envisaged the possibility of more than one officially recognized provincial association, the separatists would not rest easy until they could be certain that their own Prussian Provincial Association of Orthodox Congregations would occupy the same status as the rival organization. Taking no chances, they submitted their own version of a draft law, one that assured the absolute autonomy of the communities in matters of suffrage and organizational affiliation.[54] If Zionist accusations had any truth to them, the separatists found allies in liberal community politicians who complained secretly to the ministry about the provisions granting suffrage to aliens.[55]

The ministry's reaction to the draft was slow in coming, and it probably was not expedited by the criticism aimed at the document from important sources of Jewish opinion. When the ministry finally acted in 1931, it came down equivocally in favor of voting rights for noncitizens and foursquare

---

53. The full text of the draft is to be found in *Verwaltungsblatt des preussischen Landesverbandes jüdischer Gemeinden,* VI (September 1, 1928), 5–7.
54. *Der Israelit,* July 26, 1928; *ibid.,* September 4, 1930.
55. "Stenographischer Bericht der sechsten Verbandstagung," *Verwaltungsblatt des preussischen Landesverbandes jüdischer Gemeinden,* VIII (July 1, 1930), 57.

against compulsory membership of communities in provincial assemblies or of forced taxation of Jews who had resigned from their congregations. A government draft incorporating those principles was submitted to the majority Prussian Jewish association, which split over whether or not to bow to official pressure. Ismar Freund warned that without the means to prevent "tax-flight" and to require membership in provincial organizations, German Jewry could not survive.[56] The Zionists fundamentally agreed, and they criticized a curious clause in the ministerial draft that permitted government officials to suspend the universal suffrage requirement in "special cases." Although many liberals were resigned to accepting the government version, nothing like a clear consensus emerged early in 1932.[57] That remained the state of affairs when Franz von Papen's rape of the Prussian government on July 20, 1932, dampened the likelihood of progress toward new legislation.

The Prussian ministry's new activism of 1931–32, inspired by impatience with the Jews' bickering and their authoritarian solution to economic pressures, likewise became apparent in the Prussian province of Hanover. There parts of the hopelessly outdated statutes on Jewish affairs had been declared invalid in July, 1931, and the Prussian Ministry of Culture asked Hanover's provincial governor, Social Democrat Gustav Noske, to supervise the preparation of new legislation that would serve as a stop-gap until a new Prussian law received final approval. On January 12, 1932, Noske presided over a meeting of Jewish community representatives that discussed the specifics of such legislation. Present were observers from the Prussian ministry, the Prussian Provincial Association of Jewish Communities, and the Berlin Jewish Community, including, for the last-named, Rabbi Leo Baeck, who indirectly chided the rest of Prussian Jewry by congratulating the Hanover Jews for demonstrating admirable unity and cooperation. Final action on this matter had not been taken by May of that year, however, and presumably it met the same fate as that of the state-wide law.[58]

The failure to form a unified Jewish organization and to modernize the Prussian laws on Jewish affairs cast light upon the profound internal divisions that

---

56. "Stenographischer Bericht der Verbandstagung," *ibid.,* X (September 28, 1932), 15–16.

57. "Vorschau auf die Tagung des Preussischen Landesverbandes jüdischer Gemeinden," in Leo Wolff Collection, 4059 III. 12; Max Kollenscher, "Zum Entwurf eines neuen Judengesetzes," *Jüdische Rundschau,* November 6, 1931; *Der Israelit,* March 10, 1932.

58. Series "Hannover" 122a, XVII, No. 374a/3-146 and 80,IIe2, No. 139, Niedersächsisches Hauptstaatsarchiv, Hanover.

were a central fact of Jewish life in the Weimar Republic. But let us not attach earth-shaking significance to either the failures or the differences. In the first place, those divisions were not really unique. For years it has been common to analyze Germany's troubled past in terms of its *Zerrissenheit*—its deeply seated regional, political, religious, and other internal cleavages.[59] Seen in the context of the German experience, internal Jewish differences reflect or parallel developments in the larger society and begin to appear more typical than singular. In the second place, the failures they engendered were not particularly damaging. A national Jewish organization would have provided more symbolic than practical advantages. German Protestants were as divided among themselves and as lacking in central direction as the Jews, without being seriously handicapped. The old Prussian legislation, although scarcely convenient, served well enough and, under normal circumstances, sooner or later would have yielded to Jewish and governmental pressures for change. What these failures did reveal was a certain lack of sensitivity among German Jews to their somewhat exposed position. An officially recognized national organization of German Jews would have had the advantage of being the vehicle for class action suits against anti-Semites accused of collective libel. In its absence, the best that could be done was to answer general attacks against the Jews with suits for the relatively minor offense of gross misconduct.[60] What is more, the Jews' contentious and self-willed approach to legal reform could not have failed to antagonize elements of the important Prussian bureaucracy.

It is always tempting to attribute the failures of organizational and legal reform to general indifference among the Jews to their own collective affairs. This is the conclusion Professor Toury reached about the collapse of early efforts at Jewish union.[61] The problem during the Weimar years, however, was an excess, rather than a dearth, of concern for Jewish matters. The primary obstacle to progress was the passionate and unbending determination of Zionist, Liberal, and Orthodox Jews to make the results of collective action reflect their own desires. They may be faulted for their intransigence, but not for indifference.

The best construction that one can put upon these failures is that the German Jews were not prepared to sacrifice deeply felt convictions about Judaism

59. For a classic statement of this analysis, see Koppel S. Pinson, *Modern Germany: Its History and Civilization* (New York, 1954), 1–11.

60. Erich Eyck, "Um die Frage der Kollektivbeleidigung," *Central-Verein Zeitung*, February 26, 1926; *ibid.*, January, 1927; [Ludwig] Foerder, "Zweierlei Mass in der Justiz?" *Israelitisches Familienblatt*, March 31, 1932.

61. Toury, "Organizational Problems of German Jewry," 90.

and Jewishness for the ideals of unity and cooperation. To the degree that it expressed liberal distrust of uniformity, this attitude inspires a certain amount of admiration. We may lament its self-indulgence; in times such as those, diversity was perhaps a luxury that German Jews should not have permitted themselves on such a lavish scale. Few will argue, however, that it belongs among the more serious errors of the day.

Conclusion

It was inevitable that the Nazi catastrophe would cast a lasting pall over efforts to make sense out of the Jewish experience in Weimar Germany. The sheer enormity of what followed the collapse of Weimar institutions challenges the credibility of Jewish faith in assimilationism. Did the Jews not see disaster coming? Why did they not save themselves while there was still time?

At the outset of this survey it was noted that the persistent liberalism of German Jews might be interpreted in one of three ways: as self-deception, as compulsion born of a lack of alternatives, or as a clear-eyed choice. The first of these has been popular among those who approach the problem from the standpoint of the historian of mass psychology. For them (but by no means exclusively for them) it is frequently compelling to regard nazism as the logical culmination of German history, and Hitlerite anti-Semitism as a natural product of all previous anti-Jewish agitation. From that premise it is but a small step to the conclusion that realism on the part of the Jews would have led them to Zionism, or else to some other alternative to hopeful-minded assimilationism.

This is the approach adopted by Sydney Bolkosky in his recent study of the Jew's perceptions of their fellow Germans in the Weimar years. Although he abjures condemnatory judgments, Bolkosky nonetheless depicts German Jewish liberal assimilationism as a monumental case of self-delusion. A neurotic passion for acceptance caused the Jews to believe "that Germany and most Germans were characterized by the values of the Enlightenment: tolerance, reason, cosmopolitanism combined with nationalism, understanding, and liberal humanism." Their willingness to see only Herders and Lessings among their fellow Germans blinded them to the presence in far greater numbers of Stöckers and Hitlers. It also prompted them to assume that the Weimar Republic was deeply rooted in pre–World War I German tradition rather than that it represented a break with historical continuity. By projecting their own liberal image on the rest of German society, "German Jews ignored the dangerous growth of antisemitism among more than just uneducated Germans and the existence of a large part of Germany that was anti-Enlightenment, racist, and irrational."[1]

No one will deny the allegiance of most German Jews to the liberal values of the Enlightenment. It has been the central thesis of this study that historical, economic, and political circumstances had cemented the most intimate union between liberalism and the Jews. However, the contention that this union existed at the expense of repressing consciousness of the antiliberalism and anti-Semitism that existed among Germans as a whole cannot be squared with the facts. Jewish awareness of the need to counteract Judeophobia was authenticated by the self-defense and anti-Nazi activities of the Centralverein. These by far exceeded the bootless apologetics described by Bolkosky, who, on this point, echoes Hannah Arendt.[2] The energies of the Centralverein were not restricted to appeals to reason and assertions of confidence in the good faith of the German people. They included direct aid to the political parties that had committed themselves to stamping out the anti-Semitic plague. The fact that this was done covertly is immaterial. What is essential is the Centralverein's acute awareness that the Nazis, among whom men with serious and murderous intentions were to be found, were increasingly successful after 1929 in influencing the German masses on issues of greater substance than the Jewish question. It understood that in the final analysis it made no difference whether people supported Hitler for anti-Jewish or other reasons; if he ever came to power, some profound change in the status of the Jews might well be expected, and hence he would have to be stopped. This was far removed from complacency and blind optimism. Countering racist lies and appealing to the Germans' good will was essential to Jewish morale, but there was no substitute for political resistance if National Socialism were to be turned back. The Centralverein and the vast majority of German Jews that it represented did everything possible to deny it power; unhappily, the best they could do was to help deny it majority support.

The Jewish response to antiliberal and anti-Jewish trends in Weimar Germany was by no means confined to the field of self-defense. On the contrary, few elements of Jewish life were untouched by the painful consciousness of unrequited love. Jewish overachievement in every area of German economic and cultural life arose from a profound wish to win respect and acceptance. In 1926 Franz Oppenheimer visited Palestine and noted that Jewish students

1. Sidney M. Bolkosky, *The Distorted Image: German Jewish Perceptions of Germans and Germany, 1918–1935* (New York, 1975), especially pp. 3–19, 180–92 (quotations, p. 10).
2. *Ibid.*, 163–76; Arendt, *The Origins of Totalitarianism*, 23–25.

there were as average as non-Jews in Europe, displaying none of the one-sided drive for outstanding intellectual achievement that was common among German Jewish pupils. As Oppenheimer observed at the time, this overcompensation went far beyond the usual bourgeois passion for success. It betrayed a powerful longing to counteract antipathy by proving the value of Jewish contributions to Germany.[3]

If German Jews neither ignored nor indulged their enemies, they were no less unsentimental in their support for the liberal tradition in Germany. They probably did overestimate its strength somewhat, but not to the point of assuming its permanence. It is even more to their credit that the majority of them did not make the error of some subsequent observers in assuming its inevitable downfall. That nazism won in the end tempts the determinists among us to conclude that it had to win, that Weimar democracy was doomed from the start, that the "real Germany" of militarists and Jew-baiters was certain to reassert itself sooner or later. Those who yield to this temptation make the very mistake Bolkosky wrongly accuses the Jews of having made—that of assuming the overwhelming preponderance of only one political tradition in Germany.

The second interpretation of the Jews' loyalty to liberal assimilationism portrays them as being preoccupied with money rather than wish-fulfillment. The Marxist historians of East Germany, Walter Mohrmann preeminent among them, stress the Jews' bourgeois class interests as determinants of their obsessive anticommunism. With their gaze fixed solely on Marxist antipathy for capitalism, the Jews failed to see that capitalism itself spawns Judeophobia and hence could not join in the Communist party's struggle against anti-Semitism, racism, and imperialism. On the contrary, their economic interests impelled them toward the opposite political pole, and only the anti-Semitism of the German right kept them loyal to the liberal center.[4]

It is not necessary to assume with the Marxist historians that the Communist party had a monopoly on antiracist virtue, or that capitalism necessarily spawns racism, to attach some credibility to the broad outlines of their argument. The left held few attractions for the majority of Jews, as much for its atheism as for its anticapitalism. Most of those who voted for the Social Democrats in the last years of the Weimar Republic did so only after the de-

3. Oppenheimer, *Erlebtes*, 217.
4. Mohrmann, *Antisemitismus, passim;* Konrad Kwiet, "Historians of the German Democratic Republic on Antisemitism and Persecution," *Leo Baeck Institute Yearbook,* XXI (1976), 173–98.

mise of the bourgeois parties. Even under those conditions liberal Jews endorsed the Social Democratic party's opposition to anti-Semitism and its compromises with liberalism, but not its ultimate goal of socialization. They could have been expected to revert to their old associations with the return of normal conditions. In the meantime the longing for a nonracist right would not have been altogether out of character. It is a well-established fact that the rest of the German bourgeoisie moved into the Nazi camp in great numbers during the early 1930s. Italian Jewish support for Mussolini, at least until he issued the "Manifesto of Fascist Racism" under the influence of the Rome-Berlin Axis in 1938, may be suggestive of potential German Jewish support for a fascism without anti-Semitism.[5] As it was, with both left and right closed to them, the Jews were left virtually alone on the sinking ship of liberalism.

This reasoning retains its plausibility only as long as it restricts its view to the larger German scene and ignores the radical alternatives to liberalism among the Jews themselves. On the one hand Zionism invited the Jews to resign from the German *Volk* and to immerse themselves in Jewishness. It offered not one but several varieties of alienation from liberal moderation, including the Marxism of the Poale Zion, the humanistic socialism of the Hapoel Hazair, the militarism of the Revisionists, the capitalist developmental mentality that was common among "General Zionists," and even the chance to escape Germany entirely by emigrating to Palestine. None of these Zionist alternatives was adopted by more than a handful of German Jews. Zionism as a whole made little headway among the Jews, except perhaps in the field of fund-raising. Even among the Zionists, the great majority settled for a version of Jewish nationalism that emphasized charity for the Eastern Jews and self-respect for German Jews. They drew psychological sustenance from it, but in their heart of hearts a great many of them remained liberal Jews thumbing their noses at anti-Semitism.

At least as viable as an alternative to liberal assimilationism was the right-wing chauvinism of Max Naumann and his League of German Nationalist Jews. It presented an opportunity for Jews who were frightened of com-

5. Israel Cohen, "Mussolini and the Jews," *Contemporary Review*, CLIV (December, 1938), 700–706; Dante L. Germino, *The Italian Fascist Party in Power: A Study in Totalitarian Rule* (Minneapolis, 1959), 89–93. In 1930 Theodor Wolff, editor of the *Berliner Tageblatt*, returned from Italy with favorable impressions; Nathan Stein, president of the Jewish High Council in Baden, recalled that the Jews there regarded Italian fascism as "interesting and not dangerous." Feder, *Heute sprach ich mit . . .* , 259; Nathan Stein, "Lebenserinnerungen" (Typescript in Leo Baeck Institute Archives, New York), VIIc.

munism or disillusioned with Weimar democracy to pursue a reactionary line. It held out the hope of counteracting anti-Semitism by canceling the equation of Jew and liberal. Unquestionably the persistent Judeophobia of most of the remaining German right made its task more difficult. So did the somewhat overbearing leadership of Naumann. On the other hand, the fascist mentality is more frequently influenced by phobias than by facts. Naumann's failure to win more than a small following shows how rare that mentality was among his fellow Jews.

German Jewish liberalism, then, was determined neither by self-deception nor by the absence of choices. Rather, it expressed a clear-sighted perception of Jewish self-interest, which the Jews understandably associated with the best interests of their country. Liberalism had emancipated them and given them opportunities for advancement that few of them had missed. Their loyalty to it represents no more a victory of transcendent virtue than it does a triumph of superior intelligence. They certainly discerned liberalism's message of universal liberation, but their conviction was fundamentally their own manumission writ large. It is equally certain that they contributed their share of blunders to the turbulent years of the Republic, not the least of which was their misapprehension of the dimensions of the Nazi threat. In that, of course, they were not alone; they should not be held too strictly accountable for the cloudiness of their crystal ball. And, as we have seen, they were far from quiescent in the face of fascism. Nor were those blunders fatal in and of themselves. It is hard to escape the conclusion that there was nothing more that this small minority could have done to save itself. Even if it had been perfectly united, scrupulously free from "unpatriotic" affiliations, and ready to a man to put money and brains to work against the Nazi foe, it could not have altered the outcome in any significant way. Nothing short of clairvoyance could have spared it from a fate that could be determined in the first place by the larger society alone, and ultimately by one man—Adolf Hitler.

The uniqueness of German Jewish liberalism arose from the anomalous situation in Germany during the early years of the great depression. In other respects, Jewish singleness was more profoundly rooted in long-standing economic and cultural developments that were, however, rapidly dissipating. For hundreds of years, and especially for the last sixty, German Jews had become more and more like their German neighbors, with good reason. Zionist Nahum Goldmann underlined an essential point when he observed that his coreligionists, having experienced "the most spectacular rise any branch of Jewry has ever achieved," had emulated virtually everything German, and particularly the Germanic propensity for analyzing, formulating, and systematizing.[6] The degree of integration that accompanied this acculturation compared favorably with that existing in any country of the world at that time. By 1928, anti-Semitism, the main obstacle to further Jewish integration, was on its way to the lingering natural death it continues to experience elsewhere in the civilized world. The trend toward the typical was well advanced when the triumph of nazism abruptly ended the era of Jewish emancipation in Germany. Adolf Hitler would destroy the German Jews for racialist reasons, or perhaps as symbols of whatever it was that tortured his disturbed psyche. And yet, somewhere in his subconscious mind, he may have sensed that the Jews could have no place in totalitarian Germany because they were the enemies, not just of his racialism, but of everything that he and his National Socialist movement represented.

6. Goldmann, *Memories*, 58–60. Stephen M. Poppel has gone so far as to attribute the *völkisch* sentiments among German Zionists to the influence of the Germanic environment. It may be closer to the point to see these sentiments as paralleling, rather than as emerging from, the German *völkisch* tradition. A comparative approach to Zionist history would be helpful in clarifying this issue. Poppel, *Zionism in Germany,* 127–30.

Bibliography

I. PRIMARY SOURCES

A. Unpublished Papers

The destruction by the Nazis of valuable Jewish archival collections, including those of both the Centralverein and the German Zionist Federation, constitutes a loss that can never fully be overcome. Hence the New York Leo Baeck Institute's careful efforts to collect the papers and unpublished memoirs of hundreds of German Jews take on added significance. Most important to this study are the memoirs of Adolph Asch, Walter Breslauer, Berthold Haase, Ernst Herzfeld, Ernst Löwenberg, Philip Löwenfeld, Alfred Neumeyer, Kurt Sabatsky, Aron Sandler, Caesar Seligmann, and Alexander Szanto. Also useful are the memoirs of Bella Carlebach-Rosenak, Fritz Goldberg, Fritz Goldschmidt, Moritz Goldstein, Leo Gompertz, Walter Heinemann, Kurt Joseph, Richard Lichtheim, Emily Livneh, Wilhelm Lustig, Herbert Nussbaum, Max Reiner, Oscar Schwartz, Friedrich Solon, Nathan Stein, Paul Tachau, Max M. Warburg, and Bruno Weil. Equally significant are the papers of Leo Baerwald, Max Dienemann, Ismar Freund, Hugo Fuchs, Ludwig Fulda, Alfred Hirschberg, Arthur Lehmann, Robert Weltsch, and Leo Wolff. The Institute's collections of pamphlets and of material on the Centralverein and the Berlin Jewish Community are likewise indispensable.

The London Wiener Library's magnificent holdings of contemporary books and pamphlets are supplemented by small collections of documents relating to the Centralverein, the Reichsbund jüdischer Frontsoldaten, the Verband nationaldeutscher Juden, and the Preussischer Landesverband Jüdischer Gemeinden. Other sources are relatively scattered. The papers of Moritz Sobernheim are at the Library of Congress, Washington, D.C.. Those of Hermann Dietrich, Georg Gothein, and Albert Südekum are found at the Bundesarchiv in Koblenz. Also at the Bundesarchiv are files of the Reich Chancellery and of the Reich Commission for the Supervision of Public Order. A few thin folders on the affairs of the Breslau Jewish Community are on file at the YIVO Institute for Jewish Research, New York. The German state and local archives contain materials limited to narrow legal and financial relations between the Jewish communities and the state governments. Those available at the Staatsarchiv Münster, the Staatsarchiv Koblenz, and the Niedersächsisches Hauptstaatsarchiv in Hanover are of some pertinence to this study.

B. Newspapers and Periodicals

Allgemeine Zeitung des Judentums. 1919. Berlin. Predecessor of the *Jüdisch-liberale Zeitung.*

Die Arbeit. 1919–1924. Berlin. Journal published irregularly by the German Hapoel Hazair.

Bayerische Israelitische Gemeindezeitung. Munich. 1925–1933. Official publication of the Association of Bavarian Jewish Communities.

Blau-Weiss Blätter. 1919, 1924–1925. Berlin. Journal of the Blue-White, the leading Zionist youth group.

Central-Vereins Dienst. 1924–1927. Berlin. House organ for Centralverein functionaries.

Central-Verein Zeitung: Blätter für Deutschtum und Judentum. 1922–1933. Berlin. The official Centralverein weekly.

Deutsche Republik. 1930. Berlin. Weekly publication of the Republican Union.

Frankfurter Zeitung. 1919–1933. Germany's leading liberal daily newspaper.

Germania. 1919–1932. Catholic Center party newspaper.

Gemeindeblatt der Deutsch-Israelitischen Gemeinde zu Hamburg. 1925–1933.

Gemeindeblatt der Israelitischen Gemeinde Frankfurt am Main. 1922–1933.

Gemeindeblatt der Jüdischen Gemeinde zu Berlin. 1919–1933.

Im deutschen Reich. 1919–1922. Berlin. Centralverein journal, monthly predecessor to the *Central-Verein Zeitung.*

Der Israelit. 1919–1933. Frankfurt-am-Main. Principal organ of separatist Orthodoxy.

Israelitisches Familienblatt. 1919–1933. Hamburg. The most widely read Jewish newspaper in Germany, with regional supplements for various parts of the country.

Der Jude. 1918–1926. Berlin. Martin Buber's journal.

Jüdische Rundschau. 1919–1933. Berlin. Central organ of the German Zionist Federation.

Jüdisch-liberale Zeitung. 1924–1933. Berlin. Publication of the Union for Liberal Judaism.

K. C. Blätter. 1919–1933. Berlin. Liberal Jewish student bulletin.

Mitteilungen aus dem Verein zur Abwehr des Antisemitismus. 1919–1931. Berlin. Publication of Germany's interconfessional antidefamation organization. Adopted the prefix *Abwehr Blätter* in 1925.

Mitteilungen des Syndikus des Centralvereins deutscher Staatsbürger jüdischen Glaubens. 1919–1922. Berlin. For Centralverein functionaries and activists.

Mitteilungsblatt des Verbandes nationaldeutscher Juden. 1922–1925. Berlin. Max Naumann's mouthpiece.

Der Morgen. 1925–1933. Berlin. Scholarly journal of the Centralverein's Philo Publishing House.

Münchener Post. 1930. Munich. Bavaria's leading Social Democratic newspaper.

Der nationaldeutsche Jude. 1925–1931. Berlin. Organ of the League of German Nationalist Jews.

Der Schild. 1922–1933. Berlin. Publication of the National League of Jewish Frontline Veterans.

Sperlings Zeitschriften- und Zeitungs- Adressbuch. 1927–1931. The standard handbook of the German press.

Verwaltungsblatt des preussischen Landesverbandes Jüdischer Gemeinden. 1924–1933. Berlin. Publication of the Provincial Association of the Prussian Jews. Includes the debates of its assembly.
Völkischer Beobachter. 1930–1933. Munich. The principal National Socialist newspaper.
Vorwärts. 1919–1933. Berlin. Central organ of the Social Democratic party.
Die Weltbühne. 1919–1932. Berlin. Independent journal of radical opinion.

C. Interviews

Dr. S. Adler-Rudel, London, August 14, 1973.
Dr. Friedrich Brodnitz, New York, June 21 and July 12, 1975.
Dr. Werner J. Cahnmann, New York, July 25, 1975.
Dr. Ernst J. Cohn, London, July 17, 1973.
Dr. Fred Grubel, New York, July 28 and 29, 1975.
Dr. Max Grünewald, New York, July 23, 1975.
Hans Jaeger, London, June 16, 1974.
Dr. Arnold Paucker, London, July 4, 1973.
Dr. Herman Pineas, New York, June 6, 1975.
Dr. Eva G. Reichmann, London, July 7 and August 26, 1973.
Dr. Hans Steinitz, New York, July 16, 1975.
Gabriele Tergit, London, June 23, 1974.
Dr. Robert Weltsch, London, August 20, 1973.

D. Published Diaries, Memoirs, and Correspondence

Ball-Kaduri, Kurt Jakob. *Das Leben der Juden in Deutschland im Jahre 1933.* Frankfurt: Europäische Verlagsanstalt, 1963.
Baumgarten, Otto. *Meine Lebensgeschichte.* Tübingen: J. C. B. Mohr, 1929.
Blumenfeld, Kurt. *Erlebte Judenfrage: Ein Vierteljahrhundert deutscher Zionismus.* Stuttgart: Deutsche Verlags-Anstalt, 1962.
Bodenheimer, M. I. *Prelude to Israel.* Translated by Israel Cohen. New York: Thomas Yoseloff, 1963.
Bonn, M. J. *Wandering Scholar.* London: Cohen and West, 1949.
Braun-Vogelstein, Julie. *Was niemals stirbt: Gestalten und Erinnerungen.* Stuttgart: Deutsche Verlags-Anstalt, 1966.
Brunner, Constantin. *Aus meinem Tagebuch.* Potsdam: Gustav Kiepenheuer Verlag, 1928.
Willi Buch [Wilhelm Buchow]. *50 Jahre antisemitische Bewegung.* Munich: Deutscher Verlag, 1937.
Ebermayer, Ludwig. *Fünfzig Jahre Dienst am Recht: Erinnerungen eines Juristen.* Leipzig and Zurich: Grethlein, 1930.
Eisner, Isi Jacob. "Reminiscences of the Berlin Rabbinical Seminary." *Leo Baeck Institute Yearbook,* XII (1967), 32–52.
Feder, Ernst. *Heute sprach ich mit . . . Tagebücher eines Berliner Publizisten 1926–1932.* Stuttgart: Deutsche Verlags-Anstalt, 1971.

Fränkel, Abraham. *Lebenskreise: Aus dem Erinnerungen eines Jüdischen Mathematikers.* Stuttgart: Deutsche Verlags-Anstalt, 1967.

Goldmann, Nahum. *Memories.* Translated by Helen Sebba. London: Weidenfeld and Nicolson, 1970.

Goldschmidt, Richard B. *In and Out of the Ivory Tower.* Seattle: University of Washington Press, 1960.

Heimann, Hugo. *Vom tätigen Leben.* Berlin: Arani Verlag, 1949.

Jungmann, Max. *Erinnerungen eines Zionisten.* Jerusalem: Rubin Mass, 1959.

Kahle, Paul E. *Bonn University in Pre-Nazi and Nazi Times (1923–1939).* London: privately printed, 1945.

Kohn, Hans. *Living in a World Revolution: My Encounters with History.* New York: Pocket Books, 1964.

Kollenscher, Max. *Jüdisches aus der deutsch-polnischen Übergangszeit: Posen 1918–1920.* Berlin: Verlag "Ewer," 1925.

Landauer, Georg. *Der Zionismus im Wandel dreier Jahrzehnte.* Tel Aviv: Bitaon Verlag, 1957.

Lessing, Theodor. *Einmal und nie wieder.* Gütersloh: Reinhard Mohn, n.d. First published in Prague: Orbis-Verlag, 1935.

Lichtheim, Richard. *Rückkehr: Lebenserinnerungen aus der Frühzeit des deutschen Zionismus.* Stuttgart: Deutsche Verlags-Anstalt, 1970.

Loewenstein, Hubertus zu. *Conquest of the Past: An Autobiography.* Boston: Houghton Mifflin, 1938.

Marcuse, Ludwig. *Mein zwanzigstes Jahrhundert.* Munich: Paul List Verlag, 1960.

Marx, Hugo. *Werdegang eines jüdischen Staatsanwalts und Richters in Baden (1892–1933).* Villingen: Neckar-Verlag, 1965.

Mayer, Gustav. *Erinnerungen: Vom Journalisten zum Historiker der deutschen Arbeiterbewegung.* Zurich: Europa-Verlag, 1949.

Morsey, Rudolf. *Die Deutsche Zentrumspartei 1917–1923.* Düsseldorf: Droste, 1964.

Oppenheimer, Franz. *Erlebtes, Erstrebtes, Erreichtes: Lebenserinnerungen.* Düsseldorf: Joseph Melzer Verlag, 1964.

Preuss, Walter. *Ein Ring schliesst sich: Von der Assimilation zur Chaluziuth.* Tel Aviv: Edition Olympia, Martin Feuchtwanger, n.d.

Rathenau, Walther. *Briefe.* Dresden: Carl Reissner Verlag, 1926.

Schoeps, Hans-Joachim. *Die letzten dreissig Jahre.* Stuttgart: Ernst Klett Verlag, 1956.

Stern, Arthur. *In bewegter Zeit: Erinnerungen und Gedanken eines jüdischen Nervenarztes.* Jerusalem: Verlag Rubin Mass, 1968.

Stern, Heinemann. *Warum hassen sie uns eigentlich? Jüdisches Leben zwischen den Kriegen.* Düsseldorf: Droste Verlag, 1970.

Straus, Rahel. *Wir lebten in Deutschland: Erinnerungen einer deutschen Jüdin 1880–1933.* Stuttgart: Deutsche Verlags-Anstalt, 1961.

Tucholsky, Kurt. *Briefe an eine Katholikin.* Hamburg: Rowohlt Verlag, 1970.

Uhlman, Fred. *The Making of an Englishman.* London: Victor Gollancz, 1960.

Walter, Bruno. *Theme and Variations.* Translated by James A. Galston. New York: A. A. Knopf, 1946.

Wasserman, Jakob. *Mein Weg als Deutscher und Jude.* Berlin: S. Fischer Verlag, 1921.

Willstätter, Richard. *From My Life.* Translated by Lilli S. Hornig. New York: W. A. Benjamin, 1965.

Wolff, Theodor. *Through Two Decades.* Translated by E. W. Dickes. London: William Heinemann, 1936.

Zondek, Hermann. *Auf festem Fusse: Erinnerungen eines jüdischen Klinikers.* Stuttgart: Deutsche Verlags-Anstalt, 1973.

E. Books, Pamphlets, and Articles from Contemporary Jewish Sources

Barth, Aron. *Orthodoxie und Zionismus.* Berlin: Welt-Verlag, 1920.

Baumgarten, Otto. *Kreuz und Hakenkreuz.* Gotha: Leopold Klotz Verlag, 1926.

Behr, Stefan. *Der Bevölkerungsrückgang der deutschen Juden.* Frankfurt-am-Main: J. Kaufmann Verlag, 1932.

Bernstein, F. *Der Antisemitismus als Gruppenerscheinung: Versuch einer Soziologie des Judenhasses.* Berlin: Jüdischer Verlag, 1926.

Blankenfeld, Fritz, et al. *Los vom Zionismus.* Frankfurt-am-Main: J. Kauffmann Verlag, 1928.

Borkumer Beobachter (Borkum). *Veröffentlichungen zum Münchmeyer Prozess.* Borkum: Borkumer Beobachter, 1926.

Brunner, Constantin. *Höre Israel und Höre Nicht-Israel.* Berlin: Gustav Kiepenheuer Verlag, 1931.

———. *Der Judenhass und die Juden.* Berlin: Österheld, 1918.

———. *Von den Pflichten der Juden und von den Pflichten des Staates.* Berlin: Gustav Kiepenheuer Verlag, 1930.

———. *Über die notwendige Selbstemanizipation der Juden.* Berlin: Georg Stilke, 1931.

Callmann, Rudolf. *Zur Boykottfrage.* Berlin: Philo-Verlag, 1932.

Centralverein deutscher Staatsbürger jüdischen Glaubens. *Deutsches Judentum und Rechtskrisis.* Berlin: Philo-Verlag, 1927.

———. *125 Friedhofsschändungen in Deutschland 1923–1932.* 6th ed., rev. Berlin, 1932.

———. *Die Kongresspolitik der Zionisten und ihre Gefahren.* Berlin: Gabriel Riesser Verlag, 1919.

———. *Die Stellung der Nationalsozialistischen Deutschen Arbeiterpartei (NSDAP) zur Judenfrage: Eine Materialsammlung vorgelegt vom Centralverein deutscher Staatsbürger jüdischen Glaubens.* Berlin, n.d. [1932].

Dienemann, Max. *Galuth.* Berlin: Philo-Verlag, 1929.

Festschrift für Jacob Rosenheim. Frankfurt-am-Main: J. Kaufmann Verlag, 1931.

Fink, Georg [Kurt Münzer]. *Mich hungert . . .* Berlin: Bruno Cassirer Verlag, 1930.

Foerder, Ludwig. *Antisemitismus und Justiz.* Berlin: Philo-Verlag, 1924.

Gronemann, Sammy. *Tohuwabohu.* Berlin: Welt-Verlag, 1920.

Holdheim, Gerhard, and Walter Preuss. *Die theoretischen Grundlagen des Zionismus.* Berlin: Welt-Verlag, 1919.

Holdheim, Gerhard, ed. *Zionistisches Handbuch.* Berlin: Berliner Büro der Zionistischen Organisation, 1923.

Holländer, Ludwig. *Deutsch-Jüdische Probleme der Gegenwart.* Berlin: Philo-Verlag, 1929.

Jüdisches Jahrbuch 1929. Berlin: Scherbel, 1929.

Kahane, Arthur. *Das Judenbuch.* Berlin: Tiergarten-Verlag, 1931.

Kahn, Fritz. *Die Juden als Rasse und Kulturvolk.* Berlin: Welt-Verlag, 1922.

Klatzkin, Jakob. *Krisis und Entscheidung im Judentum.* 2nd ed., rev. Berlin: Jüdischer Verlag, 1921.

Kohn, Hans, and Robert Weltsch. *Zionistische Politik.* Mährisch-Ostrau, Czechoslovakia: Verlag Dr. R. Färber, 1927.

Kuttner, Erich. *Pathologie des Rassenantisemitismus.* Berlin: Philo-Verlag, 1930.

Lessing, Theodor. *Der jüdische Selbsthass.* Berlin: Jüdischer Verlag, 1930.

———. *Untergang der Erde am Geist.* 3rd ed., rev. Hanover: Wolf Albrecht Adam Verlag, 1924.

Levy, Jacob. *Die Schächtfrage unter Berücksichtigung des neuen physiologischen Forschungen.* 2nd ed., rev. Berlin: Philo-Verlag, 1929.

Lichtheim, Richard. *Revision der zionistischen Politik.* Berlin: Kommissionsverlag, 1930.

Marcus, Alfred. *Die wirtschaftliche Krise der deutschen Juden.* Berlin: Georg Stilke, 1931.

Marx, Hugo. *Was wird werden? Das Schicksal der deutschen Juden in der sozialen Krise.* Wiesbaden: Verlag Westdruckerie, 1932.

Marx, Jakob. *Das deutsche Judentum und seine jüdischen Gegner.* Berlin: Philo-Verlag, 1925.

Möhring, Ernst. *Gegen völkischen Wahn.* Berlin: Philo-Verlag, 1924.

Naumann, Max. *Ganz-Deutsche oder Halb-Deutsche?* Berlin: Deutsche Verlagsgesellschaft für Politik und Geschichte, 1921.

———. *Vom mosaischen und nicht-mosaischen Juden.* Berlin: Deutsche Verlagsgesellschaft für Politik und Geschichte, 1924.

———. *Vom nationaldeutschen Juden.* Berlin: Verlag Albert Goldschmidt, 1920.

———. *Sozialismus, Nationalsozialismus und nationaldeutsches Judentum.* N.p., "Als Manuskript gedruckt," 1932.

———. "Der Weg zum Deutschtum," In *Der Jud ist Schuld...? Diskussionsbuch über die Judenfrage.* Basel: Zinnen Verlag, 1932.

———. *Von Zionisten und Jüdisch-nationalen.* Berlin: Deutsche Verlagsgesellschaft für Politik und Geschichte, 1921.

Oppenheimer, Franz. *Die Judenstatistik der preussischen Kriegsministeriums.* Munich: Verlag für Kulturpolitik, 1922.

Pappenheim, Bertha. *Sisyphus Arbeit.* Leipzig: P. E. Linder, n.d. [1924].

Peyser, Alfred. *Der Begriff "nationaldeutsch" in unserer Erziehungsarbeit.* Berlin: n.p., n.d. [*ca.* 1922].

Rathenau, Walther. "Höre, Israel!" In *Impressionen*. Leipzig: S. Hirzel, 1902.

Schoeps, Hans-Joachim. *Wir deutschen Juden*. Berlin: Vortrupp Verlag, 1934.

Segall, Jacob. *Die deutschen Juden als Soldaten im Kriege 1914–1918*. Berlin: Philo-Verlag, 1922.

Silbergleit, Heinrich. *Die Bevölkerungs- und Berufsverhältnisse der Juden im Deutschen Reich*. Berlin: Akademie-Verlag, 1930.

Theilhaber, Felix A. *Der Untergang der deutschen Juden: Eine volkswirtschaftliche Studie*. 2nd ed., rev. Berlin: Jüdischer Verlag, 1921.

Tucholsky, Kurt. *Deutschland, Deutschland über Alles*. Berlin: Neuer Deutscher Verlag, 1929.

Weltsch, Felix. *Nationalismus und Judentum*. Berlin: Weltverlag, 1920.

Weltsch, Robert. "Die Judenfrage für den Juden," in *Der Jud ist Schuld . . . ? Diskussionsbuch über die Judenfrage*. Basel: Zinnen Verlag, 1932.

Wiener, Alfred. *Das deutsche Judentum in politischer, wirtschaftlicher und kultureller Hinsicht*. Berlin: Philo-Verlag, 1924.

————. *Juden und Araber in Palästina*. Berlin: Philo-Verlag, 1929.

————. *Kritische Reise durch Palästina*. 3rd ed. Berlin: Philo-Verlag, 1928.

Zentralwohlfahrtsstelle der deutschen Juden. *Führer durch die Jüdische Wohlfahrtspflege in Deutschland*. Berlin: Verlag Dr. Fritz Scherbel, 1929.

Zweig, Arnold. *Bilanz der deutschen Judenheit 1933: Ein Versuch*. Amsterdam: Querido Verlag, 1934.

F. Other Primary Sources

Andersen, Friedrich. *Der deutsche Heiland*. Munich: Deutscher Volksverlag, 1921.

————. *Zur religiösen Erneuerung des deutschen Volkes*. Hamburg: Deutschvölkischer Schutz-und-Trutzbund, 1920.

————. *Weckruf an die evangelischen Geistlichen in Deutschland*. Hamburg: Deutschvölkischer Schutz-und-Trutzbund, 1920.

Armin, Otto [Roth, Alfred]. *Die Juden im Heere: Eine statistische Untersuchung nach amtlichen Quellen*. Munich: Deutscher Volks-Verlag, 1919.

Bahr, Hermann. *Der Antisemitismus*. Berlin, 1894.

————, et al. *Der Jud ist Schuld . . . ? Diskussionsbuch über die Judenfrage*. Basel: Zinnen Verlag, 1932.

Blüher, Hans. *Die Erhebung Israels gegen die christlichen Güter*. Hamburg: Hanseatische Verlagsanstalt, 1931.

————. *Deutsches Reich: Judentum und Sozialismus*. Prien: Anthropos Verlag, 1920.

Braun, Heinz. *Am Justizmord vorbei: Der Fall Kölling-Haas*. Magdeburg: W. Pfannkuch & Co., 1928.

Buber, Martin. *Der Jude und sein Judentum: Gesammelte Aufsätze und Reden*. Cologne: Joseph Melzer Verlag, 1963.

————. *On Judaism*. New York: Schocken Books, 1967.

Coudenhove-Kalergi, Heinrich Johann Maria. *Das Wesen des Antisemitismus*. With an introduction by R. N. Coudenhove-Kalergi. Vienna and Leipzig, 1929.

Deimling, Berthold von. *Aus der alten in die neue Zeit.* Berlin: Verlag Ullstein, 1930.

Deutschvölkischer Schutz-und-Trutzbund. *Sigfried und Ahasver.* Hamburg, 1919.

———. *Deutschkritischer Gottesgeist.* Leipzig: Adolf Klein Verlag, 1931.

Ehrenthal, Günther. *Die deutschen Jugendbünde.* Berlin: Zentral Verlag, 1929.

Eisfeld, Carl. *Jüdischer Antisemitismus und Arbeiterschaft.* Hagen: Buchhandlung "Neue Freie Presse," 1922.

Fahrenkrog, Ludwig, ed. *Das Deutsche Buch.* 2nd ed., rev. Berlin: Verlag Kraft und Schönheit, 1921.

Falck, H. *Wie die Bibel entstand.* Berlin: Verlag der Deutschkirche, 1932.

Feist, Sigmund. *Stammeskunde der Juden.* Leipzig: J. C. Hinrichs'sche Buchhandlung, 1925.

Fendrich, Anton. *Der Judenhass und der Sozialismus.* Freiburg-im-Breisgau: Ernst Günther Verlag, 1920.

Fiebig, Paul. *Juden und Nichtjuden: Erläuterungen zu Th. Fritschs "Handbuch der Judenfrage."* Leipzig: Verlag von Dörfling & Franke, 1921.

———. *Wie stehen wir Christen zum Alten Testament? (Christentum und Judentum).* Göttingen: Vandenhoeck & Ruprecht, 1926.

Fischer, Eugen, and Hans F. K. Günther, *Deutsche Köpfe nordischer Rasse.* Munich: J. F. Lehmanns Verlag, 1927.

Frank, Josef Maria. *Volk im Fieber.* Berlin: Sieben Stässe Verlag, 1932.

Friedrichs, Johannes. *Eine Lösung der Judenfrage?* Detmold: Meyersche Hofbuchhandlung, 1922.

Fritsch, Theodor. *Handbuch der Judenfrage: Die wichtige Tatsachen zur Beurteilung des jüdischen Volkes.* 30th ed., rev. Leipzig: Hammerverlag, 1931.

Gerecke, Karl. *Biblischer Antisemitismus: Der Juden weltgeschichtlicher Charakter, Schuld und Ende in des Propheten Jona.* Munich: Deutscher Volks-Verlag, 1920.

Grabowsky, Adolf. *Politik.* Berlin: Industrieverlag Späth & Linde, 1932.

Günther, Albrecht Erich, ed. *Was wir vom Nationalsozialismus erwarten.* Heilbronn: Eugen Salzer, 1932.

Günther, Hans F. K. *Rasse und Stil.* Munich: J. F. Lehmanns Verlag, 1926.

———. *Rassenkunde des deutschen Volkes.* 10th ed., rev. Munich: J. F. Lehmanns Verlag, 1926.

———. *Rassenkunde des jüdischen Volkes.* Munich: J. F. Lehmanns Verlag, 1930.

Hauser, Otto. *Der blonde Mensch.* 2nd ed. Danzig: Verlag der Mensch, 1930.

———. *Geschichte des Judentums.* Weimar: Alexander Duncker Verlag, 1921.

———. *Rassebilder.* Braunschweig: Georg Westermann, 1925.

Hellpach, Willy. *Politische Prognose für Deutschland.* Berlin: S. Fischer Verlag, 1928.

Hitler, Adolf. *Mein Kampf.* Translated by R. Manheim. Boston: Houghton Mifflin, 1943.

Kaulla, Rudolf. *Der Liberalismus und die deutschen Juden: Das Judentum als konservatives Element.* Munich and Leipzig: Verlag Von Duncker & Humblot, 1928.

Lamparter, Eduard. *Das Judentum in seiner Kultur- und Religionsgeschichtlichten Erscheinung.* Gotha, 1928.

_____. *Evangelische Kirche und Judentum: Ein Beitrag zu christlichem Verstandnis von Judentum and Antisemitismus.* Berlin, n.d.

Landauer, Georg. *Der Zionismus im Wandel Dreier Jahrzehnte.* Tel Aviv: Bitaon-Verlag, 1957.

Landesarchivverwaltung Rheinland-Pfalz. *Dokumentation zur Geschichte der jüdischen Bevölkerung in Rheinland-Pfalz und im Saarland von 1880 bis 1945.* Koblenz: Selbstverlag der Landesarchivverwaltung, 1971.

Löhr, Max. *Alttestamentliche Religions-Geschichte.* 3rd ed., rev. Berlin and Leipzig: Walther de Gruyter & Co., 1930.

Maier, Friedrich Wilhelm. *Israel in der Heilsgeschichte nach Römer 9–11.* Münster: Verlag der Aschendorffschen Verlagsbuchhandlung, 1929.

Messer, August. *Der Fall Lessing.* Bielefeld: Verlag Gustav Wittler, 1926.

Meyer, Hermann. *Der Deutsche Mensch.* 2 vols. Munich: J. F. Lehmanns Verlag, 1925.

Oppeln-Bronikowski, Friedrich von. *Gerechtigkeit! Zur Lösung der Judenfrage.* Berlin: Nationaler Verlag Joseph Garibaldi Huch, 1932.

Przywara, Erich. "Judentum und Christentum." *Stimmen der Zeit,* III (1926), 81–99.

Reichmann, Eva G. *Grösse und Verhängnis deutsch-jüdischer Existenz: Zeugnisse einer tragischen Begegnung.* Heidelberg: Verlag Lambert Schneider, 1974.

Rosenberg, Alfred. *Die Spur des Juden im Wandel der Zeiten.* Munich: Eher Verlag, 1920.

Roth, Alfred. *Geheime Fäden im Weltkriege.* Hamburg: Deutschvölkischer Schutz-und-Trutzbund, 1919.

_____. *Judas Herrschgewalt: Die Deutschvölkischen im Lichte der Behörden und des Staatsgerichtshofes.* Hamburg: Deutschvölkische Verlagsanstalt Arthur Gölting, 1923.

Schlatter, Adolf. *Wir Christen und die Juden.* Velbert-im-Rheinland: Freizeiten Verlag, 1930.

Schmidt, Wilhelm. *Rasse und Volk.* Munich: Verlag Josef Kosel & Friedrich Pustet, 1927.

Sombart, Werner. *The Jews and Modern Capitalism.* Translated by M. Epstein. Glencoe, Ill.: Free Press, 1951.

Stapel, Wilhelm. *Antisemitismus und Antigermanismus: Über das seelische Problem der Symbiose des deutschen und des jüdischen Volkes.* Hamburg: Hanseatische Verlagsanstalt, 1928.

_____. *Sechs Kapitel über Christentum und Nationalsozialismus.* Hamburg and Berlin: Hanseatische Verlagsanstalt, 1931.

Was muss das schaffende Volk vom politischen, wirtschaftlichen, religiösen Juden- und Rassenhass Wissen? Hanover: Sozialdemokratischer Partei Deutschlands, Ortsverein Hannover, [1924].

Wrisberg, Ernst von. *Heer und Heimat, 1914–1918.* Leipzig: Koehler Verlag, 1921.

Wundt, Max. *Deutsche Weltanschauung: Grundzüge völkischen Denkens.* Munich: J. F. Lehmanns Verlag, 1926.

――――. *Der ewige Jude: Ein Versuch über Sinn und Bedeutung des Judentums.* Munich: J. F. Lehmanns Verlag, 1926.

II. SECONDARY SOURCES

A. Selected Books and Articles

Abel, Theodore. *The Nazi Movement: Why Hitler Came into Power.* New York: Prentice-Hall, 1938.

Adler, H. G. *Die Juden in Deutschland: Von der Aufklärung bis zum National-sozialismus.* Munich: Kösel Verlag, 1960.

Adler-Rudel, S. *Ostjuden in Deutschland, 1880–1940.* Tübingen: J. C. B. Mohr, 1959.

Allen, William Sheridan. *The Nazi Seizure of Power: The Experience of a Single German Town, 1930–1935.* Chicago: Quadrangle Books, 1965.

Altmann, Alexander. "The German Rabbi: 1910–1939." *Leo Baeck Institute Yearbook,* XIX (1974), 31–49.

Angress, Werner T. "Das deutsche Militär und die Juden im Ersten Weltkrieg." *Militärgeschichtliche Mitteilungen,* No. 19 (1976), 77–146.

Arendt, Hannah. *The Origins of Totalitarianism.* Rev. ed. New York: Harcourt, Brace, and World, 1966.

Arnsberg, Paul, *Die Jüdischen Gemeinden in Hessen.* Darmstadt: Eduard Röther Verlag, 1973.

Asaria, Zvi, ed. *Die Juden in Köln von den ältesten Zeiten bis zur Gegenwart.* Cologne: Verlag J. P. Bachem, 1959.

Asch, Adolph. *Geschichte des KC im Lichte der deutschen kulturellen und politischen Entwicklung.* London: privately printed, 1964.

Baron, S. W. "Modern Capitalism and Jewish Fate." In *History and Jewish Historians,* edited by Arthur Hertzberg and Leon Feldman, pp. 43–64. Philadelphia: Jewish Publication Society of America, 1964.

Baumgardt, David. "Looking Back on a German University Career." *Leo Baeck Institute Yearbook,* X (1965), 239–65.

Beradt, Charlotte. *Paul Levi: Ein demokratischer Sozialist in der Weimarer Republik.* Frankfurt-am-Main: Europäische Verlagsanstalt, 1969.

Berglar, Peter. *Walther Rathenau.* Bremen: Schünemann Universitätsverlag, 1970.

Bermann, Tamar. *Produktivierungsmythen und Antisemitismus.* Vienna: Europa Verlag, 1973.

Bettelheim, Bruno, and Morris Janowitz. *Dynamics of Prejudice.* New York: Harper, 1950.

Bieber, Hans-Joachim. "Zur bürgerlichen Geschichtsschreibung und Publizistik über Antisemitismus, Zionismus und den Staat Israel." *Das Argument,* No. 75 (1972), 231–74.

Bienenfeld, Franz R. *The Germans and the Jews.* Translated by R. H. Pender. London: Seeker and Warburg, 1939.

Blau, Bruno. "The Jewish Population of Germany 1939–1945." *Jewish Social Studies*, XII (1950), 161–72.

Bleuel, Hans Peter, and Ernst Klinnert. *Deutsche Studenten auf dem Weg ins Dritte Reich*. Gütersloh: Sigbert Mohn Verlag, 1967.

Bleuel, Hans Peter. *Deutschlands Bekenner: Professoren Zwischen Kaiserreich und Diktatur*. Bern: Scherz Verlag, 1968.

Böhm, Franz, and Walter Dirks, eds. *Judentum: Schicksal, Wesen und Gegenwart*. 2 vols. Wiesbaden: Franz Steiner Verlag, 1965.

Bolkosky, Sidney M. *The Distorted Image: German Jewish Perceptions of Germans and Germany, 1918–1935*. New York: Elsevier, 1975.

Bondy, Louis W. *Racketeers of Hatred: Julius Streicher and the Jew-Baiters' International*. London: Newman Wolsey Limited, n.d.

Bracher, Karl Dietrich. *The German Dictatorship: The Origins, Structure, and Effects of National Socialism*. Translated by Jean Steinberg. New York: Praeger Publishers, 1970.

Cahnmann, Werner J. "The Nazi Threat and the Central Verein—A Recollection." In *Conference on Anti-Semitism, 1969*, edited by Herbert A. Strauss, pp. 27–36. New York: American Federation of Jews from Central Europe, 1969.

Carlebach, Alexander. *Adass Yeshurun of Cologne*. Belfast: William Mullan & Son, Ltd., 1964.

———. "A German Rabbi Goes East." *Leo Baeck Institute Yearbook*, VI (1961), 60–121.

Clark, Ronald W. *Einstein: The Life and Times*. New York: World Publishing Co., 1971.

Cohn, Haim. "Joseph Carlebach." *Leo Baeck Institute Yearbook*, V (1960), 58–72.

Cohn, Norman. *Warrant for Genocide: The Myth of the Jewish World-Conspiracy and "The Protocols of the Elders of Zion."* New York: Harper and Row, 1966.

Dawidowitz, Lucy S. *The War Against the Jews 1933–1945*. New York: Holt, Rinehart and Winston, 1975.

Deak, Istvan. *Weimar Germany's Left-Wing Intellectuals: A Political History of the Weltbühne and Its Circle*. Berkeley and Los Angeles: University of California Press, 1968.

Doskow, Ambrose, and Sidney B. Jacoby. "Anti-Semitism and the Law in Pre-Nazi Germany." *Contemporary Jewish Record* (1940), 498–509.

Dubnov, Simon. *History of the Jews from the Congress of Vienna to the Emergence of Hitler*. Translated and revised by Moshe Spiegel. 10 vols. New York: Thomas Yoseloff, 1968.

Dunker, Ulrich. *Der Reichsbund jüdischer Frontsoldaten 1919–1938: Geschichte eines jüdischen Abwehrvereins*. Düsseldorf: Droste Verlag, 1977.

Edinger, Dora. *Bertha Pappenheim: Leben und Schriften*. Frankfurt-am-Main: Ner-Tamid-Verlag, 1963.

Epstein, Klaus. *The Genesis of German Conservatism*. Princeton, N.J.: Princeton University Press, 1966.

Esperstedt, Joachim *et al*. *Die Juden im ihrem Gemeindelichen und öffentlichen Leben*. Koblenz: Selbstverlag der Landesarchivverwaltung Rheinland-Pfalz, 1972.

Fischer, Ruth. *Stalin and German Communism.* Cambridge, Mass.: Harvard University Press, 1948.

Flechtheim, Ossip K. *Die Kommunistische Partei Deutschlands in der Weimarer Republik.* Offenbach-am-Main: Bollwerk-Verlag, 1948.

Franze, Manfred. *Die Erlanger Studentenschaft 1918–1945.* Würzburg: Kommissionsverlag Ferdinand Schöningh, 1972.

Fuchs, Eduard. *Die Juden in der Karikatur: Ein Beitrag zur Kulturgeschichte.* Munich: Albert Langen Verlag, 1921.

Gay, Peter. *Freud, Jews, and Other Germans: Masters and Victims in Modernist Culture.* New York: Oxford University Press, 1978.

————. *Weimar Culture: The Outsider as Insider.* New York and Evanston: Harper and Row, 1968.

Germino, Dante L. *The Italian Fascist Party in Power: A Study in Totalitarian Rule.* Minneapolis: University of Minnesota Press, 1959.

Gilon, Meir, ed. *Perspectives of German-Jewish History in the 19th and 20th Century.* Jerusalem: Academic Press, 1971.

Glatzer, Nahum N., ed. *On Judaism.* Translated by Eva Jospe. New York: Schocken, 1967.

Goldstein, Moritz. "German Jewry's Dilemma before 1914." *Leo Baeck Institute Yearbook,* II (1957), 236–54.

Gombrich, E. H. *Aby Warburg: An Intellectual Biography.* London: Warburg Institute, 1970.

Greive, Hermann. *Theologie und Ideologie: Katholizismus und Judentum in Deutschland und Österreich 1918–1935.* Heidelberg: Verlag Lambert Schneider, 1969.

Gross, Walter. "The Zionist Students' Movement." *Leo Baeck Institute Yearbook,* IV (1959), 143–64.

Grünewald, Max. "The Jewish Teacher." *Leo Baeck Institute Yearbook,* XIX (1974), 63–69.

Grunfeld, Isidor. *Three Generations: The Influence of Samson Raphael Hirsch on Jewish Life and Thought.* London: Jewish Post Publications, 1958.

Gutteridge, Richard. *The German Evangelical Church and the Jews, 1879–1950.* New York: Barnes and Noble, 1976.

Hamel, Iris. *Völkischer Verband und nationale Gewerkschaft: Der Deutschnationale Handlungsgehilfen-Verband 1893–1933.* Frankfurt-am-Main: Europäische Verlagsanstalt, 1967.

Hamburger, Ernest. "Hugo Preuss: Scholar and Statesman." *Leo Baeck Institute Yearbook,* XX (1975), 179–206.

————. "One Hundred Years of Emancipation." *Leo Baeck Institute Yearbook,* XIV (1969), 1–66.

Hannover, Heinrich, and Elisabeth Hannover-Drück. *Politische Justiz 1918–1933.* Frankfurt-am-Main: Fischer Bücherei, 1966.

Hearst, E. "When Justice Was Not Done: Judges in the Weimar Republic." *Wiener Library Bulletin,* XIV (1960), 10–11.

Heberle, Rudolf. *From Democracy to Nazism*. Baton Rouge: Louisiana State University Press, 1945.

Herrmann, Klaus J. *Das dritte Reich und die deutsch-jüdischen Organisationen 1933–1934*. Cologne: Carl Heymanns Verlag, 1969.

Hertzman, Lewis. *DNVP: Right-wing Opposition in the Weimar Republic, 1918–1924*. Lincoln, Neb.: University of Nebraska Press, 1963.

Herzig, Arno. *Judentum und Emanzipation in Westfalen*. Münster: Aschendorffsche Verlagsbuchhandlung, 1973.

Hodes, Aubrey. *Martin Buber: An Intimate Portrait*. New York: Viking Press, 1971.

Infield, Leopold. *Albert Einstein*. New York: Charles Scribner's Sons, 1950.

Jäckel, Eberhard. *Hitler's Weltanschauung: A Blueprint for Power*. Middletown, Conn.: Wesleyan University Press, 1972.

Jay, Martin. *The Dialectical Imagination: A History of the Frankfurt School and the Institute of Social Research, 1923–1950*. Boston: Little, Brown and Co., 1973.

Jospe, Alfred. "A Profession in Transition: The German Rabbinate 1910–1939." *Leo Baeck Institute Yearbook*, XIX (1974), 51–59.

Kaplan, Marion A. "German-Jewish Feminism in the Twentieth Century." *Jewish Social Studies*, XXXVIII (1976), 39–53.

Kater, Michael H. *Studentenschaft und Rechtsradikalismus in Deutschland 1918–1933*. Hamburg, 1975.

Katz, Jacob. *Jews and Freemasons in Europe 1723–1939*. Cambridge, Mass.: Harvard University Press, 1970.

———. *Out of the Ghetto: The Social Background of Jewish Emancipation, 1770–1870*. Cambridge: Harvard University Press, 1973.

Kaznelson, Siegmund, ed. *Juden im deutschen Kulturbereich*. Berlin: Jüdischer Verlag, 1959.

Kessler, Harry. *Walther Rathenau: His Life and Work*. Translated by W. D. Robson-Scott and Lawrence Hyde. New York: Harcourt, Brace and Co., 1944.

Klemperer, Klemens von. *Germany's New Conservatism: Its History and Dilemma in the Twentieth Century*. Princeton: Princeton University Press, 1957.

Koonz, Claudia. "Nazi Women Before 1933: Rebels Against Emancipation." *Social Science Quarterly*, LVI (1976), 553–63.

Knütter, Hans-Helmuth. *Die Juden und die deutsche Linke in der Weimarer Republik 1918–1933*. Düsseldorf: Droste Verlag, 1971.

Kreutzberger, Wolfgang. *Studenten und Politik 1918–1933: Der Fall Freiburg im Breisgau*. Göttingen: Vandenhoeck & Ruprecht, 1972.

Kruck, Alfred. *Geschichte des Alldeutschen Verbandes 1890–1939*. Wiesbaden: Franz Steiner Verlag, 1954.

Kuhn, Helmut. "Die deutsche Universität am Vorabend der Machtergreifung." In *Die deutsche Universität im Dritten Reich*, pp. 13–43. Munich: R. Piper & Co., 1966.

Kwiet, Konrad. "Historians of the German Democratic Republic on Antisemitism and Persecution." *Leo Baeck Institute Yearbook*, XXI (1976), 173–98.

Lamberti, Marjorie. "The Attempt to Form a Jewish Bloc: Jewish Notables and Politics in Wilhelmian Germany." *Central European History*, III (1970), 73–93.

_____. *Jewish Activism in Imperial Germany: The Struggle for Civil Equality.* New Haven and London: Yale University Press, 1978.

Lamm, Hans, ed. *Von Juden im München: Ein Gedenkbuch.* Munich: Ner-Tamid-Verlag, 1958.

Lane, Barbara Miller. "Nazi Ideology: Some Unfinished Business." *Central European History,* VII (1974), 3–30.

Laqueur, Walter. *A History of Zionism.* London: Weidenfeld and Nicolson, 1972.

_____. *Out of the Ruins of Europe.* London: Alcove Press, 1972.

_____. *Weimar: A Cultural History, 1918–1933.* New York: G. P. Putnam's Sons, 1974.

_____. *Young Germany: A History of the German Youth Movement.* New York: Basic Books, 1962.

_____, and George L. Mosse, eds. *Literature and Politics in the Twentieth Century.* New York: Harper and Row, 1967.

Levy, Richard S. *The Downfall of the Anti-Semitic Political Parties in Imperial Germany.* New Haven and London: Yale University Press, 1975.

Liang, Hsi-Huey. *The Berlin Police Force in the Weimar Republic.* Berkeley, Cal.: University of California Press, 1970.

Liebe, Werner. *Die Deutschnationale Volkspartei 1918–1924.* Düsseldorf: Droste-Verlag, 1956.

Liebeschütz, Hans. "Between Past and Future: Leo Baeck's Historical Position." *Leo Baeck Institute Yearbook,* XI (1966), 3–27.

_____. "Hermann Cohen and His Historical Background." *Leo Baeck Institute Yearbook,* XIII (1968), 3–33.

_____. *Von Georg Simmel zu Franz Rosenzweig: Studien zum Jüdischen Denken im deutschen Kulturbereich.* Tübingen: J. C. B. Mohr, 1970.

Liptzin, Solomon. *Germany's Stepchildren.* Philadelphia: Jewish Publication Society of America, 1944.

Lohalm, Uwe. *Völkischer Radikalismus: Die Geschichte der Deutschvölkischen Schutz- und Trutz-Bundes 1919–1923.* Hamburg: Leibniz Verlag, 1970.

Lotan, Giora. "The Zentralwohlfahrtsstelle." *Leo Baeck Institute Yearbook,* IV (1959), 185–207.

Lowe, Adolf. "In Memoriam Franz Oppenheimer." *Leo Baeck Institute Yearbook,* X (1965), 137–49.

Lowenthal, E. G. "The Ahlem Experiment." *Leo Baeck Institute Yearbook,* XIV (1969), 165–79.

Lowenthal, Marvin. *The Jews of Germany.* New York: Longmans, Green and Co., 1936.

Lutzhöft, Hans-Jürgen. *Der Nordische Gedanke in Deutschland 1920–1940.* Stuttgart: Ernst Klett Verlag, 1971.

Mann, Golo. *Der Antisemitismus: Wurzeln, Wirkung und Überwindung.* Munich and Frankfurt-am-Main: Ner-Tamid-Verlag, 1960.

Marcus, A. "Jews as Entrepreneurs in Weimar Germany." *YIVO Annual of Jewish Social Science,* VII, 175–203.

Massing, Paul W. *Rehearsal for Destruction: A Study of Political Anti-Semitism in Imperial Germany.* New York: Harper and Brothers, 1949.

Meier-Cronemeyer, Hermann. "Jüdische Jugendbewegung." *Germania Judaica,* VIII (1969), No. 27/30, 1–122.

Merkl, Peter H. *Political Violence Under the Swastika: 581 Early Nazis.* Princeton: Princeton University Press, 1975.

Mitchell, Allan. *Revolution in Bavaria, 1918–1919: The Eisner Regime and the Soviet Republic.* Princeton: Princeton University Press, 1965.

Mohler, Armin. *Die Konservative Revolution in Deutschland 1918–1932.* Stuttgart: Friedrich Vorwerk Verlag, 1950.

Mohrmann, Walter. *Antisemitismus: Ideologie und Geschichte im Kaiserreich und in der Weimarer Republik.* Berlin: Deutscher Verlag der Wissenschaften, 1972.

Moses, Sigfried. "The Impact of Leo Baeck's Personality on His Contemporaries." *Leo Baeck Institute Yearbook,* II (1957), 3–7.

_____. "Salman Schocken: His Economic and Zionist Activities." *Leo Baeck Institute Yearbook,* V (1960), 73–104.

Mosse, George L. *The Crises of German Ideology: Intellectual Origins of the Third Reich.* New York: Grosset and Dunlap, 1964.

_____. *Germans and Jews: The Right, the Left and the Search for a "Third Force" in Pre-Nazi Germany.* New York: Howard Fertig, 1970.

_____. "German Socialists and the Jewish Question in the Weimar Republic." *Leo Baeck Institute Yearbook,* XVI (1971), 123–50.

Mosse, Werner E., and Arnold Paucker, eds. *Deutsches Judentum in Krieg und Revolution 1916–1923.* Tübingen: J. C. B. Mohr, 1971.

_____. *Entscheidungsjahr 1932: Zur Judenfrage in der Endphase der Weimarer Republik.* Tübingen: J. C. B. Mohr, 1966.

Nebel, Theobald. *Die Geschichte der jüdischen Gemeinde in Talheim.* Talheim: Gemeinde Verlag, 1963.

Niewyk, Donald L. "The Economic and Cultural Role of the Jews in the Weimar Republic." *Leo Baeck Institute Yearbook,* XVI (1971), 163–73.

_____. "Jews and the Courts in Weimar Germany." *Jewish Social Studies,* XXXVII (1975), 99–113.

_____. *Socialist, Anti-Semite, and Jew: German Social Democracy Confronts the Problem of Anti-Semitism, 1918–1933.* Baton Rouge: Lousiana State University Press, 1971.

Noakes, Jeremy. *The Nazi Party in Lower Saxony, 1921–1933.* London: Oxford University Press, 1971.

Osborne, Sidney. *Germany and Her Jews.* London: Socino Press, 1939.

Paderborn, City of. *Baun wir doch aufs neue das alte Haus: Judisches Schicksal in Paderborn.* Paderborn, 1964.

Paucker, Arnold. *Der jüdische Abwehrkampf gegen Antisemitismus und Nationalsozialismus in den letzten Jahren der Weimarer Republik.* Hamburg: Leibnitz-Verlag, 1968.

_____. "'Gerechtigkeit!' The Fate of a Pamphlet on the Jewish Question." *Leo Baeck Institute Yearbook,* VIII (1963), 238–45.

————. "Jewish Defense Against Nazism in the Weimar Republic." *Wiener Library Bulletin*, XXVI (1972), 21–31.

Phelps, Reginald H. "Theodor Fritsch und der Antisemitismus." *Deutsche Rundschau*, (May, 1961), 442–49.

Philipson, David. *The Reform Movement in Judaism*. Rev. ed. New York: Macmillan, 1931.

Pierson, Ruth. "Embattled Veterans: The Reichsbund jüdischer Frontsoldaten." *Leo Baeck Institute Yearbook*, XIX (1974), 139–54.

Pinson, Koppel S. *Modern Germany: Its History and Civilization*. New York: Macmillan, 1954.

Plaut, W. Gunther. *The Rise of Reform Judaism*. New York: World Union for Progressive Judaism, 1963.

Pollack, Fritz, ed. *50 Jahre Blau-Weiss*. Naharia, Israel, 1964.

Poor, Harold L. *Kurt Tucholsky and the Ordeal of Germany, 1914–1935*. New York: Charles Scribner's Sons, 1968.

Poppel, Stephen M. *Zionism in Germany 1897–1933*. Philadelphia: Jewish Publication Society, 1977.

Pridham, Geoffrey. *Hitler's Rise to Power: The Nazi Movement in Bavaria, 1923–1933*. Princeton: Princeton University Press, 1973.

Pulzer, Peter G. J. *The Rise of Political Anti-Semitism in Germany and Austria*. New York: John Wiley and Sons, 1964.

Ramm, Thilo, ed. *Die Justiz in der Weimarer Republik: Eine Chronik*. Neuwied and Berlin: Hermann Luchterhand Verlag, 1968.

Reich-Ranicki, Marcel. *Über Ruhestörer: Juden in der deutschen Literatur*. Munich: R. Piper & Co., 1973.

Reichmann, Eva G. *Hostages of Civilisation: The Social Sources of National Socialist Anti-Semitism*. London: Victor Gollancz, 1950.

Reinharz, Jehuda. "*Deutschtum* and *Judentum* in the Ideology of the Centralverein Deutscher Staatsbürger Jüdischen Glaubens 1893–1914." *Jewish Social Studies*, XXXVI (1974), 19–39.

————. *Fatherland or Promised Land: The Dilemma of the German Jew, 1893–1914*. Ann Arbor: University of Michigan Press, 1975.

Richards, Donald Ray. *The German Bestseller in the 20th Century: A Complete Bibliography and Analysis, 1915–1940*. Berne: Herbert Lang, 1968.

Richarz, Monika. *Der Eintritt der Juden in die akademischen Berufe: Jüdische Studenten und Akademiker in Deutschland 1678–1848*. Tübingen: J. C. B. Mohr, 1974.

Ringer, Fritz K. *The Decline of the German Mandarins*. Cambridge, Mass.: Harvard University Press, 1969.

Ritter, Frederick. "Constantin Brunner und seine Stellung zur Judenfrage." *Bulletin des Leo Baeck Instituts*, XIV (1975), 40–79.

Rosenthal, Berthold. *Heimatgeschichte der badischen Juden*. Bühl: Konkordia A. G., 1927.

Rosenthal, Erich. "Trends in the Jewish Population in Germany, 1910–39." *Jewish Social Studies*, VI (1944), 233–74.

Rotenstreich, Nathan. *Jewish Philosophy in Modern Times: From Mendelssohn to Rosenweig.* New York: Holt, Rinehart and Winston, 1968.

Rürup, Reinhard. *Emanzipation und Antisemitismus: Studien zur "Judenfrage" der bürgerlichen Gesellschaft.* Göttingen: Vandenhoeck und Ruprecht, 1975.

_____. "Emancipation and Crisis: The 'Jewish Question' in Germany, 1850–1890." *Leo Baeck Institute Yearbook,* XX (1975), 13–25.

Ruppin, Arthur. *Soziologie der Juden.* 2 vols. Berlin: Jüdischer Verlag, 1930–31.

_____. *The Jews in the Modern World.* London: Macmillan and Co., 1934.

Ryder, A. J. *The German Revolution of 1918.* Cambridge: Cambridge University Press, 1967.

Sandler, Ahron. "The Struggle for Unification." *Leo Baeck Institute Yearbook,* II (1957), 76–84.

Schechtman, Joseph B. *History of the Revisionist Movement.* 2 vols. Tel Aviv: Hader, 1970.

Schilling, Konrad, ed. *Monumenta Judaica Handbuch.* Cologne: Stadt Köln, 1963.

Schiratzki, Selma. "The Rykestrasse School in Berlin." *Leo Baeck Institute Yearbook,* V (1960), 299–307.

Schoeps, Hans-Joachim. *Unbewältige Geschichte: Stationen deutschen Schicksals seit 1763.* Berlin: Haude & Spenersche Verlagsbuchhandlung, 1964.

Schönhoven, Klaus. *Die Bayerische Volkspartei 1924–1932.* Düsseldorf: Droste Verlag, 1972.

Schorsch, Ismar. "German Antisemitism in the Light of Post-War Historiography." *Leo Baeck Institute Yearbook,* XIX (1974), 257–71.

_____. *Jewish Reactions to German Anti-Semitism, 1870–1914.* New York: Columbia University Press, 1972.

Schüddekopf, Otto-Ernst. *Linke Leute von Rechts: Die nationalrevolutionären Minderheiten und der Kommunismus in der Weimarer Republik.* Stuttgart: W. Kohlhammer Verlag, 1960.

Schwartz, Jürgen. *Studenten in der Weimarer Republik.* Berlin: Duncker & Humblot, 1971.

Schwarz, Stefan. *Die Juden in Bayern im Wandel der Zeiten.* Munich: Günther Olzog Verlag, 1963.

Sellenthin, H. G. *Geschichte der Juden in Berlin und des Gebäudes Fasanenstrasse 79/80.* Berlin: Jüdische Gemeinde zu Berlin, 1959.

Simon, Ernst. *Brücken: Gesammelte Aufsätze.* Heidelberg: Verlag Lambert Schneider, 1965.

Sontheimer, Kurt. *Antidemokratischer Denken in der Weimarer Republik: Die politischen Ideen des deutschen Nationalismus zwischen 1918–1933.* Munich: Nymphenburger Verlagshandlung, 1962.

Steinberg, Michael Stephen. *Sabers and Brown Shirts: The German Students' Path to National Socialism, 1918–1935.* Chicago and London: University of Chicago Press, 1973.

Sterling, Eleonore. *Judenhass: Die Anfänge des politischen Antisemitismus in Deutschland (1815–1850).* Rev. ed. Frankfurt-am-Main: Europäische Verlagsanstalt, 1969.

Stern, Fritz. *The Politics of Cultural Despair.* Berkeley: University of California Press, 1961.

Stern, Rudolf. "Fritz Haber." *Leo Baeck Institute Yearbook,* VIII (1963), 70–102.

Tal, Uriel. *Christians and Jews in Germany: Religion, Politics, and Ideology in the Second Reich, 1870–1914.* Ithaca, N. Y.: Cornell University Press, 1975.

Thimme, Annelise. *Flucht in den Mythos: Die Deutschnationale Volkspartei und die Niederlage von 1918.* Göttingen: Vandenhoeck und Ruprecht, 1969.

Toury, Jacob. "Organizational Problems of German Jewry: Steps Towards the Establishment of a Central Organization (1893–1920)." *Leo Baeck Institute Yearbook,* XIII (1968), 57–90.

————. "Ostjüdische Handarbeiter in Deutschland vor 1914." *Bulletin des Leo Baecks Instituts,* XXI (1963), 14–22.

————. *Die politischen Orientierungen der Juden in Deutschland: Von Jena bis Weimar.* Tübingen: J. C. B. Mohr, 1966.

Trepp, Leo. *Die Landesgemeinde der Juden in Oldenburg.* Oldenburg: Oldenburger Balkenschild, 1965.

Wandel, Eckhard. *Hans Schäffer: Steuermann in wirtschaftlichen und politischen Krisen.* Stuttgart: Deutsche Verlags-Anstalt, 1974.

Weinryb, Sucher B. *Der Kampf um die Berufsumschichtung: Ein Ausschnitt aus der Geschichte der Juden in Deutschland.* Berlin: Schocken Verlag, 1936.

Wiener, Max. *Abraham Geiger and Liberal Judaism.* Philadelphia: Jewish Publication Society of America, 1962.

Wilhelm, Kurt. "The Jewish Community in the Post-Emancipation Period." *Leo Baeck Institute Yearbook,* II (1957), 47–75.

Williamson, John G. *Karl Helfferich 1872–1924: Economist, Financier, Politician.* Princeton: Princeton University Press, 1971.

Winter, David Alexander. *Geschichte der Jüdischen Gemeinde in Moisling/Lübeck.* Lübeck: Verlag Max Schmidt, 1968.

Wolfsberg-Aviad, Oskar. *Die Drei-Gemeinde: Aus der Geschichte der Jüdischen Gemeinden Altona-Hamburg-Wandsbek.* Munich: Ner-Tamid-Verlag, 1960.

Zechlin, Egmont. *Die deutsche Politik und die Juden im ersten Weltkrieg.* Göttingen: Vandenhoeck & Ruprecht, 1969.

Zelzer, Maria. *Weg und Schicksal der Stuttgarter Juden.* Stuttgart: Ernst Klett Verlag, n.d.

Zeman, Z. A. B., and W. B. Scharlau. *The Merchant of Revolution: The Life of Alexander Israel Helphand (Parvus), 1867–1924.* London: Oxford University Press, 1965.

B. Unpublished Studies

Bernstein, Reiner. "Zwischen Emanzipation und Antisemitismus: Die Publizistik der deutschen Juden am Beispiel der C.V.-Zeitung, Organ des Centralvereins deutscher Staatsbürger jüdischen Glaubens, 1924–1933." Ph.D. dissertation, Free University of Berlin, n.d.

Hackett, David A. "The Nazi Party in the Reichstag Election of 1930." Ph.D. dissertation, University of Wisconsin, 1971.

Kaplan, Marion A. "German-Jewish Feminism: The Jüdischer Frauenbund, 1904–1938." Ph.D. dissertation, Columbia University, 1977.

Markreich, Max. "Die Juden in Ostfriesland. Zweige sephardischen und askenasischen Judentums 1348–1945." Unpublished manuscript, Leo Baeck Institute, New York.

————. "Geschichte der Juden in Bremen und Umgegend." Unpublished manuscript, Leo Baeck Institute, New York.

Pierson, Ruth. "German Jewish Identity in the Weimar Republic." Ph.D. dissertation, Yale University, 1970.

Rheins, Carl J. "German Jewish Patriotism 1918–1935: A Study of the Attitudes and Actions of the *Reichsbund jüdischer Frontsoldaten,* the *Verband nationaldeutscher Juden,* the *Schwarzes Fähnlein, Jungenschaft,* and the *Deutscher Vortrupp, Gefolgschaft deutscher Juden.*" Ph.D. dissertation, State University of New York at Stony Brook, 1978.

Rühl, Manfred. *"Der Stürmer* und sein Herausgeber." Diplom-Volkswirt, Hochschule für Wirtschafts- and Sozialwissenschaften in Nürnberg, 1960.

Wiener, Alfred. "The Centralverein deutscher Staatsbürger jüdischen Glaubens—Its Meaning and Activities." Typescript on file in the Wiener Library, London.

Index